pd 2/7/08

# Extreme

# Metal

# Extreme Metal

*Music*

*and*

*Culture*

*on the*

*Edge*

## Keith Kahn-Harris

**BERG**

Oxford • New York

First published in 2007 by
**Berg**
Editorial offices:
1st Floor, Angel Court, 81 St Clements Street, Oxford, OX4 1AW, UK
175 Fifth Avenue, New York, NY 10010, USA

Berg is the imprint of Oxford International Publishers Ltd.

**Library of Congress Cataloguing-in-Publication Data**
Kahn-Harris, Keith, 1971-
    Extreme metal : music and culture on the edge / Keith Kahn-Harris.
        p. cm.
    Includes bibliographical references (p.   ) and index.
    ISBN-13: 978-1-84520-398-6 (cloth)
    ISBN-10: 1-84520-398-4 (cloth)
    ISBN-13: 978-1-84520-399-3 (pbk.)
    ISBN-10: 1-84520-399-2 (pbk.)
    1.  Extreme metal (Music)—History and criticism. 2.  Extreme metal
(Music)—Social aspects. I. Title.

    ML3534.K28 2007
    781.66—dc22                                                    2006027931

**British Library Cataloguing-in-Publication Data**
A catalogue record for this book is available from the British Library.

ISBN-13    978 184520 398 6 (Cloth)
ISBN-10    1 84520 398 4 (Cloth)

ISBN-13    978 184520 399 3 (Paper)
ISBN-10    1 84520 399 2 (Paper)

Typeset by Avocet Typeset, Chilton, Aylesbury, Bucks
Printed in the United Kingdom by Biddles Ltd, King's Lynn

**www.bergpublishers.com**

# CONTENTS

## ILLUSTRATIONS

## ACKNOWLEDGEMENTS

In writing and researching this book I have been greatly touched by the support and encouragement I have received from a wide range of people.

This book has its origins in my (2001) PhD thesis 'Transgression and Mundanity: The Global Extreme Metal Music Scene'. The Department of Sociology at Goldsmiths College was a supportive and intellectually vibrant environment within which to conduct research. I would like to thank in particular my supervisor Professor Chris Jenks for guiding my work with subtlety and good humour. I also acknowledge the help of the Economic and Social Research Council, whose award (R00429924515) made the completion of the thesis possible.

I would like to thank the many scene members I met and interviewed in the course of my research. Their willingness to talk and to listen to my sometimes ill-informed theories helped to make the process of research a great pleasure. I would particularly like to thank those who copied tapes for me, sent me CDs and fanzines for free and introduced me to other scene members. Nick Terry showed great patience and support to me at a crucial stage of the research, as I negotiated the process of becoming an informed scene member. Yishai Schwartz gave up his time to ensure that my visit to Israel was a productive and unforgettable experience. Jonathan Seltzer and others at *Terrorizer* magazine have helped and inspired me in numerous ways.

I would like to thank those members of the academic 'scene' who helped me in developing my ideas and providing me with stimulation and support. The International Association for the Study of Popular Music (IASPM) was a welcoming and sustaining community for a new researcher. Motti Regev provided intellectual and financial help during my fieldwork in Israel. Michael Forsman and Ove Sernhede ensured that my fieldwork in Sweden was similarly well supported. My thoughts on the extreme metal scene were clarified and challenged at numerous conferences and seminars over the years. I want to thank in particular those who attended my lectures at Turku University in October 2003 and I am grateful to Henri Terho and Janne Mäkelä for facilitating my visit. I am also grateful to those who attended my joint seminar with Geoff Stahl at the Advanced Cultural Studies Institute of Sweden, Norrköping in March 2005 and to Johan Fornäs who arranged my postdoctoral fellowship.

I want to thank those whose suggestions, conversation and support have helped me over the years, in particular: Les Back, Andy Bennett, Harris Berger, Thomas

Bossius, Kosta Economou, Ben Gidley, Paul Gilroy, Ingemar Grandin, Dave Hesmondhalgh, Paul Hodkinson, Lutgard Mutsaers, Giovanni Porfido, Tim Rapley, Geoff Stahl, Will Straw, Phil Tagg, and all metal researchers from across the world.

Hannah Shakespeare at Berg showed enthusiasm for this project from the beginning and has been an unfailingly supportive editor.

My wife Deborah has shown great fortitude in coping with me during the process of completing this book and the PhD that preceded it and has provided an excellent 'sounding board' for my emerging ideas.

Finally, I want to thank my parents, whose unfailing love and support has helped to make this book possible. *Extreme Metal: Music and Culture on the Edge* is dedicated to them.

Mention the words 'heavy metal' to someone even casually acquainted with contemporary popular music and you are likely to trigger some strong associations: long hair, headbanging, screaming vocals and guitars, outrageous behaviour and excess, over the top machismo, black leather. The semiotics of metal are so well known that they have an almost iconic position in popular culture. Metal divides people. The music boasts some of the most devoted music fans across the world and many of its practitioners are stars. But at the same time metal has always attracted virulent and intense dislike, even hatred and fear. In the 1980s, metal attracted condemnation from right and left and was the subject of media- and state-sponsored 'moral panics' (Miller 1988; Richardson 1991).

This iconic representation of metal has become out of step with reality. Although metal was always more diverse than it was given credit for, there has been a significant fragmentation of metal since the early 1990s. In the early 1990s, the rise of grunge, sparked off by the success of Nirvana's *Nevermind* (1991), had a profound effect on metal. It is no hyperbole to state that an entire generation of bands had their careers ended almost overnight. This was particularly true of 'pop metal' bands such as Poison, but even some of the biggest 'classic' metal bands such as Judas Priest and Iron Maiden suffered a considerable loss of popularity in the 1990s. However, grunge's connection with the history of metal was much greater than some of its protagonists might have liked to admit. This connection has become ever more evident as subsequent generations of grunge-influenced bands, such as Nickelback, have produced music that sounds increasingly similar to the classic metal and hard rock bands of the 1970s and 1980s.

Another hugely successful 1990s offshoot of heavy metal was nu metal, which began to constitute itself in the latter half of the 1990s with the success of bands such as Korn and Limp Bizkit. Such bands built on the early funk metal work of bands such as Faith No More by combining metal with rap and dance music. Nu metal also built on grunge and punk by lyrically emphasizing pain and personal alienation.

As the twenty-first century has progressed, nu metal has begun to exhaust itself artistically and 'emo' bands such as Funeral For A Friend and My Chemical Romance, that draw on both nu metal and impassioned versions of 1990s hardcore punk, have become more popular. There has been an increased re-evaluation and renaissance of 1980s-style heavy metal. Pop metal bands such as Mötley Crüe and

Poison have reconvened and bands such as Iron Maiden and Judas Priest have re-formed their original line-ups to wide acclaim. Metal has come to be thought of much more affectionately and nostalgically, with artists such as The Darkness and Andrew WK developing an ironic, exaggerated take on metal's more ludicrous elements. Even Ozzy Osbourne, the subject of ferocious attacks from the Christian right in the 1980s, has been reinvented as a loveable clown in the highly successful MTV programme *The Osbournes*. On the other end of the scale, so-called 'new wave of American heavy metal' bands such as Killswitch Engage, which are much more musically ferocious, are also challenging nu metal's popularity.

Although metal has fragmented and does not generally attract the notoriety and controversy that it once did, metal remains an important and recognizable form of popular music. Yet on the edge of metal culture, forms of metal that are much more obscure and that attract much less attention are thriving. These forms of metal represent the most diverse, the most artistically vibrant, the most dynamic and also the most problematic aspects of metal culture. Collectively they are known as extreme metal.[1]

### What is Extreme Metal?

Heavy metal was developed in the late 1960s and early 1970s by bands such as Black Sabbath, Deep Purple and Led Zeppelin. But it was in the 1980s that heavy metal reached the apex of its popularity. Whereas the bands that emerged in the 1970s often had roots in rhythm and blues, from the late 1970s there emerged a generation of bands that took their primary inspiration from metal itself. The so-called 'new wave of British heavy metal', led by bands such as Saxon, Def Leppard and Iron Maiden in the early 1980s, contributed enormously to the distinctiveness of metal. This moment of coalescence in the early 1980s, in which many of the most identifiable aspects of heavy metal came together, was also the moment that began the process of the fragmentation of metal that was to reach its apotheosis in the 1990s. As Deena Weinstein (2000) has shown, this fragmentation initially occurred in two directions. One was towards the mainstream with the 'pop' or 'glam' metal popularized by bands such as Poison. The other direction was towards what Weinstein calls the 'fundamentalism' of what became known as 'thrash' or 'speed' metal.

Fundamentalism implies a disgust at decadence (in this case the decadence of pop metal) and a desire to return to a perceived prior state of purity. In 1981 the British band Venom released *Welcome To Hell*, which, followed by 1982's *Black Metal*, inspired a new generation of bands. Venom reacted to the increasingly burlesque nature of metal by presenting more extreme occult imagery than other metal bands. Venom also reacted to the burgeoning emphasis on technical virtuosity in metal by presenting a speeded-up and stripped-down version of the genre. Their lack of technical competence meant that they were simply unable to emphasize traditional notions of musicianship as heavy metal bands did. In emphasizing speed and simplicity, the band, like the other thrash metal bands that followed, were influenced by punk, in particular the 'hardcore' punk that was developed in the early 1980s by bands such as Discharge and Black Flag. Inspired by Venom, punk and the new wave of British heavy metal, a host of thrash metal bands quickly emerged. Metallica's *Kill 'Em All* (1983) and Slayer's *Show No Mercy* (1983) were landmark releases characterized by speed, aggression and an austere seriousness. Later releases by bands such as Anthrax and Megadeth further cemented thrash metal's place as a commercially popular form of metal.

Thrash engendered a variety of ever more radical extreme metal genres. In the mid 1980s, bands such as Death and Possessed created death metal out of thrash metal. Vocals became less and less intelligible, songwriting became more complex and guitar 'riffs' (chord sequences) sounded increasingly austere and 'dark'. Death metal, played by bands such as Cannibal Corpse, Obituary (see Figure 1) and Morbid Angel, features growled vocals and fast, complicated guitar work with few solos. Death metal lyrics (decipherable only with the aid of a lyric sheet) deal with themes such as violence, war and the occult. Grindcore emerged at a similar time as death metal and was developed in the mid to late 1980s by bands such as Siege, Repulsion and Napalm Death (see Figure 2). A punk-influenced radicalization of death metal,

1: The death metal band Obituary photographed around the time of their debut album *Slowly We Rot* (1989). Reproduced with the kind permission of Roadrunner Records.

grindcore utilizes extremes speed, often featuring extremely short songs. Contemporary grindcore bands such as The Dillinger Escape Plan and Agoraphobic Nosebleed have developed avant-garde versions of the genre incorporating frequent time signature changes and complex sounds that at times recall free jazz.

Doom metal also emerged in the 1980s, building on the work of 1970s bands such as Pentagram and Black Sabbath. Bands such as St Vitus and The Obsessed played an extremely slow form of metal with long, epic song structures and melancholic lyrics. Doom metal was refined further in the 1990s, with bands such as My Dying Bride and Paradise Lost employing exaggeratedly 'depressed' vocals and tortuous song structures, often influence by gothic rock. In the 1980s the term 'black metal' had begun to be used to refer to overtly Satanic forms of metal pioneered by bands such as Bathory and Hellhammer. In the early 1990s Norwegian bands such as Emperor, Mayhem, Burzum and Darkthrone developed a highly distinct and influential form of black metal, characterized by screamed, high-pitched vocals, extremely rapid tempos, 'tremolo' riffs, a 'trebly' guitar sound, and simple production values. Black

2: Napalm Death in the late 1980s. Reproduced with the kind permission of Earache Records.

metallers embraced Satanism wholeheartedly and on occasions, fascism and racism too. In the early 1990s, Norwegian black metal became notorious for a spate of murders, suicides and church burnings linked to its main protagonists (Moynihan & Søderlind 1998). Subsequently, black metal became more diverse, with bands such as Cradle Of Filth and Dimmu Borgir introducing keyboards and sung vocals.

The above-mentioned genres are frequently referred to collectively as extreme metal. All share a musical radicalism that marks them out as different from other forms of heavy metal. All forms of extreme metal share fans, musicians and institutions. In contrast to heavy metal's mainstream commercial reach, extreme metal is disseminated through small-scale 'underground' institutions that extend across the globe. The differences between extreme metal and most other forms of popular music are so pronounced that those who are not fans may not see its considerable internal differences. Extreme metal music frequently teeters on the edge of formless noise. Whereas heavy metal was at least intelligible to its detractors as 'music', extreme metal may not appear to be music at all and its attendant practices may appear terrifying and bizarre. On the edge of music, on the edge of the music industry, extreme metal thrives.

### Why a Book on Extreme Metal?

Sometime in 1987 I tuned into BBC Radio 1's John Peel show and heard a sound that was to change my life: short, incomprehensible bursts of unlistenable guitar noise overlaid with a series of brutal grunts. The sound was utterly different from anything that I had ever heard before, completely bewildering yet at the same time strangely compelling. The band I heard was Napalm Death (pictured in Figure 2) and in subsequent months Peel was to play other, similarly extraordinary bands such as Carcass and Bolt Thrower. This exposure to pioneering UK grindcore bands led me to completely re-evaluate my feelings about metal, which save for a brief flirtation in the early 1980s, were largely negative. As a consequence I discovered the burgeoning death metal scene, which instantly fascinated me just as grindcore did.

This simultaneous fascination and bewilderment has never left me. Extreme metal's sheer difficulty as a musical form, its aestheticization of sounds that many people find repellent, has always entranced me. At the same time, its problematic politics, its occasional misogyny and in particular the fascism of some black metallers has always worried me. My discovery of the social sciences as an undergraduate gave a shape to my inchoate interests: I had found a topic for research, a source of involving and complex questions.

I have always been an ambivalent fan of extreme metal, but as a sociologist I have tried to use my ambivalence to productive ends. As an MA and then a PhD student, I delved further and further into extreme metal music and culture, moving back and forth from critical insider to sympathetic outsider. This continual movement offers, I believe, the ideal (shifting) standpoint from which to conduct research. To my continual shifting between the standpoints of fan and researcher, I added the stand-point of critic when I began writing for the British extreme metal magazine *Terrorizer* in 1997. I completed my PhD thesis on extreme metal in 2001 (Harris 2001) but I was never quite able to 'leave the field'. I have continued writing for *Terrorizer* on and off, to listen to extreme metal music and to write and research articles (Harris 2000; Kahn-Harris 2002, 2003, 2004a, 2004b). This book stems from a desire to commu-nicate the findings of my engagement with extreme metal. More ambitiously, it stems from a desire to communicate my findings outside the academic world so as to spark a debate about the politics of extreme metal both within and without the extreme metal world. As I will show in chapters 7 and 8, a debate of this kind is sorely needed.

Eyebrows are often raised when I tell strangers about my research. As with research on other forms of popular music, it is sometimes seen as a frivolous pursuit. Yet there are a number of reasons why extreme metal is a significant phenomenon:

### Extreme Metal Is Influential

Extreme metal is much more influential than its relative obscurity might suggest. In the 1980s in particular, the boundaries between heavy metal and extreme metal were relatively porous. Extreme metal has provided a crucial, if sometimes unacknowl-edged, motor of innovation within metal. It is increasingly becoming a source of inspiration for cutting edge artists in a number of musical fields.

### Extreme Metal Is Artistically Challenging

In pushing conventional musical aesthetics to the point where music collapses into what is conventionally classed as noise, extreme metal challenges notions of what music is. Extreme metal musicians have pioneered sounds that can be heard nowhere else and developed new musical fusions that challenge accepted musical boundaries.

### Extreme Metal Is Diverse

More than any other kind of metal, extreme metal is exceptionally diverse. There has been a continual process of musical experimentation that has expanded the possibil-ities of metal. Extreme metal culture is equally diverse, with musicians and fans located across the world.

### Extreme Metal Is Reproduced through Innovative Social Practices

From its inception, extreme metal fans and musicians have developed complex prac-tices and institutions for the music's reproduction. These practices and institutions have allowed the music to be spread worldwide and to thrive despite its modest popu-larity.

Asserting that extreme metal is a significant and interesting phenomenon does not necessarily confer value on it. In fact, it is precisely the value of extreme metal that is in question in this book. It is hard to know how to respond to lyrics dealing with murder, sexual assault and violence. Even harder to understand how to treat instances of flirtation and sometimes outright embrace of fascism and racism. The dividing line between fantasy and reality has at times been extremely porous for extreme metal protagonists. This book then is not a history or an 'appreciation' of extreme metal music and culture – there are other books that deal with this (e.g. McIver 2000; Moynihan & Søderlind 1998; Mudrian 2004). Rather it explicitly seeks to ask difficult questions with the aim of providing new perspectives on the politics of extreme metal.

### Investigating Extreme Metal

Extreme metal is a tricky phenomenon to pin down. It consists of a cluster of genres with different histories, which are constantly developing and reconfiguring. It is produced and consumed across the world through a wide variety of institutions in a wide variety of contexts. The first, largely theoretical, chapter in this book examines the challenges of asking questions about extreme metal and approaching it as a multi-faceted phenomenon. The chapter reviews existing writing on the subject and goes on to draw on a wide literature in order to develop the concept of 'scene' as the framework for the analysis of extreme metal music and culture.

Chapter 2 looks at what is 'extreme' about the extreme metal scene. The concept of 'transgression' is introduced to examine those aspects of the extreme metal scene that are most visible to non-scene members: the music that appears to challenge notions of what music is; the problematic discourses and practices that have involved racism, arson and murder. The chapter shows how transgression within the extreme metal scene is accompanied by great ambivalence – the scene sets up rigid boundaries even as it transgresses others. Chapter 3 puts transgression into the context of the experience of the scene within the everyday life of its members. Scene members orient their practices both towards the experience of transgression through the body and towards the mundane experience of community.

Chapters 4 to 6 are concerned with hierarchy, status and power within the scene. Chapter 4 introduces Pierre Bourdieu's concept of 'capital' and then goes on to look at how and whether the scene's institutions 'refract' capital from outside the scene. The chapter also examines what sorts of 'habitus' members come to the scene with. Chapter 5 investigates the complexities of location in the scene, the emergence of cores and peripheries within the global scene and how location in a particular country or region may or may not confer certain privileges on scene members. Chapter 6 looks at how the scene produces its own forms of 'subcultural capital'. The chapter shows how the tension between 'mundane subcultural capital' and 'transgressive subcultural capital' has provided a productive source of tension in the historical development of the scene.

Chapter 7 investigates the workings of and limitations of 'reflexivity' within the scene. The chapter argues that scene members practise a form of 'reflexive anti-reflexivity' that is used to resist the encroachment of 'politics' onto the scene and to provide a source of playful, ironic pleasures. Chapter 8, the final chapter, then goes on to reflect on the problematics of the scene's politics and its simultaneous resistance to and retrenchment of forms of power. The book concludes with some tentative explorations as to how the scene might be opened up so that its more conservative aspects might be challenged while still retaining its considerable radicalism.

For many who encounter it, extreme metal simply provokes incomprehension, disgust and ridicule. But for some, extreme metal generates *questions*. As we will see in Chapter 3, this is as true for fans of extreme metal as it is for academics. Such questions include: what is extreme metal? Why is it relatively obscure? Who plays and listens to it? Why do they play and listen to it? What does it all mean? Does it have any value? Such questions are difficult given extreme metal's considerable complexity. Extreme metal features a complex of closely interrelated and continuously cross-fertilizing genres, all of which relate in complex ways to heavy metal and to other genres. It is played and consumed across the world in a wide variety of contexts. Extreme metal culture involves people in a variety of ways from musician and fan; in a variety of institutions such as bands, record labels and fanzines; in a variety of contexts such as concerts, rehearsals and offices. How can we understand this complexity and diversity?

## Metal Studies

Such is the notoriety of metal's more mainstream manifestations that for a long time, the diversity of metal and its post-1990s development were marginalized or ignored. Over the last couple of decades a modest amount of interest in extreme metal has developed. There has been a little coverage in the general media (e.g. Campion 2005; Cayton 1999; Heller 1992), in the music press (e.g. Pouncey 2005; Steinke 1996; Wells 1998), by fiction writers (Elbom 2004; Richter 1999; White 1999), by non-fiction writers (Christie 2003; Moynihan & Søderlind 1998; Mudrian 2004); by writers of memoirs (Hunter 2004; Klosterman 2001), as well as by academic researchers. There is no unanimity as to terminology in such writing. The term extreme metal alternates with black metal, death metal or thrash metal. These generic terms are often assumed to cover other genres (with death metal treated as a part of thrash metal, for example) or the genres are assumed to be discrete (with black metal discussed as entirely distinct from death metal, see for example Purcell 2003). This fragmentation and marginalization of extreme metal has begun to change but, inevitably given the complexity of the subject matter, certain aspects of extreme metal tend to be foregrounded at the expense of other aspects.

Perhaps the most striking aspect of extreme metal culture is 'the music itself'. Simon Reynolds and Joy Press (1995) have argued that the emphasis on death and mutilation in death metal lyrics is mirrored by a musical style that revels in the breakdown of conventional musical structures into primal formlessness. Similarly, Ronald Bogue (2004a, 2004b) has used Deleuzian theory to examine the 'deterritorializing' power of death metal music. Phillip Tagg (1994) has argued that metal's raucous sounds are connected to the infant's desire to dominate the soundscape. He has also examined (1998) the 'tritone' (the augmented fourth interval) that dominates metal, which was demonized by the Catholic Church in the Middle Ages as the *diabolus in musica* and is also used to signify danger and mystery in the incidental music of detective films and television shows. Such works appear to account for metal and extreme metal's reputation as a disturbing and 'evil-sounding' music.

Robert Walser (1993) identifies 'the dialectic of freedom and control' as the defining element of metal. In the same way as metal guitar solos transcend the narrow confines of their musical backing, so metal fans escape the oppressive confines of deindustrialized capitalism through participation in metal culture. Walser's study is one of the most comprehensive and thought provoking of the few musicological studies of metal.[1] However, he virtually ignores extreme metal, instead focusing on the more popular heavy metal genres of the 1980s.

Harris Berger (1999a, 1999b) has used phenomenology in his investigation of metal music. His most extensive piece of analysis is of the song 'The Final Silencing' by the US death metal band Sin Eater (1999a). Together with the song's composer, Dann [*sic*] Saladin, he explores in microscopic detail how Saladin experiences the piece. In particular, he focuses on the piece's lack of tonal centre and on the bewildering array of tonal structures that appear to be a common feature of death metal (see also Bjornberg 1996). The complexities of tonal structure help to evoke a range of emotions surrounding the theme of death. Berger builds on this analysis to argue that the music provides a source of individual empowerment, responsibility and community among people who have suffered in the transition to post-industrial capitalism.

Empowerment is a key theme in studies of metal. Jack Harrell finds in death metal music 'an unofficial expression of industrialism's emotional isolation and violence' (1994: 91) and Anne Petrov argues that 'Death metal could be seen as a direct product of the ongoing urbanization of suburbia, as one of the forms which suburban violence takes' (1995: 5). Deena Weinstein (2000) also emphasizes the empowering effect heavy metal has on its disenfranchised audience. Thomas Bossius (2003) has argued that black metal is a powerful form of 'here and now religion', providing meaning in a complex world. Jeffrey Arnett (1995) also sees involvement in metal as a form of survival in an insecure world, but for him this is not a cause of celebration. He postulates that 'metalheads' resort to the music as a result of the failure of US society to socialize its adolescent members 'properly'.

Detailed information on metal audiences is limited. There is a tradition of American psychological research that attempts to establish the possible 'harm' that metal can cause (for a useful survey, see Hemming 2003). There has been some quantitative work on the US heavy metal audience in the 1980s suggesting that metal fans are predominantly white and working class (Epstein, Pratto & Skipper 1990; Hakanen & Wells 1990). There is also some evidence that German metal fans are likely to be young, undereducated and to live in rural areas (Niketta 1998). The antipathy of many women towards most forms of metal has also been partly demonstrated (Shepherd 1991). This very limited data suggesting that metal is predominantly white, male, heterosexual and working class has been taken as fact by many researchers and applied indiscriminately to all metal genres. Recently there have been some suggestive studies of metal and extreme metal in a number of non-American global contexts, including Nepal (Greene 2001; In Press), Bali (Baulch 2003), Indonesia and Malaysia (Wallach 2003, In Press) and Brazil (Avelar 2003). These studies are beginning to complicate some of the more simplistic understandings of metal. What they often lack, however, is a sense of the overall global context, of the links between sites of metal production and consumption.

Research on metal has offered some intriguing insights, but has been tentative and fragmentary and has only erratically looked at extreme metal. As yet little attention has been paid to such key metal institutions as record labels, tape trading and fanzines. There has also been insufficient appreciation of the interconnections between different elements of metal culture and in particular of extreme metal culture. How can we begin to appreciate the intricate ways in which different aspects of extreme metal music and culture fit together? There are real methodological difficulties in combining research on musical production, consumption and aesthetics. I want to argue that in order to better understand and ask searching questions of extreme metal, we need to find a way of approaching extreme metal *holistically* and *spatially*.

### A Spatial and Holistic Approach to Extreme Metal

Holism can be defined as 'the notion that all of the institutions, beliefs and morals of a society are interrelated as a whole' (Cohen 1968: 34). Holism provides a perspective that recognizes the interconnection between different elements of social phenomena and that avoids the fragmentation of the subject area that studies of metal have suffered from. Holism has been associated with Parsonian functionalism, whose shortcomings – its tendency towards teleological explanations, its inability to understand change, its convoluted complexity and its empirical unwieldiness – are well known (Craib 1984). Yet it does not seem unreasonable to argue that, holistically speaking, extreme metal needs to be considered as the locus for a huge range of interconnected practices, texts, institutions and social phenomena.

A number of different conceptual apparatuses potentially allow us to navigate extreme metal music and culture in a holistic manner. The literature on 'genre', as developed within popular music studies, provides a potential source for a holistic framework. In more traditional forms of musicology, genre signifies a mode of producing music (e.g. 'ballads'), whereas 'style' signifies the specific mode of producing those genres (e.g. 'heavy metal ballads'). Nonetheless, in both lay and academic forms of popular music writing, genre has taken on a more holistic meaning, covering both the music that is produced and the style in which it is produced. Genre is both a set of musical events and the social processes and communities that constitute those events. According to Franco Fabbri (1982), generic rules are defined by communities and include sociological and economic variables. Keith Negus argues that 'genre cultures [arise] from the complex intersection and interplay between commercial organizational structures and promotional labels; the activities of fans, listeners and audiences; networks of musicians; and historical legacies that come to us within broader social formations' (1999: 29–30). Similarly, Simon Frith (1996) argues that genres are produced through a complex interplay between music, markets and ideologies. Genres are not and cannot be static. Indeed, as Charles Hamm (1994) has shown, the genre within which a particular song is positioned can change from performance to performance. Furthermore, what constitutes a genre is the subject of considerable debate. Robert Walser shows how the bands and songs to which the label heavy metal should be applied are forcefully contested by musicians and fans. Indeed, genres are constituted precisely through these struggles.

However broad the concept of genre might be, taking genre as the basis of popular music studies privileges musical events as the starting point for analysis. However, if we privilege the social processes through which genre is constituted, there is a risk of treating music simply as the contingent outcome of social processes. In his study of punk, Dave Laing (1985) argues that the concept of discourse describes the point at which social conditions and signifying practices meet. Johan Fornäs (1995) has looked at how rock as a genre is contested and constructed by various competing discourses. Similarly, Walser argues that heavy metal should be understood as discourse. Discourse pervades all areas of popular music text and practice and therefore, to investigate discourse is to investigate 'everything'. In this way, the concept has holistic tendencies.

While concepts such as discourse and genre point in a holistic direction, they are ultimately rooted not in social, but in textual abstractions. They lack a sense of locatedness in real existing social relations. The question of where to locate social phenomena is an important issue in sociology. Social interaction is both something that occurs on an intensely parochial, 'micro' level and something that is structured by complex, large-scale 'macro' social structures. Yet both micro and macro are inadequate as a way of locating social phenomena. As a unit of analysis, 'society' (or 'culture') is simply too broad, whereas focusing on the micro may dissolve the social altogether. Understandably therefore, sociology has developed a whole range of 'middle range' concepts (Merton 1957) that describe the social contexts within which interaction takes place. Such concepts include 'community', 'field', 'network', 'system' and 'social world'. Each has generated a rich tradition of research and each emphasizes different aspects of the social and the ways in which individuals relate to each other. While there is a danger that such concepts may lead us to lose sight of the overall 'meta' importance of the social (Jenks 2005), it is only through conceptually breaking down the intimidating size of society that the social becomes navigable, recognizable and 'visible'.

Some of these mid-range concepts such as community are 'spatial' in that they provide metaphors for a particular kind of location. Such metaphors have become increasingly common in sociology (Keith & Pile 1993). Contemporary discussions of space emphasize that space is not an easily visible, containable, mappable 'thing' (Massey 1994). Space is both an epistemological and a material concept; both real and imagined; both representation and practice (Lefebvre 1991). Space is not static, but multiple, fluid and overlapping (Soja 1989), relating in complex ways to 'place' (Lash & Urry 1994). Space is also inextricably linked to time in a continually shifting relationship (Giddens 1984; Harvey 1990). In 'late modernity', modern systems of communication lead to a 'separation' of time and space, through a 'disembedding' of social systems from their location in space (Giddens 1990). Lash and Urry (1994) and Castells (1996) show how contemporary capitalism is constituted as a global network of 'flows' of capital and information, structured around certain key hubs.

Contemporary work on space, place and time helps to make sense of the ways in which globalization has made available a wide range of musical resources that are used across the globe by individuals and groups in the construction of ethnicity, identity and location (Stokes 1994). Globalization is facilitated by music's 'malleability' (Taylor 1997) and is important in the creation and dissemination of new musical forms. In our contemporary globalized world, processes of musical export and import occur ever more extensively and rapidly, giving rise to new forms of appropriation and syncretism. As Motti Regev (1997) has argued, popular musics have the potential to provide temporary resolutions to the apparent contradiction between participation in the global and the local. However, globalization is by no means unproblematic. Global flows of music are facilitated by global flows of capital that are subject to severe inequalities.

By grounding a holistic approach in the materiality of space, place and time, we are constantly reminded that to understand extreme metal music and culture we cannot limit our attempts at understanding to a single site at a single point in time. Rather, it needs to be rooted in an appreciation of the constantly shifting, multifaceted nature of the contemporary globalized world. It is necessary then to locate extreme metal music and culture within a particular kind of space.

## Exploring Scenes

One spatial concept used by participants in extreme metal culture is 'scene'. The term is used in a variety of ways to describe the context within which extreme metal music, practices and discourses are produced. Consider the following extracts from an interview with a young, male, death metal fan that I conducted in an earlier project (Harris 1997):

> I go to loads of gigs now, I like the underground that's a good scene it's friendly, social. You wouldn't think so by looking at the people who go there but it is . . . I'm one of the youngest, in like most of the people I hang around with, but, there's also younger, I've got friends who are younger than me as well who [are] like in the scene as well.

In this extract 'scene' is constructed in two slightly different ways to describe a particular kind of space. The scene is used in a very loose way to identify 'the underground' as 'a good scene'. The term is also used more specifically to describe something of which he and his friends are members. In other extracts from interviews conducted for the same study, scene was also used to describe something larger and more diffuse. Consider this extract from an interview with a young, female fan of the death metal band Obituary:

> KKH: . . . there was rumours recently that they'd split up
>
> R:    Yeah, yeah they did split up
>
> KKH: Yeah, does that make you sad?
>
> R:    Not really because, I don't think, it's because like, the musical scene has progressed so much I don't think Obituary could come with anything, very, you know significant . . . I mean I would, I would accept them anytime but in a scene it changes it change too much.

Here, the interviewee argues that it was not sad that Obituary split up, since the 'musical scene' had developed to the point where the band could no longer come up with anything relevant or new. Scene refers to a space within which music making takes place, with strong connotations of genre. But later in the same interview, the use of scene shifts slightly as she defines it more specifically:

> R:    What I mean by music scene is, in general commercial side of it, business side of it and musical side of it, and that . . . they're very important line between it you know between business and between musical scene, you know, you know what I'm trying to say?
>
> KKH: Yeah
>
> R:    That that's what I and when I say music scene I consider both of that sides, when I said Obituary wouldn't do anything if they released a new album, I mean they wouldn't do anything in a, in a whole scene in general, like in a business they wouldn't sell any records.

The scene has a 'musical side' and a 'commercial side' but the relationship between the two is confused. There is a 'line between' the two, yet on the other hand the reason why Obituary shouldn't release another record is that they would be redundant in 'the whole scene in general'. For this interviewee, the scene is constructed as something that is a collection of texts *and* a collection of institutions. But it is neither of these things alone. Similarly, for the other interviewee, the scene is a collection of people that socialize, but 'scene' is not used in any clear sense, and the 'underground' is another term that has similar connotations.

For all its vagueness, scene seems to be implicitly holistic in defining something that encapsulates music making, production, circulation, discussion and texts. The term 'scene' originated in the theatre, denoting the space within which action is performed (Giovanni Porfido, personal communication). The metaphor of the theatre has long been important in Western thought, originating in ancient Greece. It became particularly important in Enlightenment ideas of 'public men' (Sennett 1996) coming together in 'public spheres' (Habermas 1989a), detached from the feminized private sphere. The public was seen as a space of performance, artifice and power, the private a space of authenticity and nurture. This idea has been challenged in contemporary critical thought. Gender is seen as being 'performed' (Butler 1997) in a world of panoptic surveillance (Foucault 1977a) in which we are never 'off stage'. That the theatrical metaphor has been reworked in each intellectual era is a testament to its adaptability.

The theatrical metaphor does not exhaust scene's resonances. As Alan Blum (2001) has shown, scene has rich connotations of the urban and of nightlife. John Irwin (1997) notes that the term can be used in two very different ways in everyday language. It can be used in the sense of 'that's not my scene', connoting vague notions of lifestyle. It can also mean something much more definite and located that connotes something 'subcultural'. However, the two senses of the term are not necessarily contradictory. They both connote something that is shared, something we choose whether or not to participate in. Scene can be both a public space and a more general way of living.

In recent years, scene has been used increasingly within studies of youth culture and popular music to connote the location for youth cultural and popular musical activity. Much of this use of scene, particularly in its less theorized forms, takes as its starting point a rejection of the competing concept of subculture. Inevitably then, an examination of the concept of scene involves a 'detour' through the extensive debates over subculture. Subculture is itself a concept with a complicated genealogy, ranging from Victorian studies of criminality to Parsonian systems theory (Gelder & Thornton 1997; Jenks 2005). According to the 'Chicago school' of sociology, subcultures are transient yet tight-knit groups that exist on the margins of 'acceptable' society. They are *sub*cultures owing both to their lowly status in social hierarchies and to the fact that they are smaller than 'communities' and other groups. Subcultures such as marijuana smokers and jazz musicians (Becker 1973) were seen as sharing a frame of reference that was distinct from that of the wider society, speaking and acting 'differently'.

The most extensively theorized definition of subculture was developed by the Birmingham Centre for Contemporary Cultural Studies (CCCS) in the 1970s. At the heart of CCCS subcultural theory was a Gramscian emphasis on subcultures as sites of counter-hegemonic resistance to dominant ideology. The contributors to Hall and Jefferson's collection *Resistance Through Rituals* (1976) argued that subcultures in post-war Britain emerged as collective responses to changes in the structure of capitalism. Through counter-hegemonic 'rituals', subcultures such as mods, bikers and skinheads 'give expressive form to their social and material life experience' (Hall & Jefferson 1976: 10). Subcultures used a variety of strategies, ranging from parody to outright aggression, to deal with the rapid changes sweeping post-war Britain. In this way, they 'penetrated' (Willis 1977) the contradictions of capitalism. However, in the end this penetration was always fleeting and doomed because it only occurred on the symbolic level, where it could easily be incorporated and deflected by dominant groups.

The subcultures studied by the CCCS theorists in the 1970s were seen as displaying distinctive and 'spectacular' 'styles'. Paul Willis (1978) developed the concept of 'homology', in order to describe the apparent 'fit' between style and subculture, arguing that the early rock and roll music preferred by the bikers he studied evoked feelings of relentless movement and fitted with the bikers' restless sexual energy. Dick Hebdige (Hebdige 1979) drew on semiotics to explain the relationship between style and subculture further. Subcultures assemble spectacular signs through 'bricolage' in a kind of 'semiotic guerrilla warfare'. Such strategies may be shocking, yet remain so only for a short period as fashions become incorporated into commercialized styles.

The CCCS conception of subculture has been subject to criticism for three decades. Such criticisms often focus on the narrowness of and exclusions inherent in the CCCS subculture studies. The CCCS concentrated on a narrowly defined version of subculture, in order to analyse a particularly tangible response to capitalist hegemony. Angela McRobbie (1991) criticized the gender imbalance in traditional accounts of subculture. Women have historically been less able to participate in the public sphere and their semiotic activities tend to take place in the home. It is possible that women were present in the subcultures that the CCCS studied, but were simply ignored (Miles 1998). Subcultural theory disparaged the activities of 'normal' working-class and middle-class people as completely incorporated and lacking in meaning (Clarke 1990). Subcultures that did not conform to strict notions of resistance, such as heavy metal (Brown 2003) were either disparaged or ignored.

Subcultural theory also assumed that subcultures were internally homogeneous. The assumption that subcultures are predominantly working class was never properly substantiated. Much (although not all) subcultural research was done without substantial contact with subcultural members themselves. Hebdige's study, for instance, is based purely on the scrutiny of media reports and the production of 'readings' from them. The subcultural members themselves are silent and lack any kind of reflexivity. They are 'read' as resistant, yet their own meanings are absent. Widdicombe and Wooffitt (1995) have shown that members of spectacular subcultures, while appearing to be implacably resistant, may construct their identities in ways that do not conform with subcultural theory. Their interviewees actively sought to resist the implication that they were members of a subculture, a finding partly replicated in my own research (Harris 1997). Furthermore, as David Muggleton (2000) shows, subcultural theory's focus on 'style' risks treating subculture members as superficial 'clothes-horses', without any sustained engagement or commitment to the social formations that they create. Subcultural theory's lack of empirical research ignores the ways in which subculture members may play with a number of styles over their lifetime, yet still be committed to the discursive construction of some sense of continuity and 'authenticity'.

Subcultural research took as its subject those who were 'other' to capitalism. Subcultures were the subject of 'moral panic' from the state and media (Cohen 1987). However, the concept also *produced* that otherness through a rigid conceptual framework that read members' activities as implacably resistant. Their interaction within 'everyday' society was only weakly explored, as subculture was assumed to be their primary context for interaction and identity formation. In fact, the otherness produced by media, state and academic constructions of subculture may be part of the process by which they are constituted (McRobbie & Thornton 1995). Constructions of subcultures as 'authentic' and resistant may collude with members' own constructions, designed to maximize prestige (Thornton 1995).

While few researchers use the CCCS concept of subculture these days, its legacy lives on. Even when researchers do not use the term subculture at all, traces of the CCCS concept may still appear. Donna Gaines (1990), for example, argues that teenagers in US suburbs are alienated and oppressed, and resist through such practices as listening to heavy metal and hardcore punk music. Researchers also frequently define the space that they are studying as subcultural, even if their use of the term is more loosely theorized than that of the CCCS. The concept of subculture has been applied in this way to rather banal analyses of heavy metal (Gross 1990) and teenage Satanism (Lowney 1995). The term subculture is also widely used in the media and in the public sphere, as Andy Bennett puts it: 'In introducing the term "subculture" into the wider public sphere, the media have completed the process begun in socio-logical work of reducing subculture to a convenient "catch all" term used to describe a range of disparate collective practices whose only obvious relation is that they all involve young people' (1999: 605).

There have been a few attempts to reclaim and re-theorize subculture. In his study of goth, Paul Hodkinson argues that the grouping produces 'subcultural substance', characterized by an intense, thick form of social organization whose key elements are 'identity, commitment, consistent distinctiveness and autonomy' (2002: 29).

However, increasingly subculture is treated as an outmoded concept, not simply for its theoretical inadequacies but also because of a prevailing view that, even if it was ever a useful concept, it is inapplicable to contemporary society. Contributors to a number of collections (Bennett & Kahn-Harris 2004; Redhead 1993, 1998; Skelton & Valentine 1998; Swiss, Sloop & Herman 1998) have emphasized the newness of subcultural, musical and popular cultural forms in the last two decades. Contemporary 'postmodern' society is characterized by such phenomena as: less commitment to membership of social groups; greater heterogeneity in society as a whole; increased possibilities for multiple social affiliations; the fragmentation of 'grand narratives'; increased globalization; growing job insecurity; greater choice of popular cultures; the multiplication of centres of power and surveillance; the blurring of the line between 'popular' and 'unpopular' cultures; and the blurring of the line between 'conservative' and 'resistant' cultures. Such changes make it hard to maintain any notion of subculture as a social formation with coherence, a firm class basis or a clear notion of resistance. It has been argued that we are now in a 'post-subcultural' era (Muggleton & Weinzierl 2003). As David Muggleton asserts: 'Post-subculturalists no longer have any sense of subcultural "authenticity", where inception is rooted in particular sociotemporal contexts and tied to underlying structural relations' (1998: 180).

Andy Bennett (1999) has suggested that in 'late modernity' identities and lifestyles are fluid and constructed rather than static and given. Bennett attempts to understand urban dance music as 'neo-tribe' rather than subculture, a term introduced by Michel Maffesoli (1996). Neo-tribes are based on eclectic and endlessly changing patterns of consumption. They are temporary, affective alliances based around temporarily shared sensibilities. They are not based on commitment or on shared political/discursive positionings, but on shared affect and shared experiences of the body as occurs, for example, in mass gatherings such as rock festivals.

It would be hard to imagine a concept less similar to subculture than neo-tribe. It highlights precisely those aspects of sociality that subculture ignores. Yet a 'neo-tribal' framework leaves out almost as much as a subcultural framework. For one thing, the concept is of little use as an analytical structure, since it is essentially a description of a form of sociality and affect that arises from such things as dancing in nightclubs and going on protest marches. There is a kind of reductive essentialism here that treats a disparate range of activities as essentially alike. This approach does not help us to understand why someone would go on a march rather than go dancing. Nor does it help us to understand the texts and institutions that particular social formations create. Advocates of the neo-tribal approach also overstate the extent to which culture has changed in recent decades. Certainly, the type of subcultures that the CCCS described may now be exceptional, and looser formations are now more common, yet this does not mean that subcultural forms do not still exist. Further, the neo-tribal approach does not take into account how the enduring quality of 'subcultural substance' (Hodkinson 2002) ensures that some formations are far from ephemeral and fleeting.

The concepts of both neo-tribe and subculture are highly restrictive. Neither recognizes the possibility that a variety of forms of involvement and interaction may coexist within a particular space. The challenge of holism is to retain the 'spatialness' that concepts such as subculture provide, without excluding any class of people or interaction by defining that space too strictly. We cannot, a priori, assume that 'casual' fans of extreme metal and those who deal with little else are two totally different classes of people. This may obscure close linkage between private, occasional and uncommitted consumption and public, intense and committed 'subcultural' practice. Those on the margins of groups that have been called subcultures may, in fact, have a crucial role to play in them (Fox 1987). It is true that, in the contemporary world, it may be possible to be a musical 'omnivore' (Carrabine & Longhurst 1999), participating in a number of musical cultures at once. However, this does not mean that musical cultures do not have an enduring quality of their own.

With subculture being largely rejected as a concept and with neo-tribe and other post-subcultural alternatives not yet in wide circulation, it is understandable that researchers, particularly in popular music culture, have looked to scene as an alternative. The advantage of scene is that it locates musical practices in specific spatial and temporal locations. The level of theorization of the concept varies dramatically. Sara Cohen (1991), for example, frequently referred to the 'Liverpool scene' in her groundbreaking study of music making in Liverpool, but does not extensively spell out what she means by the term. Scenes are often associated with specifically local contexts of music making, as in Barry Shank's study of the music scene in Austin, Texas (1994). Shank argues that: 'A scene itself can be defined as an overproductive signifying community; that is, far more semiotic information is produced than can be rationally passed (1994: 122). Shank's notion of scene has a certain amount in common with the idea of neo-tribe. He focuses on affect, the body and the way individuals lose themselves within a mass, albeit a transitory one. He argues that: 'These are the necessary conditions for the development of a scene: a situated mass of transformative signs and sweating bodies, continually reconstructing the meaning of a communion of individuals in a primary group' (1994: 128). Although in practice Shank concentrates on music makers and live performance, his emphasis on the circulation of signs allows his definition of scene to incorporate both production and reception. Shank also looks at the position of scenes within capitalist economics, arguing that scenes are born through a struggle between 'the fierce desire to remake oneself through musical practice, and the equally powerful struggle to affirm the value of that practice in the complexly structured late-capitalist marketplace' (1994: x). Shank's book marries a detailed look at the locally situated practices that constitute the Austin scene with an appreciation of the way scenes create affect, pleasure and identity. He appreciates both the enduring quality of scenes and their constant struggle and change. Yet Shank, despite acknowledging the issue in footnotes and asides, largely ignores the way local scenes relate to national and global scenes. Moreover, it is unclear how Shank would deal with music making that does not take place within the kind of local scene that he describes.

Holly Kruse has argued that scene implies 'something less stable and historically rooted than a "community"' and that this allows us to look at 'the relationship between situated music practices and the construction of identity' (1993: 38). She posits that scenes are 'connected rather abstractly through shared tastes . . . and quite concretely through social and economic networks' (1993: 36). Although her use of the concept is less theoretical than Shank's, she does attend to the issue of how scenes relate to other scenes. In the case of alternative music, she argues that local scenes link up with other local scenes to create trans-local scenes. A record label may be based in one particular town but have links with networks of labels in other towns. In this way, local and trans-local identities and histories coexist.

For Will Straw scenes are distinct from older notions of a 'musical community' (1991: 373). Whereas the latter are based on 'a population group whose composition is relatively stable . . . and whose involvement in music takes the form of an ongoing exploration of one or more musical idioms said to be rooted within a geographically specific historical heritage', a music scene is defined as: 'that cultural space in which a range of musical practices coexist, interacting with each other within a variety of processes of differentiation, and according to widely varying trajectories of change and cross-fertilisation' (1991: 373). Music scenes continually form temporary musical alliances, both locally and trans-locally, and these can produce senses of community. Straw analyses scenes according to their particular 'logics of change', driven by scene members' struggles for prestige, which occur within the context of larger processes of social change. Straw's paper is important in that it characterizes scenes as sites of heterogeneity and permanent change and he attempts to understand how different scenes relate trans-locally in his analysis of the alternative-rock and dance-music scenes. The 'logic' of alternative rock is that each local scene has a self-sustaining infrastructure, yet each local scene is musically similar to other local scenes. The logic of dance-music scenes is based to a far greater extent around autonomous local 'sounds'.

Mark Olson has criticized Straw for depicting scenes as 'merely empty vessels within which certain practices interact', without a 'productivity' of their own (1998: 271). Scenes, for Olson, are 'territorializing machines' (1998: 281) that are productive of particular kinds of relationship to geographic location. Scenes 'mobilize' people in peculiar ways, based on migrancy, pilgrimage and diaspora, creating new ways of belonging. Scenes such as that of Seattle, Washington are based 'not upon already being there, upon an arrival, but in terms of a common desire to be there, a common belonging to a trajectory of investment towards a particular place: a movement' (1998: 283). Scenes can never be stable; they are in permanent motion.

The concept of scene may also be used to attend to important issues of difference and exclusion. Scene may connote performance, but it does not necessarily connote public performance within an exclusive and bounded space. Sara Cohen (1997) has shown how the concept of the 'Liverpool scene' may be used to deconstruct its gendered nature. Using the work of Judith Butler, she shows how gender is 'enacted' in the Liverpool scene in ways that exclude or marginalize women. The scene concept may also be used to incorporate insights from research into feminized 'riot grrrl' scenes (Kearney 1997; Leonard 1997, 1998). Such scenes challenge conventional constructions of women in music and subculture. They do not denigrate the private sphere, they provide support and empowerment to young women struggling with their gender identity and they eschew many of the trappings of the music industry, such as 'stardom'.

The use of scene to describe a variety of musical spaces shows that the concept need not be based on predetermined ideas of what scenic involvement consists of. The heterogeneity of the use of the scene concept facilitates the spatiality and holism that I have argued a study of extreme metal music and culture requires. As Will Straw (2001) has argued, its anti-essentialism produces a fruitful ambiguity. In contrast, David Hesmondhalgh (2005) has argued that the concept has simply been used in too many, fundamentally contradictory ways for it to be useful and that its rootedness in everyday uses is not necessarily an advantage in social analysis. Furthermore, he rejects the search for a 'master concept' in the study of youth and popular music, which he identifies as motivating those who advocate the concept. To a certain extent this is a matter of personal preference, as one person's creative ambiguity is another's confusion. Yet I would argue that it is precisely the ambiguity of the concept that allows for it to be tailored to the specific conditions of the phenomenon to which it applies. The concept of scene allows researchers to produce work that is empirically grounded in specific contexts yet is open to connections with other pieces of research and to everyday language.

### Defining the Extreme Metal Scene

One of the fundamental issues with any spatial concept is the question of boundaries – who and what is 'inside' and 'outside'? Extreme metal practitioners apply the term scene to a huge variety of spaces, not always consistently and unanimously. Boundary-maintaining questions such as 'is this a scene?' or 'is this person a scene member?' may well be crucial aspects of extreme metal practice but can disable sociological analysis. Moreover, asking 'is this a scene?' obscures the essential constructedness of conceptual frameworks. The act of defining the scene must be inclusive and draw attention to the process of definition.

Let us make the initial assertion that *all* musical and music-related activity takes place within a scene or scenes. By asserting that everything takes place within a scene, the question 'is this a scene?' becomes redundant. The assertion also creates an inclusive scene, encompassing everything from tight-knit local musical communities to isolated musicians and occasional fans, all contributing to and feeding from a larger space(s) of musical practice. Even the simple action of buying a CD means to become 'involved' in the scene, in however slight a way, by virtue of causing some sort of effect within it. One cannot make a rigid distinction between 'active' and 'passive' membership. The nature of membership in the scene is a question that can only be resolved through research.

The consequence of this primary assertion is that everything within a scene may exist within a number of scenes. A musical text, for example, may circulate within a number of scenes at once. Texts and individuals may move through scenes on a variety of trajectories, as they also move along particular individual 'pathways' (Finnegan 1989). Similarly, it follows that scenes with varying degrees of autonomy may exist within other scenes. Scenes themselves are constantly shifting, splitting and combining – any coherence can only be temporary.

Scene has no privileged 'centre'; not local music making, not committed fans, not production, consumption or the texts themselves. No analysis of popular-music culture is entirely satisfactory without a holistic analysis of all these factors. At the same time, holism does not predetermine the interrelationship of the elements of the scene. The concept also allows for pragmatism and holism in its combination of a variety of theoretical perspectives. Scene is both an emergent feature of everyday interaction and a construct of the researcher. The scene concept is a fairly flexible sign, gathering several types of analysis together. Yet one cannot assume that different types of analysis are collapsible into each other – on the contrary, they may be incompatible. Therefore, one possible way of drawing connections between the incommensurable empirical and theoretical elements of the scene is to use the concept of homology. Homology connects two completely different 'things' by suggesting that they are similar, perhaps modelled on each other, yet entirely different. For example, the use of scene in everyday life and the use of scene by the researcher are homologous.

So what is the extreme metal scene? A 'map' of the extreme metal scene overlaps considerably with mappings of the genre of extreme metal, but is not confined to it. The extreme metal scene is a global music scene that contains local scenes within it. It also contains other scenes based on the production and consumption of particular forms of extreme metal genres, such as black metal and death metal. However, the considerable musical and institutional overlap between these scenes allows us to talk about the extreme metal scene as a totality. There is also considerable overlap between the scene and the heavy metal scene. This is particularly the case at the scene's less extreme margins where, for example, power metal is a hybrid of thrash and heavy metal. Above all, the extreme metal scene remains a part of a wider metal scene that contains a wide variety of metal styles, such as heavy metal. Although metal has fragmented, different metal scenes still have much in common (Roccor 2000).

The extreme metal scene also relates in complicated ways to other music scenes. As I mentioned in the introductory chapter, hardcore punk has been important in the development of extreme metal. There is considerable overlap between the harder elements of punk and some elements of extreme metal. Indeed, there is an entire genre, metalcore, based on the cross-fertilization between the two scenes. Despite this, the two scenes remain distinct. The same is true with the relationship to goth. While goth has proved a considerable influence on elements of extreme metal in the 1990s and beyond, members of the goth scene are generally highly ambivalent about this development and seek to maintain their distinctiveness (Hodkinson 2002). Other scenes that also have a productive relationship with the extreme metal scene include the industrial scene and elements of hardcore dance music.

### Mapping the Extreme Metal Scene

A holistic approach necessitates that judgement be reserved on the relative importance of particular features of the scene. A mode of investigation is required that avoids isolating features of the scene as separate 'topics' (music, social practices, etc.), without losing all analytic purchase through collapsing everything into everything else. Holism is not produced through a 'complete' study of the scene – something that is, of course, impossible – but through a process of 'mapping' by which we become aware of what we do and do not know about the scene.

While, as I noted in the previous chapter, my interest in extreme metal goes back a long way, my most intensive period of research took place between 1997 and 2000 during which I conducted my PhD fieldwork. During this major fieldwork period I conducted interviews and collected extreme metal musical and other texts. From an early stage in the process I defined myself as an ethnographer. Ethnography attempts to engage with the lives of members as they are lived out in all their complexity. Although I had casual dealings with the scene previously, I wished to develop a much closer relationship. My attempt to do this was facilitated when in early 1997 I wrote to Nick Terry, then editor of the British extreme metal magazine *Terrorizer*, asking whether we could meet to discuss my research. In the course of our meeting, he offered me the chance to write for the magazine. As a result, I began to be exposed to a large amount of music that I would not otherwise have heard and this exposure changed many of my ideas about extreme metal and the scene. Through writing for the magazine I got an inside look at the workings of an important scenic institution and got to know a range of scene members at concerts and other events. In addition to this process of ethnography, I also conducted semi-structured interviews with about fifty scene members in order to ask the kinds of questions that do not arise in everyday interaction within the scene.

In order to investigate the workings of the scene in more detail, I focused my research on particular case study areas. National and local difference is a key topic within the global scene and members often discuss the nature of local 'sounds' and scenes. In my main fieldwork period I concentrated on Israel, Sweden and the United Kingdom. Clearly, the UK was a convenient case-study area and writing for *Terrorizer* inevitably made my choice for me. Further, the UK has had an important historical role in the development of extreme metal and a number of important scenic institutions are based in the country. Israel and Sweden are countries that are similar in terms of population size, albeit in vastly different geopolitical circumstances, and were chosen to provide two extremes for comparative purposes. Israel has a small extreme metal scene and only a few of its bands are known within the global scene. It is also a country with considerable social, political and cultural conflict. The Swedish scene, conversely, is one of the most productive and well known in the world, within a stable prosperous country. In extreme metal terms the UK scene comes somewhere between Israel and Sweden. It has produced many important extreme metal acts, but in the 1990s the size of the scene has declined and the scene contains fewer extreme metal bands and fans than formerly.

Each country itself contains a number of local scenes, necessitating further case studies. Deciding which of these to cover was least difficult in Israel, where the size of the scene enabled me to contact almost every band in the country. At the time of my research in Israel the scene was concentrated in Jerusalem and the Tel Aviv area. In Sweden I conducted case studies in Gothenburg and Stockholm, cities that have strong local scenes producing extremely distinctive music. The difference between these scenes provided the core of the case study. In the UK I conducted interviews in the South-East and London, from Brighton up as far as East Anglia, however my work for *Terrorizer* meant that I knew a considerable amount about the scene throughout the country. Within each case-study area I tried to interview a reasonable balance of fans, bands (of varying degrees of success and of different genres), record labels (large and small), fanzines and distributors. I also made an effort to look for minority groups within the scene, interviewing a number of women (who are often marginalized within the scene) as well as seeking out Christians, homosexuals and ethnic minorities.

The principal case-study areas were by no means the only sources of information in this research. Given its importance in the global scene, I also made a special effort to investigate the US metal scene, conducting a small number of further interviews, as well as taking a particular interest in reports and articles on scenes in the developing world. I also collected fanzines, CDs and demos from throughout the global scene. In order to explore the parameters of the scene, I actively sought out recordings and fanzines with unusual features or from unexpected sources, such as a demo tape from Pakistan. The Internet also allows for a more global perspective on the scene.

Relating to the Extreme Metal Scene

Ethnographic sociological research inevitably involves complicated questions about how to relate to those who are the subjects of research. Becoming a writer for a well-respected scenic publication made these issues even more complex and ambiguous. In writing for the magazine I held a position of power within the scene and gained 'subcultural capital' (Thornton 1995; see also Chapter 6). This helped give me access to those who might otherwise have been hard to reach, particularly the more famous bands. A number of interviewees specified that they had only consented to be interviewed because I wrote for *Terrorizer*. Often, it was unclear how far interviewees understood the purposes for which I was speaking to them. On occasions, band members looked to me to review and publicize their music in the magazine – something that I was not always able to do.

At the heart of the problem of writing for *Terrorizer* was the issue of how far to become an 'insider' within the scene (Hodkinson 2002). I was frequently treated by interviewees as a fellow scene member and often recorded comments such as 'you're a metaller, you know what it's like'. Furthermore, in my life outside the scene, my choice of PhD topic often marked me out as a part of the scene. Certainly, taking part in the life of the scene was often exhilarating. I met and enjoyed the company of people I would otherwise not have met, enjoyed music I otherwise would not have heard and came to know some of the pleasures of 'belonging' to the scene. However, I was ambivalent about this membership. Politically, I found certain elements of the scene very hard to accept, such as casual sexism, homophobia and racism. On one occasion, a member of an English black metal band told a 'humorous' anecdote about how his bandmate pursued some 'Jew-boys' down the street with a pig's head. Such incidents were uncommon, but they were enough to make me uncomfortable.

The response I chose in such cases was to stay neutral, neither approving nor condemning. The problems with such a response are acute, as my supposed 'neutrality' could actually reinforce prejudices by allowing silences to be read as approval (Griffin 1991). However, my own capacity to change deep-rooted patterns of thought and behaviour was not great. Upbraiding people would have jeopardized my access within the scene and might have provoked confrontation with the more extreme members of the scene. I also believe strongly that respect for the subjects of research applies equally to people of all views. Interviews, in their suspension of the 'normal' rules of interaction, force the interviewer, who may normally wish to challenge the interviewee, actually to listen to the voice of the 'other'. For all its dangers, a temporary suspension of moral evaluation during the interview is a strategy more amenable to sociological understanding (Jackson 1987).

While I may have suspended judgement at times in my interactions with scene members, such judgements are certainly not suspended in this book. Indeed, as I stated in the introduction, this book actively seeks to make value judgements about the extreme metal scene. The aim is to develop a 'critical' perspective on the scene, based on an awareness of dominating practices and power relations within the scene. Power is a crucial issue in this book. Power is an inevitable part of capitalist modernity, but it can also be negotiated, used, abused and resisted. As will be seen, the particular ways in which power works within the scene constitutes the scene's politics. In examining power and politics, this book attempts to provoke debate about the scene, both inside and outside it. An unflinching look at the problems of the scene is combined with an equally searching look for the positives and potentials nested within the negatives.

Even if this book attempts to offer a sober, politically sensitive response to the scene, the best intentions of writers are often subverted. There is much about the scene that is shocking and worrying to those who are not scene members. Given the history of attacks on and censorship of metal, there is always the possibility that this book may be misused by those with a less subtle agenda. While I do not censor myself when writing about the more problematic aspects of the scene, I also attempt to show how the more exotic and offensive practices of the scene take place within the context of the mundanity of everyday life. I have tried to appreciate how the scene fits into the complexities and ambiguities of people's lives. Further, I have actively tried to search for change and heterogeneity in the scene. Most accounts of metal, however well intentioned, seem to ignore the diversity and fluidity of metal. This book will not seek to elevate extreme metal artistically or reify its culture, but to recover its complexity in a world that tends to ignore it.

## Fear of Metal

Metal has historically provoked strong reactions. The 1980s heavy metal scene was noteworthy for the sustained attention it attracted in the USA, where it was a bête noire for the 'religious right' (Miller 1988; Walser 1993; Weinstein 2000). A classic 'moral panic' (Cohen 1987) developed around heavy metal, stimulated by powerful political groups that saw it as a dangerous influence on the nation's youth. The Parents' Musical Resource Center (PMRC), founded in the early 1980s, sought to provide 'information' about the dangers posed to young people by certain forms of music, and rap and metal in particular (Chastagner 1999). In 1985 the PMRC's influence on the political process culminated in a series of senate hearings, to which a number of heavy metal musicians were called to give evidence. This inquiry resulted in the music industry being pressurized into putting labels on records warning of 'offensive' lyrical content.

The strongest charge made against heavy metal was that it caused murder and suicide. In a number of US murder trials, heavy metal was cited as the 'cause' and, on occasion, being under the influence of heavy metal was accepted as a 'diminished-responsibility' defence in criminal trials (Richardson 1991). Christian groups claimed that subliminal messages and 'backwards messages' on heavy metal recordings could lead impressionable young people to murder and suicide. In 1990, the band Judas Priest were unsuccessfully sued for causing the suicide of two young men from Reno, Nevada, through the placing of backwards messages on their 1978 album *Stained Class*. Such attacks, based on flimsy evidence, have not gone away. The documentary film *Paradise Lost* records how in 1993, an interest in metal led to 3 young men (the so-called 'West Memphis 3') being convicted on dubious grounds of the murders of three eight-year-old boys.[2]

Attacks on heavy metal did not come only from right-wing groups with links to powerful authorities. Heavy metal was also the focus of considerable anxiety in more liberal quarters. Jeffrey Arnett's book *Metalheads* (1995) was written in response to liberal worries about heavy metal. Whereas right-wing groups saw heavy metal music as inherently dangerous, Arnett suggested that heavy metal was a symptom of a disturbing alienation among US youth. While Arnett's conclusions do not lead him to recommend censorship, his work still represents a view held widely by both left- and right-wing observers – that heavy metal cannot in and of itself be worthwhile.

Much of the pressure on metal eased in the 1990s. Furthermore, as it is more obscure than more mainstream forms of metal, extreme metal has always escaped much of the attention. However, there have been some notable exceptions. The 1998 Norwegian documentary *Satan Rides the Media* shows how a classic moral panic developed in Norway during the spate of murders and church burnings committed by black metallers in that country in the early 1990s. Cloonan (1996) has recounted some attempts to censor death metal in the United Kingdom. In 1991 Nottingham's Earache Records had stock seized by police in an ultimately unsuccessful attempt to prosecute the label for obscenity. In the same year customs officials tried unsuccessfully to prevent Oxford's Plastic Head Distribution from importing the album *Like an Ever Flowing Stream* (1991) by the Swedish band Dismember. Isolated incidents of this kind have occurred throughout the world, although none have been given a high profile by the media. For example, the US band Cannibal Corpse had to produce 'censored' versions of their cover art in order for their albums to be stocked in various countries. The Christian right has occasionally and erratically attacked extreme metal. For example, one Christian schoolteacher in Germany made a concerted attempt to ban Cannibal Corpse from playing certain venues during their 1995 tour. In 1996, in a speech that received some media coverage, US presidential candidate Bob Dole attacked Cannibal Corpse as part of a general attack on the media. The attack rebounded when Dole admitted he had never heard the band. In 1999, presidential candidate Gary Bauer attacked a number of 'anti-Catholic' artists, including 'the homosexual music group Rotting Christ'. Rotting Christ is a Greek black metal band with no known connections to homosexuality.

In countries more marginal to the global scene, attacks on extreme metal may have more serious consequences. A number of Israeli scene members have complained of police investigations and surveillance following press articles accusing black metallers of being Nazis and of sacrificing animals. The most serious attack on extreme metal occurred in Egypt in 1997 (Swedenburg 2000). A large group of middle- and upper-class Egyptian young people were arrested under blasphemy laws and accused of devil worship after extreme and heavy metal recordings were found in their homes. Most were released fairly quickly, but potentially they faced heavy sentences. The arrests were the product of a cultural war between Islamic hardliners and the more Westernized sectors of Egyptian society (di Giovanni 1997). There have also been instances of censorship of metal in Syria (www.freemuse.org/sw9020.asp; accessed November 2005) and other Islamic countries (see Chapter 5). More generally, in authoritarian countries that attempt to create an 'official' musical culture, metal can be treated with official disapproval, as in the case of Cuba (Roach 1999).

Extreme metal's relative obscurity undoubtedly affords it a good deal of 'protection' from attacks and censorship. However, the vehemence of attacks when extreme metal is exposed, together with the notoriety that heavy metal has attracted despite producing much less extreme material, shows that extreme metal is still shocking, worrying stuff. In the rest of this chapter I want to look at what is extreme, shocking and worrying about extreme metal.

## Transgression

What is 'extreme' about extreme metal? Extremity has become a ubiquitous and vague concept in contemporary popular culture. The term extreme is widely used in the scene as a term of approbation and a vague way of delineating death metal, black metal, grindcore and other metal genres as special. In this chapter, the much more rigorous concept of 'transgression' will be used as a way of analysing what is extreme about the scene.

Transgression, like extremity, implies a sense of testing and crossing boundaries and limits. For structuralists, such as Mary Douglas (1984), binary oppositions such as good–bad, pure–impure, moral–immoral, clean–unclean structure our world and the boundaries between these oppositions are the source of anxiety. Yet at the same time, structuralists have argued that there is a constant desire to transgress boundaries as well as to protect them. In traditional societies, such transgression may be ritualized, for example in initiation practices in which initiates retreat for a time from the everyday, ordered world, before returning to that world with a new status. Similarly, Bakhtin (1984) and Stallybrass and White (1986) show how in the medieval carnival, the everyday order was turned upside down, for example in the practice of crowning the village fool 'king'. Victor Turner (1974) has shown how, through highlighting the artificiality of boundaries, 'liminal', transgressive practice allows people to escape power and authority, if only for a time. Even if transgression has always been the source of concern to authorities, it always had a place in pre-modern societies, if only for short periods of time. In contrast, in modernity, as Jervis (1999) argues, transgressive practice has increasingly been legislated against and marginalized.

Ultimately, transgression is dangerous. Georges Bataille (1985, 1993) emphasized transgression's engagement with mortality and eroticism. Transgression involves the embrace of carnality, allowing humans to 'lose themselves' in the 'totality' – the infinity of death. Ironically, only through losing themselves in the totality can humans experience 'sovereignty' over their being, escaping everyday utilitarian considerations. Transgression both dissolves and affirms being. As Foucault (1977b: 30–52) argued, it sets 'limits' even as it challenges others. The intimate relationship between the practice of transgression and the practice of setting limits can be seen in the ambivalence with which transgressive practice treats the 'abject' (Kristeva 1982). The abject is that which is formless, disgusting, terrifying and threatening. Abjection is associated with 'vile' bodily fluids, but may be displaced elsewhere: to women, to Jews, to animals, etc. The abject has to be removed from orderly society and/or destroyed. At the same time, as Stallybrass and White argue, 'disgust always bears the imprint of desire' (1986: 191). As Kristeva argues, the abject is deeply alluring, based on a desire to return to the primal formlessness of the mother–child union. This desire may be intolerable, particularly for men in societies that emphasize the importance of self-control over the body (Theweleit 1987). Consequently, transgressive behaviour, while it revels in the abject, may also displace abjection elsewhere to loathed 'others'. Nonetheless, 'edgework' (Jenks 1998), transgressive practice that occurs on the edge of acceptability, at the edge of society, still excites and fascinates.

This is all rather heady stuff! Much of the literature on transgression is based on the assumption that everyone would want to indulge in transgressive behaviour. Whether or not this is a reasonable assumption is a matter for debate. What is not in doubt is that the transgressive is an important category of human experience. Further, the concept of transgression captures the central elements of the extreme metal practices that I will describe in this chapter: they are excessive, testing and breaking boundaries, invoking the joys and terrors of formless oblivion within the collective, while simultaneously bolstering feelings of individual control and potency. In the next section I will present three 'ideal types' of scenic transgression: 'sonic transgression', 'discursive transgression' and 'bodily transgression'.

### Types of Transgression

### Sonic Transgression[3]

Walser (1993) has argued that heavy metal music is based on a dialectical relationship between musical 'freedom' (embodied in the guitar solo) and 'control' (embodied in the 'riff'). He shows how the music explores a wide and complex set of themes, drawing on a complex set of sources, including Western classical music (particularly baroque) and the blues. Heavy metal, for all the outrage it attracted in the 1980s, was musically at least strongly connected to the mainstream of Western music, producing a kind of 'cross-cultural', iconoclastic dialogue.

The history of extreme metal music represents a radical and systematic process of removing metal from this kind of cultural dialogue. The blues roots of metal are virtually imperceptible in extreme metal. Additionally, the connection with baroque music has been weakened (although not severed) as the importance of guitar solos has declined. While, as we shall see in Chapter 6, extreme metal has increasingly reinstituted a dialogue with a number of other kinds of music, the principal musical trajectory of the scene in its formative period in the 1980s was to close itself off in a self-conscious attempt to explore the radical potential of metal. Extreme metal has transgressed a number of musical boundaries that were only gingerly explored in heavy metal and even then were 'leavened' by heavy metal's more conventional aspects. Extreme metal represents a systematic 'musical deterritorialization of musical conventions' (Bogue 2004b: 114), producing ' . . . an aggressive sonic machine of destruction, an electronic, nonhuman sound shredder' (Bogue 2004a: 91).

Extreme metal may sound unmusical and unpleasant to its detractors. Indeed, its sounds have allegedly been used in 'soft torture' by the US military (Weinstein In Press). Some of the music's initiators in the early 1980s such as Hellhammer and Venom, had a very low level of technical proficiency. Yet extreme metal rapidly developed in complexity so that today its apparent unmusicality is the product of carefully made sonic choices and even virtuosity (Rodel 2004). Far from being a chaotic noise, extreme metal systematically offers transgressive alternatives to the principal elements of Western music:

*Modes*   Modes are eight-note, one-octave scales featuring particular arrangements of tones and semitones. Walser points out that: 'Most heavy metal is either Aeolian or Dorian, for example, although Speed Metal is usually Phrygian or Locrian; most pop songs are either major (Ionian) or Mixolydian' (1993: 46). Extreme metal, of which speed or thrash metal is a constituent part, is also dominated by the Phrygian and Locrian modes. The significance of this is that certain modes have long had particular associations and connotations, with the Phrygian and Locrian seen to have the 'darkest' sounds. Both Phrygian and Locrian are used sparingly in Western music. The Phrygian is associated with oriental musics, such as flamenco. The Locrian is the only mode to contain a flattened fifth – the so-called 'tritone'. Famously, the use of this interval was discouraged by the medieval Catholic Church and referred to as the *diabolus in musica*. Ever since, the tritone has been employed in classical music to signify evil and danger (for example, in Mussorgsky's *St John's Night on the Bare Mountain* (1867)). As Philip Tagg points out (1998), the tritone has also been used extensively in the music for detective and adventure films (a notable example being the main theme for the *Pink Panther* films of the 1960s–80s). Where extreme metal appears to differ from such musics is that it 'lightens' these modes to a far lesser extent. In detective-film music, for example, a 'bluesy' flattened third is frequently added to the Locrian to create a 'burlesque' feel. Extreme metal represents a sustained and austere exploration of 'darker' modes that have long been associated with danger and evil.

*Guitars*   The distorted guitar has always been the key signifier of metal. As Walser argues: 'distortion functions as a sign of extreme power and intense expression by overflowing its channels and materialising the exceptional effort that produces it' (1993: 42). In heavy metal the oppressive dominance of distorted guitar is leavened by the liberating guitar solo, thereby producing what he understands as the dialectic of freedom and control. Similarly, Steve Waksman (2001) shows how hard rock and heavy metal guitars produce a sense of 'phallic mastery' but one that always threatens to break down. In contrast, extreme metal aims for total mastery and total control.

In extreme metal, solos take on a diminished importance – they are briefer and indeed some bands never use them – and sequences of guitar chords, or 'riffs', take on an even greater importance. Extreme metal guitarists tend to use one- or two-note 'power chords' and prevent the other strings sounding through the technique of 'palm muting'. Combined with overdriven vocals and frequent bursts of speed, there is little to detract from the 'wall' of guitar noise.

One common metal guitar technique is downtuning, in which the pitch of the guitar is lowered by one or two steps. Extreme metal bands have taken downtuning to extremes, with the bottom E string often tuned as low as B or A. This level of downtuning requires the use of a heavier string gauge, together with specialist amplification and production techniques. Different extreme metal sounds are put together in different ways. Some may be based on extremely 'clear', compressed but still heavily distorted sounds, such as the famous 'Florida sound' of death metal, developed in the late 1980s at Morrissound Studios, Tampa, by the producer Scott Burns with bands such as Deicide and Obituary. During the same period Thomas Skogsberg of Sunlight Studios, Stockholm, pioneered a totally different death metal guitar sound with bands such as Entombed and Dismember. The 'Sunlight sound' utilized extremely downtuned guitars with a far 'fuzzier' form of distortion. This sound was characterized by its lack of clarity even to the extent that it can be difficult to hear chord changes. Black metal guitars are generally not downtuned and are often played at a higher register and produced with considerable treble. When played fast, this trebly sound can be highly indistinct. Yet, no matter how indistinct extreme metal guitars may sound, uncontrolled feedback rarely appears.

*Vocals*   Heavy metal vocalists employ forms of vocal distortion. As Walser explains, 'Heavy metal vocalists project brightness and power by overdriving their voices (or by seeming to), and they also sing long sustained notes to suggest intensity and power; sometimes heavy vibrato is used for further intensification' (1993: 45). Extreme metal voices are also overdriven, but vocalists generally do not use sustain or vibrato, neither is there any 'brightness' in their vocals. Extreme metal takes vocal distortion further than heavy metal by abandoning practically all elements of melody in the voice. Instead, vocals are screamed or growled in ways that generally make lyrics impossible to decipher without the aid of a lyric sheet. There are a variety of vocal styles. Generally speaking, death metal bands use growled vocals and black metal bands use screamed vocals. Vocals may also be semi-spoken, chanted or simply shouted.

*Rhythm and Tempo*   Most forms of extreme metal appear to stick to basic 4–4 time, but some forms employ greater rhythmic complexity. Some forms of death metal and grindcore have incorporated unusual time signatures and jazz influences. Whatever the time signature, extreme metal drumming is often exceedingly complex. Drummers often play intricate patterns using double-bass drums and generally make more use of the whole kit than heavy metal drummers do.

Tempo is one of the most transgressive elements of extreme metal. Songs often range between 150 and 250 beats per minute (BPM). Extreme metal bands also pioneered the 'blast beat', drumming at 300–400 BPM and above. With blast beats and other fast tempos, the drummer is generally restricted to simple bass–snare–hi-hat sequences. The tempo of the guitars may not necessarily match that of the drums. Often, guitars play to a more reasonable tempo, while the drummer plays blast beats. Conversely, guitarists may play 'tremolo' riffs of 500–600 BPM while the drummer plays at slower tempos. The use of tempos of 200 BPM and above can create an odd effect of stasis in the music. This paradoxical stasis, together with the simultaneous combination of fast and slow tempos on drums and guitar, can make the music seem both fast and slow. Indeed, slowness can itself be practised to extreme degrees in some forms of doom metal.

*Songwriting* Walser argues that 'melody is relatively less important in metal than in many other kinds of music' (1993: 50). However, heavy metal still retains recognizable melodic structures, particularly in the vocals. In extreme metal, any conventional sense of melody is almost completely jettisoned. Instead, songs are put together from sequences of riffs that are often only tenuously connected to each other harmonically or modally (Bjornberg 1996). Songs may be punctuated by sudden changes in tempo and time signature. Song structures frequently eschew conventional verse–chorus–verse forms. Themes may be introduced once and never recapitulated, meaning that songs may lack a sense of progression from start to finish. This can create an unsettled sound, lacking the conventional forms of closure and cadence common in popular music (McClary 1991). In some forms of extreme metal, songs may appear to be little more than an arbitrary collection of riffs. Yet extreme metal songs are not put together arbitrarily. Indeed, musicians within the scene take songwriting very seriously.

Not all forms of extreme metal practise all these forms of sonic transgression. For example, in the 1990s some forms of black metal and doom metal began to employ keyboards and melodic vocals. Furthermore, the ways in which sonic transgression has been practised have changed throughout the history of the scene. For example, in the 1980s there was a far greater emphasis on fast tempos than today. Nevertheless, all forms of extreme metal are predicated on a commitment to practise at least some kind of sonic transgression, in the process producing extremity.

At the same time, the scene has strict limits on the boundaries of sonic transgression. For all its exploration of transgressive sounds, the scene constantly emphasizes musical control. Extreme metal bands almost never improvise on stage and strictly control guitar feedback. They also set strict limits on the use of solos, never letting them dominate the songs themselves. The extent to which extreme metal has excluded the African American musical influences of metal is striking. Not only is there virtually no detectable blues element in the music, there is a near-total absence of syncopation and other rhythms common in forms of funk, soul and other African American influenced dance music. As we will see in Chapter 7, those bands that have incorporated the aforementioned forms of music, such as nu metal bands, are often strongly criticized. The partial exception to this is jazz, which is sometimes incorporated by the more 'technical' death metal and grindcore groups. However, the jazz forms that are incorporated tend to be more 'intellectual', free jazz rather than forms more closely associated with Afro-Americans. Intriguingly, the renowned free jazz musician John Zorn has collaborated with grindcore drummer Mick Harris in the band Painkiller.

Simon Reynolds and Joy Press (1995) have identified fear of and attraction to the abject as a crucial theme in rock music. In extreme metal the abject is identified with musical forms that appear uncontrolled, limitless and are associated with the feminized body. Feedback, syncopation, excessive guitar solos and melody are all abjectified and have to be tightly controlled. As we have seen, Walser argues that the musical dialectic between freedom and control is a key theme in heavy metal. Extreme metal reduces musical freedom still further, until it appears only in order that it can be controlled. Extreme metal often sounds close to being a formless noise, but backs away from doing so at the last moment. Of course, as Jacques Attali (1985) argues, all music is simply a form of socially organized noise. If noise were to become 'formless', it would cease to have any kind of social organization. This constant flirtation with the formless sonic abject produces dominance of the abject. In doing so, extreme metal is associated with a form of masculinity that is based on a fear of feminine weakness. The 'musical fundamentalism' that Deena Weinstein identifies in extreme metal can be seen in its strict discipline, and its obsessiveness. The abject cannot simply be controlled once; dominance has to be proven again and again. This obsessiveness produced extreme metal as its logical conclusion and produces thousands of identical-sounding recordings to this day.

Discursive Transgression

The extreme metal scene produces an enormous amount of non-musical discourse through a variety of media: lyrics, song titles, fanzines and other publications, record sleeves, band names and, of course, everyday talk. Transgressive discourses are repeatedly reproduced in these different media. Once again, there are continuities with the forms of transgression practised in heavy metal. Walser defends heavy metal's preoccupation with violence, the occult and other 'dark' themes, arguing: 'In their free appropriation of symbols of power, and in their material enactments of control, of hanging on in the face of frightening complexity . . . heavy metal bands suggest to many that survival in the modern world is possible, that disruptions, no matter how unsettling, can be ridden out and endured . . .' (1993: 159). Walser acknowledges that metal deals with dark fantasies, but posits that those fantasies 'stand for' certain very real problems in capitalist society and that, by controlling those unsettling fantasies, an element of empowerment and control over the threats of the modern world can be assured. This argument, also advanced in a different way by Harris

Berger (1999b), depends on a sympathetic reading of heavy metal texts and fantasies as attempts to deal with contemporary anxieties in complex, coded ways. This kind of reading is not difficult, given that heavy metal texts tend to have a somewhat overblown quality that marks them out as fantastic. Extreme metal texts, however, frequently revel in fantasies that are far more sinister.

Consider, for example, the controversial association between heavy metal and suicide. In the 1980s Ozzy Osbourne's song 'Suicide Solution' (off *Blizzard Of Oz* (1980)) was attacked for promoting and encouraging suicide and he himself was attacked as a supposed Satanist. Walser's analysis of the song (1993: 148–50) finds it to be a more complex meditation on depression and self-destruction. Now, look at an extreme metal song that talks of suicide, 'Sacrificial Suicide', from the eponymous album by the US death metal band Deicide (1990). The song contains the lines:

> Damned to hell, end my life
> Wrath of God – Satan
> Sin my soul blessed with fire
> Throne of stone – Satan
> I must die, in my wake
> Seventh gate – Satan
> Suicide, end my life
> I must die – Satan

The lyrics are explicitly satanic and explicitly glorify suicide. The lyrics are accompanied by Deicide's fast and dense form of death metal, which contains no levity or possibility for ironizing the lyrics (as Walser argues occurs in 'Suicide Solution'). The vocalist of Deicide, Glen Benton has consistently proclaimed his uncompromising Satanism over the years and he has an inverted cross branded on his forehead. At one time, the band even claimed to have made a pact to commit suicide when they reached a certain age.

Whereas heavy metal may have played with such themes, in extreme metal they are made much more vivid and unambiguous. Death, killing and mutilation provide a constant source of inspiration within the scene, particularly, of course, in death metal. The names of the bands themselves are an indicator of this: Cannibal Corpse, Death, Dismember, Obituary, etc. Album titles speak for themselves – *Butchered at Birth, Scream Bloody Gore, Cause of Death*, etc. – and album covers often depict scenes of torture and suffering. Some death metal and grindcore bands use the destruction of the body as their major lyrical resource. For example, the lyrics of the (now defunct) British band Carcass are a catalogue of bizarre and disgusting things that can happen to the human body. They are often lengthy and use extremely explicit medical terminology. The following example is a verse from the song 'Cadaveric Incubator of Endo-Parasites', from the album *Symphonies of Sickness* (1989):

> The inset [*sic*] of rigor mortis, ulcerous corruption and decay
> Saponified fats lather as soap as you slowly eat yourself away . . .
> Organs savaged by rotten enzymes, rennin and rancorous cysts
> A festering abcess [*sic*] immersed in ravenous autolysis . . .

As Reynolds and Press suggest, such lyrics treat the body and its manifold constituents as ludicrous and revolting but endlessly fascinating. They are 'a testament to the threat and the almost voluptuous allure posed by the abject' (1995: 95).

Abjection is a key theme in extreme metal lyrics, but the way Carcass treat the abject is relatively rare. More commonly, the abject is something that has to be mastered and dominated. One extreme example of this dominance is found in the early lyrics of the US death metal band Cannibal Corpse (discussed in more detail in Kahn-Harris 2003). The following extract comes from the song 'Fucked with a Knife', from their album *The Bleeding* (1994) (see Figure 3):

> Tied tight to the bed
> Legs spread open
> Bruised flesh, lacerations
> Skin stained with blood
> I'm the only one you love
> I feel her heart beating
> My knife deep inside

Unlike the Carcass lyric, in which the gender of the body that is being destroyed and the agency by which it is destroyed is unknown, this lyric dwells on the ability of a male protagonist to control and conquer a subject female 'other'. Such explicit descriptions of sexual violence are extremely rare in popular music and virtually unknown in heavy metal. In death metal they are also relatively uncommon and they only represent part of Cannibal Corpse's work (and their earlier work, at that). Yet this lyric represents two crucial traits of extreme metal discourse. One is an obsession with fantasies of control. The other is the unflinchingly explicit way in which violence is described. Like Carcass, Cannibal Corpse demonstrate one of the ways in which extreme metal discourse has systematically transgressed the boundaries of 'the acceptable' in art.

Walser suggests that heavy metal is ultimately empowering and acts as a form of social criticism. Conversely, extreme metal appears to offer no possibility of hope or redemption. Doom metal bands have long dwelt on the inevitability of mortality and decay. Nick Terry (1998) has argued that extreme metal and hardcore in the 1990s are characterized by an obsession with the apocalypse and millenarianism. War, particularly nuclear war, has long been an obsession in all forms of metal. Some bands, such as the British band Bolt Thrower display a detailed knowledge of military tactics and technology. Bullet belts and other military paraphernalia have long

3: The cover of Cannibal Corpse's *The Bleeding*. Reproduced with the kind permission of Metal Blade Records.

been associated with metal fashion. Many bands have shown an interest in swords and some wield them on stage.

Extreme metal also continues heavy metal's interest in Satanism and the occult. A fascination with the devil has been a feature of rock and roll, from Robert Johnson to the Rolling Stones (Baddeley 1999). From its inception, heavy metal was closely associated with the occult, with Black Sabbath's lyrics in particular dwelling on such themes. Walser treats the fascination with the occult in 1980s heavy metal as part of an eclectic, postmodern use of symbols from a variety of ancient cultures. He suggests, rightly in my opinion, that it is misplaced to ask whether 1980s metallers were 'really' Satanists as occult themes were simply a powerful resource for song-writing. However, the extreme metal scene is characterized by a far more sustained engagement with occult ideas. Whereas heavy metal musicians generally denied being Satanists or tried to evade the question, some extreme metal musicians claim to be committed Satanists. Early extreme metal bands, such as Venom, were fascinated by the occult, but for the most part the scene avoided wholeheartedly embracing its philosophy or practice. This changed in the early 1990s when the black metal scene emerged.

Lyrically, many black metal bands have been unambiguous in their commitment to Satanism. Consider the first verse of the eponymous title track from the Swedish band Dark Funeral's *The Secrets of the Black Arts* (1996):

> Lucifer
> Show me the secrets enshrined
> The hidden source of eternal wisdom
> That dwells within the abyss
> Infernal majesty
> Guide me in my eternal search
> Lead me to the ancient empire
> Of dark treasures that once were lost

Black metal is often treated as a kind of ritualistic medium for personal transformation. As one Israeli black metaller explained to me:

> When you play black metal you don't play it like you were a human . . . no no no, you play it like you're a warrior. (Raffi[4])

To this end, black metallers often wear warrior-like clothing, such as armour, bullet belts and swords (see Figure 4). To create a sense of the inhuman, some black metallers don 'corpse paint', painting the face white, with dark black rings about the eyes and mouth. Black metallers also draw on other symbols such as the inverted cross, the pentagram and the baphomet (goat's head). Pseudonyms are also popular. The 'infernal names' that Anton LaVey (1969) lists in *The Satanic Bible* are particularly popular: Ahriman, Euronymous and Fenriz have all been used as pseudonyms; Azazel, Behemoth and Marduk have all been band names.

Black metallers have also articulated an ideology of black metal, which is less a coherent doctrine than a common set of reference points (Kahn-Harris 2005). One belief that is universally shared is opposition to Christianity as embodied in the common slogan 'Support the war against Christianity'. For some, Christianity is opposed for its association with corrupt and hypocritical churches. As one scene member put it to me: 'I'm not anti-Christian, I'm anti human manipulation' (Tom). Ironically though, Christianity, and in particular contemporary American evangelical Christianity, supplies the very symbols and discursive frameworks that scene

4: 'You play it like a warrior': Legion, vocalist of Marduk, live at Norway's No Mercy festival 2003. Reproduced by kind permission of Rachel Rijdisjk (http://www.rachelrijsdijk.com).

members seek to transgress. Extreme metal is part of what Lynn Schofield Clark (2003) calls 'the dark side of evangelism' in which Christianity's deepest fears are made flesh. This strange reliance on one's supposed enemy is characteristic of transgressive practice.

One common way of describing Christianity is as weak or submissive, as in the following interview extract:

> . . . it's submission, total submission and it's total opposite of the human nature
> I think. The whole moral, Christian moral is complete opposite of the of the
> natural way for us to act, you know
> KKH: So what is the natural way for us to act?
> R:    Like an animal. (Eric)

Rather than being a literal personality, Satan is a potent symbol of man's (*sic*) lustful nature. Christian civilization has repressed this true nature and, as a consequence, men neglect their true potential.

Satanism is generally more concerned with liberation from the perceived constraints of humanity than with worshipping the devil. Some black metallers have participated in satanic rituals of the sort pioneered by Anton LaVey's 'Church of Satan'. However, there remains a strong suspicion of anything that might turn Satanism into anything resembling a religion. As one female black metal musician put it to me:

> . . . I'm not, I'm not into all this like collecting up shitloads of fucking books
> and the occult. That doesn't make you a Satanist. You're a Satanist because you're
> a Satanist. You don't, you don't need anyone else's words to tell you what you
> are. I'm me, I don't need anybody else to tell me what I am. (Zara)

Another common feature of black metal Satanism is misanthropy, often expressed in very extreme ways. For example, the US fanzine *Wheresmyskin* (late 1990s, no date or issue number) proclaimed: 'Kill everything holy, kill everything else, then kill yourself'. Dani, the lead singer of Cradle of Filth, is quoted in an interview with *Terrorizer* magazine as saying 'if I was in control of the world, I would wipe out half of it instantly and indiscriminately without any remorse' (April 1996: 28). Misanthropy involves a determined effort to set oneself apart from the world. Many black metallers claim to avoid social interaction as far as possible, as one told me: 'I'm only trying to fit into my own world' (Eric). This misanthropy is often related to a self-conscious elitism, based on contempt for the 'weakness' of most humans.

Such elitism is frequently accompanied by a yearning for a pagan past. Scandinavian black metal bands often invoke the Vikings and mourn the arrival of Christianity in the Middle Ages, almost claiming themselves to be colonized people. Pagan society is constructed as lacking the 'weakness' that characterizes contemporary society. Scandinavian bands are also fascinated by the Scandinavian countryside.

Drawing on an ideology of romanticism (Mønk In Press), the wildness of the forests and mountains is contrasted with the effete cosmopolitanism of contemporary cities. These themes have also been incorporated by black metallers from other countries, with varying degrees of success. For example, the band Melechesh, who are of Turkish–Armenian–Syrian (Christian) descent, draw on the history of ancient Mesopotamia. An interest in mythology and ancient history is not confined to black metal. The stories of H. P. Lovecraft and Robert E. Howard have provided inspiration to many across the extreme metal scene.

An interest in pagan mythology can easily become an interest in racism and fascism. The apparently uncritical celebration of pagan pasts, the obsession with the 'unpolluted' countryside and the distrust of the cosmopolitan city were common features in nineteenth- and twentieth-century fascist and racist movements (Beckwith 2002). Indeed, Nazism contained a strong anti-Christian, mystical strain (Goodrick-Clarke 1985). Many black metallers are fascinated by social Darwinism and eugenics:

> . . . I mean just look at nature, the strong are surviving, you know, like the strong eats the weak, and that's just the way it is, you know. So you can't really go against that. I mean of course in modern day society has gone against it, you know, but I think that's a bit foolish because I mean it's natural selection, it's a law and there is a reason why it has been like this, you know, and why it's like that in the natural world, you know. (Jane)

In many ways, the Nazis are *the* pre-eminent transgressive symbol in the modern world. Unsurprisingly, there has been much interest in the Nazi period within the black metal scene and the extreme metal scene as a whole. One example is the Swedish black metal band Marduk's *Panzer Division Marduk* (1999). In interviews, the band have spoken of their obsession with tank warfare and with the German Panzer tank in particular. The album cover features the gun barrel of a Panzer tank pointing at the viewer and the music features artillery and battle sounds (see Figure 5). The appropriation of Nazi symbols has always been a feature of extreme metal. Slayer not only used an SS 'S' in their logo, they also named their fan club the 'Slaytanic Wehrmacht'. However, in black metal these appropriations have been accompanied by discourses that are highly conducive to the incorporation of Nazi ideologies. Unsurprisingly, perhaps, a number of black metal bands, such as Norway's Burzum and Poland's Graveland, have become involved in far-right politics and others have expressed some sympathy with fascist and racist ideas. Since the 1990s a fully-fledged Nazi black metal scene has developed, existing in a complicated relationship with both the Nazi music scene and the black metal scene (Burghart 1999).

The black metal scene is the most radically transgressive space within extreme metal, but commonalities exist between black metal discourse and other discourses

5: The cover of Marduk's *Panzer Division Marduk*. Reproduced with the kind permission of Osmose Productions.

within the scene as a whole. Christianity is widely reviled, as are other forms of authority. It is also common for scene members to proclaim a radical individualism, even if this is not associated with elitist misanthropy as in black metal:

> I think there's too much bullshit about how you should act, that's bullshit, how you should be and all that. Just be yourself, if you are sick, you are sick, you know, it's nothing you can do about it. (Johan)

This kind of radical individualism is similarly to that articulated in punk and other alternative music scenes (Duncombe 1997; Widdicombe & Wooffitt 1995).

The discursive transgressions of the extreme metal scene, like its sonic transgressions, reveal concerns about abjection. The abject is associated with human weakness, mortality and the voluptuousness of the human body. The abject is a source of fascination and of terror, leading to an obsessive, 'fundamentalist' preoccupation in extreme metal discourses with the details of the abject and of its control. Lyrics by bands such as Cannibal Corpse show a delight in the abject but also a repetitive desire to control it. Extreme metal discourse represents a departure from heavy metal discourse in that the fantasies it explores are less obviously 'fantastic'. Heavy metal discourses are generally lurid, theatrical, baroque and often satirical. Extreme metal discourses are detailed, repetitive and apparently serious. This progression mirrors a progression seen in 'horror' films from the 1970s to the early 1990s, as explicit 'slasher' movies replaced more traditional, gothic horror films (Badley 1995; Clover 1992; Crane 1994). In both traditional horror films and heavy metal, the abject is liberated and animated within a colourful fantasy world. In extreme metal the abject is repetitively examined, only to be destroyed and suppressed.

### Bodily Transgression

The scene's transgressive discourses have implications for and are influenced by particular bodily practices. Metal has always been associated with excessive drinking and the abuse of illicit drugs. The attitude to alcohol and drugs within the extreme metal scene is more complex. On the one hand, some sections of the scene have embraced self-destructive behaviour even more fully than heavy metal did. Some bands, such as Germany's Tankard, sing about little other than alcohol and mention little else in interviews. Some scene members delight in alcoholic self-destruction. Consider this interview extract:

> KKH: What plans do you have for your life and for (*name of band*)?
>
> R: More metal, more alcohol, more drugs, um, I don't know, let's just see how much I can fuck myself up before I die.
>
> KKH: You say you're an alcoholic, is that in the literal sense?
>
> R: I hope so (*laughs*) you know, there's no point in fucking, no point in kidding yourself, is there (*laughs*)
>
> KKH: You do drugs, is that what, dope or . . .
>
> R: Whatever I can get my grubby little mitts on. (Zara)

While alcohol tends to be the drug of choice in the scene, cannabis is also popular. Death metal and grindcore bands, in particular, are often heavy cannabis smokers and some bands such as the American death metal band Six Feet Under, have celebrated the drug in songs and interviews. Drugs such as ecstasy, heroin and cocaine rarely openly appear within the scene. Some scene members who have a close relationship with punk may have histories of speed and glue, but this is similarly rare. Furthermore, there are sections of the scene that abstain from alcohol and other drugs or use them only sparingly. The black metal scene in particular contains a strong element of asceticism.

Nor is excessive sexual indulgence generally celebrated within the extreme metal scene – a striking contrast to heavy metal. Black metallers, in particular, may be very suspicious of overt displays of sexuality, even if those displays of sexuality involve images of women in subordinate positions. The popular British black metal band Cradle Of Filth have been criticized in the scene for featuring scantily clad female dancers on stage and images of naked women on their T-shirts and publicity material (see Figure 9, p. 75).

Thus, while some forms of excessive indulgence are practised, often to self-consciously suicidal lengths, scene members also resist indulgence. The threat of the abject is raised in any loss of control over the body. Similarities abound with 'straight edge' punks who are celibate, do not drink or take drugs and are vegan. Both scenes are based around ideologies of personal empowerment, independence and self-control (Wood 1999).

The same ambivalence about bodily excess can be seen with regard to dancing and movement. The academic literature on music has shown how music is experienced 'erotically' in the body (DeNora 1997). Outsiders who attend extreme metal gigs are often struck by the extreme forms of movement that are practised (Heller 1992; Petrov 1995). Audiences often headbang and 'mosh', a form of dancing involving intense and violent physical activity; slamming into other audience members and throwing mock punches and kicks. To outsiders, these activities may look like an uncontrolled battle. Audience members also 'stage-dive' from the stage into the audience (although this has become less fashionable). Such activities represent some of the most extreme bodily responses to any form of music and carry with them the threat of injury. However, moshing, headbanging and stage-diving are also intensely controlled activities. Harris Berger describes moshing as 'the tension between violence and order' (Berger 1999b: 71). The violence is accompanied by 'the subtle awareness that this [is] a mosh pit and not a riot' (72). Berger points out that moshers are careful to take care of other moshers. Within the mosh pit, people who fall are quickly picked up. When someone stage-dives, they are always met by outstretched hands in the audience waiting to catch them. Those who do not control themselves and cause too much hurt may be forcibly ejected from the mosh pit. It is tempting to understand moshing as a kind of expression of communal solidarity. However, William Tsitsos argues that for straight edge punks 'the moshpit is a sort of proving ground in which those who are too weak must be forcibly eliminated' (Tsitsos 1999: 412). The mosh pit is certainly a tough place to be.

The emphasis on control also manifests itself in an avoidance of the mosh pit. Berger writes amusingly of the 'silent men' who stand, arms folded, at the edge of the mosh pit, a phenomenon also noted by Wendy Fonarow (1997) at alternative music gigs. This phenomenon is partly explained by audience members being too old, tired or bored to enter the mosh pit. However, there are other reasons why people stand still. As we have seen, extreme metal is a music whose claustrophobic speed can produce a kind of paradoxical stasis. The music also tends to be amplified to incredibly loud volumes at gigs. Moreover, extreme metal is a difficult music to reproduce in live performance and can often come out as an indistinct noise. If audience members are unwilling to mosh, the sheer wall of noise may 'paralyse' people, rooting them to the spot. It is virtually impossible to find a middle ground between frantic movement and no movement. Often, bands are also virtually static on stage. The speed and technical demands of the music make impossible the sorts of expansive movements practised in heavy metal. Frequently, band members are only able to headbang or move their heads in a whirlwind motion. Only in slower forms of extreme metal is 'putting on a show', in a conventional sense, possible.

However, over and above the very real practical difficulties of movement to extreme metal, some scene members actively refuse to move. Some early 1990s black metal adopted the slogan 'No Fun, No Mosh, No Core' (the 'Core' refers to hardcore). Black metallers were reacting to the contemporary popularity of death metal. At the time, death metal shows resembled hardcore shows, featuring large, communally oriented mosh pits. This communal solidarity, together with the bonhomie that death metallers frequently expressed, was seen as being contrary to the 'seriousness' required to be a satanic metaller. As a result, black metallers adopted an exaggeratedly humourless attitude and scorned moshing. This attitude has lessened with time, but this extreme position revealed a very real ambivalence towards the body and dance, which affects the entire scene. Once again, scene members yearn for a deep engagement with the body; yet actively resist it as well.

Scene members have also been involved in less consensual violent incidents, including fights between scene members. Generally speaking, this sort of behaviour is no more or less prevalent within the scene than in any other space that is full of young men. However, in the early 1990s the Norwegian black metal scene was accompanied by a level of violence previously unknown in metal and which has been described in detail by Michael Moynihan and Didrik Søderlind (1998). Between 1992 and 1998 around fifty churches were burnt (Mønk In Press) and a number of prominent black metal musicians were convicted of arson and spent time in prison. In 1994 Varg Vikernes (aka Count Grisnakh), of the band Burzum, murdered Øystein Aarseth (aka Euronymous) a prominent musician with the band Mayhem and an important scene figure. Vikernes subsequently received a 21-year prison sentence (see Figure 7). Mayhem were already notorious following the suicide of their vocalist Dead in 1991, after which Euronymous took photographs of the scene (later used as the cover to a Mayhem bootleg release) and, allegedly, ate some of his brain. One of Mayhem's subsequent vocalists, Maniac, frequently engaged in self-cutting on stage. In the mid 1990s, another musician, Bård 'Faust' Eithun, a member of the band Emperor (see Figure 6), was belatedly convicted of the apparently motiveless murder of a homosexual stranger in 1992. Violence and church burnings have continued sporadically. In 1998 Jon Nödtveit, of the Swedish band Dissection, was imprisoned for being an accessory to the murder of an Algerian homosexual. (It is unclear whether there were racial motives to this murder: the person who committed the murder to which Nödtveidt was an accessory was of Iranian origin.) Nödtveidt killed himself in August 2006. In 2005, Gaahl, the vocalist of the Norwegian band Gorgoroth, was convicted for beating a man up and threatening to drink his blood. Violence has not been confined to Scandinavia, with church burnings (and attempted church burnings) occurring in France, the UK, Australia and elsewhere. Murders by people with connections to the extreme metal scene have also occurred in Germany, Italy and the United States. However, none of these cases have involved people as integral to the scene and its music as in Scandinavia.

6: Emperor (featuring 'Faust' on drums) at the height of the Norwegian black metal scene's violent period, c. 1993. Reproduced with the kind permission of Nocturnal Art Productions.

# Burzum
## The Wolf Caged

The Nordic Metal scene was rocked asunder when *Varg Vikernes* was jailed for the murder of Euronymous of Norwegian Black Metallers MAYHEM, as well as starting church fires. Now serving a 21-year sentence in a Norwegian prison, Varg, alias Count Grishnackh remains the most controversial figure in Black Metal. *Roberto C. Sanchez* took advantage of visiting hours and went to meet the man behind the music of *Burzum*.

7: Varg Vikernes in his jail cell in 1996 – from an article in *Terrorizer* magazine, 28 March 1996. Reproduced with kind permission of Dark Arts Ltd.

Putting Transgression in Context

While the literature on transgression suggests that it is a universal human desire, there are many other ways to practise transgression than participate in the extreme metal scene. As Paul Greene (In Press) shows, music that may sound transgressive in one culture may not in another. The interest in the occult in particular is rooted in the wider Western revival of what Chris Partridge (2005) calls 'occulture'. Although extreme metal is produced across the world, its transgressive practices are always, at least in part, aimed at specifically Western targets. Although black metallers have been known to make racist statements in interviews, Islam for example has never been the object of aesthetic transgression.

Nor is the extreme metal scene the only transgressive music scene. Not unnaturally given that the two scenes interact and cross-fertilize extensively, there are strong similarities between the extreme metal scene and elements of the punk scene. Evaluating the differences between transgression as practised in the punk scene and as practised with the extreme metal scene is complicated by the internal differences in both scenes – some elements of the extreme metal scene, such as thrash, may have more in common with elements of the punk scene than they do with other elements of the extreme metal scene such as black metal. Nevertheless, punk has always been much more concerned with social criticism than extreme metal, with some punks actively involved in political struggles (O'Conner 2002). While some elements of the punk scene, particularly in the 'straight edge' scene are as obsessed with self-control as members of the extreme metal scene, there are also elements of the punk scene that embrace a 'bohemian', cosmopolitan and artful lifestyle, a very different kind of dissolution than is practised within the extreme metal scene. It is also the case that much of the punk scene is opposed to the technical virtuosity that characterizes extreme metal music.

Punk has always delighted in practising transgression much more visibly, more 'spectacularly' than extreme metal. While the appropriateness of the concept of 'resistance' (Hebdige 1979) as applied to punk is a matter of debate, the concept certainly fits much better to punk than it does to extreme metal. The extreme metal scene produces transgression of a much more rigid, solipsistic kind, hiding from the limelight in the effort to sustain self-control. The same is true in comparing the extreme metal scene to the rap scene. Like extreme metal, rap has been associated with murder and has actively revelled in discourses of violence and eroticism. Yet, like punk, the rap scene embraces opposition and spectacle (embodied in the obsession with 'bling') in a way that extreme metal does not. Again, the extreme metal scene is much more rigidly self-controlled.

While the purpose of the scene is the production of transgression, the practice around which it coheres, the next chapter will show that this does not mean that most scene members live lives that are transgressive in their entirety. Only a tiny minority have ever taken things as far as those in the early 1990s black metal scene did. Yet the power of transgression ensures that the most transgressive scene members, practices and texts take on a kind of mythic significance. While the inescapable *telos* of the most transgressive practices in the oblivion of death is not what most scene members want, it retains an overwhelming allure. In the next chapter, we will examine this allure more closely and look at how the transgression that the scene represents fits into the everyday lives of scene members.

## Music and Talk

What do scene members get out of participation in the extreme metal scene? One obvious answer might be 'pleasure from music'. Talking about music is an important practice in the scene, carried out in fanzines, magazines, websites, e-groups as well as in face-to-face contexts such as gigs. As Simon Frith (1983, 1996) has argued, part of the pleasure of popular music consists in talking about it. Music fans' accounts of the music they like can be passionate and moving (Crafts, Cavicchi & Keil 1993). Indeed, scene members often talk of music as an essential part of life:

> . . . I have always lived only for the music, you know, it's only for the hard rock and heavy metal. (Lars)

> Oh music was my life, oh yeah music was my life since I was thirteen, or even younger. I bought my first record when I was eleven (Dave)

> KKH: How important is music to you then?
> R:  It's very important, very. I didn't have a stereo when I lived in London and for the last few days we didn't even have a tape recorder, and that was horrible . . . I almost went crazy, you know . . . I have to listen to music, I have to. I can't live without it, so it's very important. (Nora)

Interestingly, members often do not specify what sort of music is so essential for life. An attachment to music is generally treated as existing prior to an attachment to any specific form of extreme metal. Indeed, scene members often emphasize the breadth of their musical tastes:

> KKH: What are you mostly into is it death metal or black metal or . . .
> R:  I like them all, everything, from classical music, to Satan, black metal, I like them all, everything right through. (Dave)

> R:  I mean I enjoy a lot of calm music . . . I mean bands like, or artists like Enya or, all the records of Enya or this folk/pop band from, play like Irish music, I can't remember – Levellers, they're great, and other bands (Henrik)

As Carrabine and Longhurst (1999) have argued, contemporary musical taste is frequently expressed as a musical 'omnivorousness'. Music is constructed in a utopian way – music is life and an absolute good. Music is placed at the discursive centre of these scene members' lives and extreme metal is constructed as a specific subset of a more general attachment to music.

The reason generally given for the importance of extreme metal in a member's life is that it fulfils a particularly valuable function within a broader musical landscape:

> . . . I like extreme music I also like soft music I like every sort of music but the music I do best is the brutal music. (Johan)

Within this musician's account, extreme metal is treated as particularly attractive as it enables him to engage deeply with music through playing it. Scene members commonly assert that they love music in general, but that extreme metal offers something that other musics do not. Often, the specific attraction of extreme metal lies in an ill-defined 'energy' that excites and charges up the body:

> KKH: Why do actually like the music you like? What it is about . . .
>
> R:    Cos it's got energy . . . I've always liked stuff that's, like even like me mum's old sixties stuff . . . I never liked ballads, I've never been one for ballads or soft stuff, I've always liked something with like . . . Yeah, stuff you can shout along to, stuff with a bit of a kick in it, you know what I mean? (John)

> R:    I think it's just like, an extreme fast death or black metal song or whatever yeah just like, stirs something inside of you, it's like fucking adrenaline you know what I mean? (Richard)

Extreme metal's vitality 'stirs up' the body. This process allows the expression of what are seen to be negative emotions. Aggression, anger, violence and brutality are seen as the essential elements of extreme metal and the source of its vitality:

> KKH: What was it about it that attracted you first?
>
> R:    (*phew*) Th- just the speed, the aggression and it was kind of a fusion of what punk and heavy metal as like one crazy intense vibe, you know. (Tom)

> KKH: Why [did you like] thrash instead of the more mainstream?
>
> R:    Cos I was always really violent and it was just the most violent fucking extreme metal at the time and I just loved it, you know. (Zara)

The pleasures of extreme metal music derive from the excitement of violence and aggression. Scene members frequently explain this pleasure in terms of catharsis. Listening to extreme metal is seen as giving voice to aggressive emotions and, in the process, reduces depression and frustration in exhilarating ways:

> KKH: What was it that appealed to you about that sort of stuff, the punk and the

metal? You said that Black Sabbath blew you away. What was it about them?

R:    I think it's something that's hard to define. I think it's really sub-subconscious type reaction to the music. There's a lot of feeling [into] it, there's a lot of aggression, there's a lot of soul and passion in it. Basically it's like a release of tension [and] emotions basically by listening to the music. (Tony)

Members often argue that this catharsis helps them to cope with personal difficulties, as in the following story:

> . . . we were playing metal you know, having long hair and rehearsing in the suburbs you know and stuff like that you had like, those hot shot kids much younger than us . . . beating people up robbing them and so on. I've been beaten up a lot of times by like fifteen people you know, five years younger than me. That pisses you off, you get angry and I'm not gonna write that fucking suburb kids beat me up, instead I write lyrics for like for a song like [name of song]. You know you get pissed off you have to deal with your aggressions. You write lyrics that put into aggressive music . . . you can live that aggression out, and you can become a much calmer person I think, cos otherwise, otherwise I think if you're not going to be able put your aggressions out that way, you're going to be, you're going to be drinking in a bar and hitting the first person that say anything wrong about you. (Johan)

Johan claims that playing death metal helped him deal cathartically with the anger that stemmed from the trials of his everyday life. In claiming that this cathartic process reduced aggression, he refutes those psychologists who argue that violent media 'prime' real-life aggression (e.g. Anderson et al. 2003) and bolsters those who see metal as a way of coping with aggression (e.g. Nahum 2004). This may or may not be true for all scene members in all situations. Certainly, a few scene members have committed violent acts, although it is always hard to tell whether these might have occurred even if the perpetrators were not fans of extreme metal. There is no doubt though that the majority of extreme metal, for all the aggression and violence of its lyrics, tends not to explicitly target particular 'real-life' people or targets. As with Johan, most scene members do not respond to the specific details of specific situations in specific ways, but through an ill-defined aggression, which provides a 'fantastic' way of coping with anger.

Within the scene, talk about musical affect tends to describe the attractive elements of extreme metal as aggression, brutality, energy, etc. The language available within the scene to talk about the nature of musical attraction and pleasure is very limited. While scene members may love to talk about music, the scene offers only limited tools for talking about how music makes scene members feel. Similarly, the scene offers only limited tools for talking about why scene members like particular forms of music. Many members are often extremely reluctant to talk about the relationship between music and self:

> KKH: What attracted you to Burzum's music?
>
> R:　I just liked it, I thought it was really good, you know. It's hard to explain, I mean why do you like chocolate, why do you like coffee, you know? It's just like matter of taste. (Jane)

Jane rejects the invitation to investigate the complex reasons why she finds the music of Burzum pleasing. The reasons are relegated to the mysteries of 'taste'; mysteries that are apparently as uninteresting as why one might like coffee or chocolate.

Another example of the reluctance to talk about the relationship between music and self can be found in an interview with a nineteen-year-old British male extreme metal fan conducted for the research project I reported in Harris (1997):

> KKH: Why d'you think it [death metal] appeals to you?
>
> R:　I don't think there is a reason it appeals to me it's just I like it you know, it's not the sort of thing you can say, I like it because . . . it's just, it's just there.

Scene members frequently seem to be 'inarticulate' when talking about their relationship with music. While music is constructed as energizing, cathartic and pleasurable, members are reluctant to delve into their reactions to the music to which they listen. Members resist being drawn into detailed, quasi-psychoanalytic discussions of music, emotion and feeling. This reveals ambivalence about the relationship between music, the self and the body. The relationship is acknowledged to exist, but beyond that most scene members prefer to leave it alone.

### The Experience of the Scene in Everyday Life

While talk about music may be a part of the pleasures that the extreme metal scene offers, it does not provide an unambiguous route into understanding what members get out of participation in the scene. A better way of approaching this question is to look more broadly at how members 'experience' the scene. For Harris Berger musical experience is a broad phenomenon: 'musical experience does not just refer to sound, but to any phenomena deemed "musical" by the people who make it and listen to it. Such experiences do not exist solely in performance, but in the full range of settings . . . where musical life is carried out' (1999b: 23). Berger shows us that 'music' is not simply a set of sounds or texts and that 'experience' is not simply an individual's reaction to those sounds and texts. I want to go further and treat *all* scenic experiences as musical experiences of some kind. As with the concept of scene, such a definition allows us to escape definitional boundary disputes over what is musical and what is not. This definition allows us to consider fully the experiential role of the huge number of institutions and practices, such as tape trading, record labels, concerts, bands, websites, etc., which exist within the scene. Time spent participating in such institutions and practices equals if not exceeds the amount of time spent listening to and playing music. Moreover, music is played and listened to in the context of such institutions and practices and we cannot disengage music from them. We can therefore reframe the question 'what do members get out of the scene?' as 'what range of experiences are possible within the scene?'

The experience of the scene does not take place in an isolated, socially abstracted environment but in the 'everyday life' of members (Douglas 1971). Everyday life encompasses the 'normal', the 'routine' and the unexceptional. As Henri Lefebvre puts it, 'The quotidian is what is humble and solid, what is taken for granted and that of which all the parts follow each other in such a regular, unvarying succession that those concerned have no call to question their sequence' (1971: 24). This taken for grantedness ensures that the everyday is the terrain in which capitalist power is reproduced, through oppressive routines that nonetheless go unquestioned. Nevertheless, as other authors have shown (Cohen & Taylor 1976; de Certeau 1984; Willis 1990), everyday life is also the terrain in which power is manipulated and contested. Through the use of what de Certeau calls 'tactics', members have the agency to shape meaningful, liberating, expressive cultures from everyday routines. Music provides a powerful means of inserting this agency into everyday life in a multiplicity of ways. As Tia DeNora argues, 'music is in dynamic relation with social life, helping to invoke, stabilize and change the parameters of agency . . . By the term "agency" here, I mean feeling, perception, cognition and consciousness, identity, energy, perceived situation and scene, embodied conduct and comportment' (2000: 20). Similarly, Lawrence Grossberg (1994) shows how rock can disrupt the rhythms of everyday life and perhaps offer liberating possibilities of escape.

The concept of everyday life draws attention to the ways in which individuals, who may spend their lives moving within a plurality of contexts, may nonetheless experience these contexts as part of a seamless flow. The experience of the scene is not necessarily an exceptional experience and, therefore, cannot always be considered as separate from the experience of everyday life. At the very least, the experience of the extreme metal scene may affect the experience of everyday life outside the scene. For example, humming a song while walking down the street or having no money for rent owing to the excessive purchase of CDs are possible intrusions of the scene into everyday life. However, it is possible that the scene *may* be experienced as removed from the rest of everyday life. Indeed, as we shall see, members *may* actively attempt to construct the scene as disconnected from everyday life. The relationship between the scene and everyday life is not a settled one and is the object of contestation and negotiation.

Accounts of members' journeys through the scene attest to this complex relationship. Accounts of members' initial exposure to extreme metal often speak of the 'overwhelming' impact of encountering something entirely different from the rest their lives up to that point. Exposure to extreme metal can be a bewildering and exciting experience:

> First time I heard Slayer, I couldn't handle it, first time I heard Slayer the first album Show No Mercy, I was fucking completely stoned in a friend's house band called [name of band] we used to go and stay with them every week in [name of town], and they had the first Slayer album like I mean, done a bunch of bongs and a load of hot knives and stuff, and they put on Show No Mercy, and I'd heard about it I knew it was fairly, totally fast totally manic, hardcore metal, and I couldn't handle it – man it was like, all this satanic stuff it's like whoa what's going on here? (Jason)

Accounts of entry to the scene are frequently constructed as rapid journeys from ignorance and horror at these strange new sounds to a knowledgeable mastery of them. Members show how the excitement generated by hearing extreme metal led them to a frantic search for more of it:

> . . . and er, I was listening to a radio show and they played a lot of heavy metal music on that programme you know . . . and one day they were interviewing a Danish guy, a phone interview they were interviewing a Danish guy this was in nineteen eighty-three, and they played a song from the guy's album, it was 'Metal Militia' you know from Metallica. So they played that one and 'Motorbreath', it just totally blew me away and I taped it . . . then I tracked down the album the *Kill 'Em All* album, then I went totally thrash crazy from there really. (Ulf)

The shock of being 'blown away' by extreme metal tends to lead to a frantic search for more of it. The search for more extreme metal inevitably brings members into contact with scenic institutions. The following extract contains many of the features of the two previous extracts and shows how Eli came into contact with the institution of demo and tape trading:

> . . . when I hear Venom, Venom my whole life changed till today . . . I received the, it was the Welcome to Hell yeah? I put it on the stereo and you know everything was like Chhhhhhhhhh, and I didn't understand nothing you know. I was so scared I put the record outside and didn't listen to this record for maybe, two weeks something like this, and then I put it again on the record and tried to listen again, and you know it was it's very noisy you know that Venom that Iron Maiden like the Motorhead and Iron Maiden but er when you get a band like Venom it, the old time it was very noisy and very . . . powerful very brutal for somebody that never listen this kind of music, and then I know I get into this and try into this and I try to find lots of bands in this kind of style, and then I

got Slayer from a friend from America and he got demos from Slayer and Metallica. (Eli)

The search for recordings similar to Venom brought Eli into contact with tape trading, through which he heard other recordings. Becoming part of the scene can be an intoxicating process. The rapid and overwhelming exposure to a new form of music is combined with an exposure to a new social space, new forms of interaction and new institutions. In the following extract, Ulf describes how the process of becoming involved in the scene takes on a momentum of its own, leading to the rapid acquisition of new forms of scenic expertise. Previously, he had described how he had begun corresponding with a more established British musician in the mid 1980s:

> . . . and then he started taping me a lot of stuff and, you know he started taping me the whole death metal thing you know, which was all these, you know the Repulsion demos and Massacre demos . . . bands like Macabre and this is like eighty-six, eighty-seven at the start of death metal . . . and I just, it just freaked me out because I just found that kind of music that . . . it had everything you know all the bands that I ever liked like the aggression of hardcore bands you know just the energy, together with like and this the guitar sounds were really, really heavy and I don't really know why maybe because they were tuned down, that's when I learned about tuning down and stuff, and using heavier gauge of strings you know and having different tunings, and it just sounded so brutal you know. And often like these tapes were kind of you know, copied loads of times so the quality was kind of really noisy and stuff which added to the attraction I guess . . . I think it was the most exciting period for me as a music fan, in my life you know . . . because it felt like it was kind of being getting in part of the scene as well, because I started up my own death metal band . . . then we did a demo (Ulf)

Ulf and the other interviewees quoted above emphasize that the process of getting involved in the scene could not have happened without the help of others. Receiving this help and contacting other scene members is an integral part of the experience of getting to know the music. However, some scene members, particularly black metallers, argue that the process of discovering the scene happened with no outside help. This finding corroborates Widdicombe and Wooffitt's findings (1995) that 'subculture' members are anxious to emphasize that they discovered scenes themselves, rather than scenes discovering them. They argue that members attempt to maintain 'biographical authenticity' by resisting the 'category ascription' that subcultural involvement means conformity to group norms. In the following extract Eric emphasizes how he only became involved in scenic institutions on his own terms:

> I started [to get involved] mainly to promote the band, that was the main reason, because I wasn't, after a while I got interested in the whole movement,

but it took a while before I really got interested in the whole scene, you know. Because I thought I am doing my own thing, I'm, who gives a shit about what other peoples do you know, but later I start to realize that someone wanna help me to promote my band, I better be loyal back to them and support the other bands as well. (Eric)

Even though Eric seeks to make his connection to the scene contingent, the extract still affirms the importance of the experience of a wide range of scenic institutions and the impossibility of disengaging from them. He accepts that he needed to maintain relations with other scene members, if only to help his band.

The dominant logic of the scene is to become heavily involved in it. The scene contains relatively few members whose engagement with extreme metal is limited simply to listening to music. For the majority of members, involvement in the scene becomes the predominant interest and commitment of members' everyday lives – indeed, it can be said to constitute the centre of their lives. The scene overwhelms members, leading them to ever-greater involvement and greater pleasures, but involvement also creates complex problems. Members still need to earn a living and maintain relationships with the world outside the extreme metal scene. At times, involvement in the scene can cause difficult clashes with other parts of members' everyday lives. Indeed, these clashes may be so difficult that the non-scenic world becomes an exceptional terrain in which the taken-for-granted assumptions that guide practice within the scene do not hold sway.

For some members, the process of becoming involved in the scene can lead to estrangement from previously close friends. Non-metal friends may react to extreme metal with incomprehension and banter:

I've still got a couple of trendy friends and they come over they're like turn it off [name] it sucks turn it off, they really don't like it. (Richard)

Estrangement from non-metal friends can make it difficult for some members to find sexual partners. Since the scene is male dominated, heterosexual scene members are forced to look outside the scene for a partner, which can be a difficult process:

. . . I meet a lot of girls but the minute they find out, what kind of person I am and what music I like, they just run out the door you know. (Shimon)

This estrangement from the world outside the scene can force members to make difficult choices, sacrifices and compromises within the worlds of work and study. Take, for example, the following extracts:

. . . they attempted to cajole me into going to university because everybody thought it was the right thing to do, but I just decided that I had so many ideas musically I wanted to do, I'd either do it now or probably never do it at all. So I mean, you know, four years at uni, it's a long time. . . . and things just got to the stage whereby music and the underlying things behind it were the main driving force in what I wanted to do. (Nathan)

. . . I only went to university because I'd got the right A levels and there was a kind of parental like 'oh, you're gonna go there now, go to university' and I could not stand it, the minute I walked in the place. I did bugger all. I mean effectively I wasn't actually sort of struck off for about a year and a half . . . They kind of like sort of didn't realize half the time, but eventually it was like 'yeah, yeah' and I just dropped out of university basically and because I was like, I don't know, I think I just didn't take to it really, further education. I was like, had my fill of it and I was just like, I was totally obsessed with early metal stuff and basically wanted to get involved in music. (Graham)

I've always been fixated on the music scene, ever since I was thirteen/fourteen there's always been my life more or less is the music scene and music and social life has always superseded work and careers throughout my life and it's no different now. (Will)

What is interesting in these accounts is that involvement in music is seen as being opposed to a sustained involvement in university, work or a conventional career. Involvement in the scene may be so overwhelming that some scene members are unable to concentrate on other involvements. The members quoted above chose to sacrifice other opportunities and, in return, achieved a satisfactory scenic career that now constitutes their everyday lives. However, this is not always possible. Some requirements of the world outside the scene cannot be put aside so easily and this can be a source of great frustration to some scene members. For instance, in Israel the parsimony of the social security system and the need to perform military service make it difficult to sustain a high level of involvement in the scene, causing frustration to some members.

### The Experience of Mundanity

Commitment to the scene makes many demands, particularly in terms of time, but only a tiny minority are able to make a living from their commitment. Virtually every scene member must earn a living by non-scenic means and, consequently, members find it difficult to prevent the rest of the world intruding on scenic involvements. Scene members have learned to limit the resulting difficulties by orienting their practice towards the experience of *mundanity*. The orientation of scenic practice towards the experience of mundanity provides a powerful 'logic' within the scene (Straw 1991).

I define the logic of mundanity as the attempt to experience 'everydayness' in all its regularity and unexceptionality within the scene itself. Most members attempt to make their experience of the scene 'normal' and uncomplicated so as to deal with the challenges of being involved in both the extreme metal scene and the non-scenic world. Members seek to be content with the experience of the scene as mundane and to make the rewards of participation worth the costs. At its most developed, the logic of mundanity ensures that the scenic and non-scenic elements of everyday life are closely integrated. In their accounts, most members do admit to struggling, at times, with the often-divergent demands of the scenic and non-scenic worlds, but for most the struggle is tolerable and worthwhile. In fact, what is more striking is how success-fully the majority of scene members manage the complex relationship between the scenic and non-scenic worlds, even while scene members may emphasize the distinc-tion between the scene and the rest of the world in their talk.

*How* individuals orient practice towards the experience of mundanity varies enor-mously, depending, in part, on the various circumstances in which members find themselves. Some may experience mundanity by the successful exclusion of much of the non-scenic world – for example, through earning one's living from the scene. However, for most this is not possible. Those who experience the scene as mundane with the greatest degree of success achieve this by the careful management of the rela-tionship between the scene and the non-scenic world. This management is achieved through the deployment of members' 'reflexivity' – the constant process of internal conversation through which the relationship between self and other is negotiated – to create a particular kind of scenic *career* (the concept of reflexivity will be discussed in more detail in Chapter 7). Career, as I use the term, implies some sense of purpose, some sense of flow that knits together the various aspects of members' lives.

Scene members reflexively negotiate careers through the scene along particular 'pathways' (Finnegan 1989). Most scene members tacitly recognize that, to be truly contented, members must aim to be contented throughout their everyday lives and not just within the scene. Members must attend to their lives as a whole, through the management of their lives as careers. A reflexively managed career does not imply rigorous planning so much as the existence of a set of robust, yet flexible techniques and strategies, which will guide an individual through a variety of scenic and other spaces. A brief examination of a highly revealing incident will help to explain the importance of a reflexively managed scenic career.

While attending the 1999 Dynamo Festival in the Netherlands, I met a British death metal musician whom I had previously interviewed. His band had recently released a self-financed CD and, when he saw that I had a backstage pass, he asked whether I could do him a favour. He wanted me to take two CDs and give them to the managers of two particular record labels. He then went on to complain, in highly disgruntled and bewildered tones, about how difficult it was to promote the band and how alienated he felt from the backstage area. This incident raises questions about scenic infrastructure and divisions of capital that will be attended to in future chapters. What is revealing here is the musician's lack of scenic knowledge. While bands do send unsolicited CDs and demos to large metal labels, this is almost never successful. Generally, bands get signed by working to build up a following first, writing countless letters to fanzines and traders and sending flyers throughout the world. My acquaintance had failed to do this work. He had taken CDs to the festival in the hope that he would bump into someone who could help him. Although this would be reasonable as a complement to other promotional strategies, without them it was an ineffectual plan. Yet in other conversations he had revealed himself to be highly committed to music. He worked part-time at unskilled jobs in order to concentrate on the band. But even in this respect he had failed to capitalize on the resultant free time, admitting that the band only rehearsed once or twice a week. He also smoked a lot of cannabis and took other drugs on a regular basis. My acquaintance had failed to achieve a reflexively managed career, since he had not developed any kind of strategy, despite his evident love of the scene and desire to succeed. The areas in which he was highly committed and active and those in which he was less so undermined each other. However, despite his lack of comfort in the scenic world, he had relegated his non-scenic life to second place. The result was a lingering sense of dissatisfaction and bewilderment.

A reflexively managed scenic career is goal-oriented without being either dogmatic or unrealistic. It is pragmatic without being unprincipled. It is this balance that some members, such as the one above, fail to achieve. However, such members are in a minority. What is more striking is how successfully most scene members attend to the multiple spaces within which they move. Scene members maintain friendships outside the scene and have non-metal interests and hobbies. Indeed, a number of scene members I interviewed were very involved in other pastimes, such as sport, comic collecting and car restoring. Furthermore, many scene members are voracious readers, particularly of books on fantasy, religion, horror, the occult and philosophy.

Another crucial space to which scene members attend is that of the family. Many accounts of scenes assume that generational conflict is a crucial aspect of them (Gaines 1990). Whether or not this is the case in other scenes past or present, generational conflict rarely appears as a central element in scenic discourse. Of course, some scene members have become estranged from their families, but such cases are rare and there is no reason to think that they are more common in the extreme metal scene than elsewhere. More prevalent, in fact, is a ready display of affection for parents and family, even from those who produce highly transgressive music. Acknowledgements on album sleeves frequently contain expressions of musicians' gratitude to parents, as in the following example from *Cult Of The Initiated* by the US satanic death metal band Pessimist (1997):

> I endlessly and profusely thank 'Pessi-Mom' and the 'Big Guy' for putting up with practice three times a week, for sleeping through countless parties and noisy late-night load-ins, for feeding and providing a crash pad for countless bands and other assorted derelicts . . . and for always supporting me 100% in everything I do . . . I love you both

Parents were frequently mentioned by interviewees as sources of support, both financial and emotional, and even as inspirations. During my interviews, parents were
occasionally present in the house or even in the room where the interview took place.
Even those parents who disapproved of extreme metal themes offered support in
other ways, a testimony to the efforts made by scene members not to antagonize
them.

The generally harmonious relationships with parents and family may possibly stem
from a deep conservatism. Many scene members are married and have children. The
support for the family within the scene is conceivably part of the ambivalence
towards sexual excess and women that I discussed in the previous chapter. Certainly,
including the family in extreme individualist and satanic discourses creates surprisingly few problems. For example, one Swedish black metal musician explained to me
that having a family did not contradict his individualism as he aimed to be like an
animal and animals have 'hoards' that they protect.

As we saw earlier, the requirements of earning a living or studying can be a source
of frustration for some scene members. However, for other scene members the world
of work and study can also be a space of personal fulfilment. While many of the more
committed scene members sacrifice promising careers to become involved in the
scene, other scene members have well-paid and satisfying jobs in a wide variety of
industries. Few scene members 'drop out' and live on the streets or in squats as is
common in the punk scene. It is perfectly common for scene members to be secure
in economic terms and to be educated to university level.

Most scene members manage the complicated negotiations of everyday life
without excessive frustration and often with considerable success. Nevertheless, for
many scene members the most effective way to manage the non-scenic elements of
everyday life is to engage with the non-scenic world as little as possible. One Swedish
scene member told me how he had very few friends, no television and little contact
with the non-scenic world, concluding: 'I live in my small world and whatever
happens outside, it doesn't bother me' (Henrik). This quotation highlights how the
experience of mundanity can frequently become the experience of solipsism. A solipsistic outlook or, at the very least, a capacity to be alone, is an important element of
a reflexively managed scenic career. Unlike other scenes, the extreme metal scene is
not based on collective experiences involving gatherings of large numbers of people.
Of course, in many parts of the world, there are frequent gigs and some members do
interact within the scene with small groups of friends. But, as we shall see in the next
chapter, the scene is so diffuse that its institutions have developed in such a way that
isolated members can easily participate. Many scene members are content to be
involved in the scene by going to gigs and listening to music at friends' houses. But
the logic of the scene propels most members towards greater levels of involvement
and, when this level of involvement is reached, members encounter institutions that
are not locally based. The backbone of all scenic institutions is writing, by letter or

email. Bands develop reputations and obtain deals with record companies by writing fanzine interviews, corresponding with other scene members and by trading demos. With few exceptions, bands cannot get a recording deal or sell their recordings solely by playing live. Live performance can help a band to develop musically and to solidify a reputation, but it is not the principal route to a scenic career. Similarly, a non-musician within the scene quickly finds that greater involvement within and enjoyment from the scene cannot come without writing letters, contributing to bulletin boards, writing fanzines and hunting them down.

The mundane, solipsistic practice par excellence is collecting. Most scene members have extremely large collections of recordings – I saw a listing of one member's collection that totalled nearly 20,000 items – and members frequently have a staggeringly detailed knowledge of the scene's music. Indeed, obscurity for its own sake is valued within the scene. Tape traders commonly seek out obscure rehearsal tapes by bands that may never have formally released a recording. Will Straw (1997) has argued that record collecting is strongly associated with particular forms of masculine practice. However, it is a masculine practice that differs markedly from the sort of transgressive displays of male power that are so prominent within the scene: 'Forms of expertise acquired through deliberate labour of a bookish or archival variety are typically so dependent upon bureaucratised institutions of knowledge that they are poor supports for ideals of masculinity as transcendent strength' (7). The pleasure of collecting comes from a desire to order and categorize: '. . . indeed, the most satisfying (albeit under-theorised) explanation of the masculine collector's urge is that it lays a template of symbolic differentiation over a potentially infinite range of object domains' (6). Collecting involves a sustained commitment to the development and organization of vast and detailed forms of scenic knowledge. Like other forms of scenic practice, it also involves participation in complex networks, the accessing of which, similarly, demands considerable commitment. Members put considerable hard work into their involvement with the scene. In their homes members often have desks and filing systems that appear little different from other kinds of workspaces. One British scene member admitted to having written 300 letters a month at the peak of his involvement in the scene. Interviews with more experienced members of the scene, who had established bands and other scenic institutions with good reputations, constantly emphasize the need to be focused, goal-oriented and hardworking, as in this account of the origin of a prominent Swedish death metal band:

> . . . I played with these guys [name of musicians] and they were much younger than me, just one year but still they were in high school very childish you know, and I had my goals set straight you know and they were like they didn't have any goals for their future they were just like playing around, having fun you know rehearsing but I was like I want to do good songs I was very . . . I know what I was going to do you know, and I felt kind of trapped with guys that were so

childish and didn't have any goals for their future. . . . So when I met [name of musician] and he was also very into making a band, coming up with a band that could get a record deal you know, so when I met with him I talked lots with him and you know he, we decided, to work together instead so I split [name of band] up and moved down to [name of city] where he lived. (Johan)

What is striking about Johan's account is the opposition he makes between 'having fun' and having a successful career within the scene. He uses a discourse of work to describe the development of his band. When he met a more acceptable musical partner they decided 'to work together'. Work dominates reflexively managed scenic careers that are oriented towards mundanity and those who manage scenic institutions constantly emphasize the need for and an expectation of 'professional' standards:

. . . my aim was to provide quality music with a fast reliable service which is what I wanted from a distro. If I ordered from someone I wanted stuff to come back straight away and not people sending out alternatives because stuff is not in stock so they just send you anything that they think you will like. (Tony)

. . . when we arrive at the venues we have a very good catering, sandwiches and all sort of stuff, you know, and then we get a hot meal before the show and we have put together a tour rider with all our demands. Sometimes we have to compromise of course but . . . we want to be treated as professional band and if we're there, to do a job, I mean I take it as a job. (Eric)

This discourse of professionalism is not, perhaps, what we might expect from a scene so devoted to the production of transgression. Other scenes frequently emphasize opposition towards the mundane world of work. For example, a frequently reported element of punk discourse is its concern about 'selling out' and negative attitudes to those who make a living from music (Fox 1987). Making a living from the scene is problematized much less in the extreme metal scene than in other scenes. Still, members commonly recognize that it is difficult to be professional within the scene:

You have to be tough, you have to be really, really tough, and I have learnt this over the years now. You must not be timid and you must not take any shit, you know. But as long as you're that, you know, that's fine. I mean I've learnt the tricks now. (Jane)

As Alex Kurtagic, who runs the British distribution service Supernal Music, commented in the fanzine *Fitted Kitchens Of The Living Damned* (Issue 1, December 1998): 'Think and act like a suit and pretend to be a Metalhead for appearance's sake'.

A tacit admission in the last and other such comments is that the necessity of orienting practice towards the experience of mundanity threatens to dominate the experience of the scene to the exclusion of all else. The experience of mundanity always threatens to become the experience of work and, consequently, the experience of boredom. One British scene member describes how he became jaded with the scene and, in response, reduced the level of his commitment:

> . . . when I started with [name of magazine] it just got too much because I was writing all these letters, I was working full-time at that time coming home and writing all these letters and I was also doing reviews of demos, interviews with bands and doing selling stuff as well and it just got too much. So basically I told a lot of people that were writing to me that I would be cutting down my mail at the time. So there was a lot of people who got cut out that were just writing letters that were two lines long and stuff like that. It was totally uninteresting just to write back to them all the time. So a lot of them just got cut out and I just concentrated on the interesting people I wanted to write to. (Tony)

For Tony, the pleasure of contributing to the scene fades as it becomes simply routine. The pleasure that many scene members feel when they start to write letters and receive demos is threatened when letter writing becomes a daily chore. There is a danger that a scenic career may simply become a job like any other. This is particularly the case for those who earn a living from the scene, who may be unable to simply leave:

> KKH: What do you listen to at home? Do you listen to death metal?
>
> R: I don't listen to anything any more because you used to sit here eight hours or ten hours and –
>
> KKH: You got fed up with it?
>
> R: Yeah. You know before I started with this thing, I played in four bands in the same time, one after the other just, well I stopped playing because it was too much, so I miss that part of it. Actually you shouldn't work with the thing you love . . . But I don't know what I would do otherwise so. I don't want to stand in the car factory. (Goran)

The process through which members become attracted into the scene can ultimately be self-defeating. Members are attracted to the scene by the exciting experience of the music, which leads inexorably to greater scenic involvement. But the dominant logic of mundane scenic involvement can remove members from the pleasures that attracted them in the first place. From being a shocking intrusion into everyday life, the scene may simply become indistinguishable from everyday life itself. While this guarantees stability and security, it also risks the experiential problems of everyday life – boredom, exhaustion, etc. This is not simply the case for those involved in the institutional work of the scene, it is also the case for those who make and listen to extreme metal music. The sheer physical demands of the music are considerable. Regular unprotected playing and listening risks tinnitus, excessive headbanging can lead to muscle problems and the speed at which the music is played can lead to various physical complaints. Some members of prominent groups such as Immortal and Nile have been forced to retire through injury.

### Transgression and the Mundane

The challenges that scene members face in balancing the requirements of the scene and of the non-scenic world may be faced by *anyone* heavily involved in *any* scene that is oriented towards 'leisure-time' activity. One might expect to find that someone heavily involved in, say, English civil war battle re-enactments, would face some of the same frustrations and difficulties as extreme metal scene members. Of course, the scene is different from other scenes owing to the presence of transgressive practices and discourses, but we cannot assume that the texts, discourses and practices 'produced' by a scene necessarily affect its experiential character. The transgressive sounds, discourses and practices discussed in Chapter 2 are so highly developed that their production has become a mundane, everyday matter. We are a long way from the image of the scene presented in the previous chapter!

Yet notwithstanding the fact that the scene is oriented towards the mundane production of transgression, it does not follow that a distinct experience of transgression is not possible within the scene. The experience of transgression is the experience of something exceptional, removed from mundane, everyday experience. It is understandable, therefore, that the power of the transgressive is felt most intensely on entry to the scene. Nonetheless, although the production of transgression may be routinized within the scene, the practice of transgression can never be completely contained. As we saw in the previous chapter, the logic of transgression is to exceed, to burst boundaries and disturb. This is particularly the case regarding what I called bodily transgression. Even long-standing scene members involved in the business side of the scene can still be excited by the experience of music through the body:

> KKH: . . . you sounded a little jaded with the music itself?
>
> E: Nah, nah, I still get fucking off on good records yeah, for sure, yeah. I thought that band the other night were that good I needed, I literally felt the physical need to go and bounce round like a [inaudible] you know, and go down the pit, fucking fall off the stage and all that sort of shit. I'm still well up for that, you know. (Will)

Will's experience demonstrates how the experience of the scene's transgressive music rejuvenates, giving new life to those jaded by mundane practice. It is the possibility of transgression that ensures that members tend to 'drop out' of the scene very slowly, if at all. Many members have been involved in the difficult, often frustrating work of scenic involvement for over two decades.

The logic of transgression pulls scene members towards both a mundane involvement in the scene and a transgressive abandonment of everyday life. Transgression has an uncontainable quality, which has brought some scene members into the greatest difficulties with the non-scenic world. As we saw in the previous chapter, the most extreme forms of transgression have led scene members to jail and to the morgue. Again as we saw in that chapter, this (self-)destructive kind of transgression is seen by some as the apotheosis of the scene's meaning, yet it is nonetheless practised comparatively rarely within the scene. Scene members may be fascinated by the likes of Varg Vikernes, but few have emulated him. The mundane logic of the scene tends to hold its transgressive logic in check. Further, as we also saw in the previous chapter, a crucial element of transgressive practice within the scene is the fear of the abject and a desire to reinforce boundaries. Transgression carries with it the fear of excess and part of the logic of transgression is the control of that excess. The logic of mundanity does not arise independently of the logic of transgression, but reinforces transgression's self-limiting tendencies. One way in which transgression is limited can be seen through a reconsideration of the reluctance of some scene members to discuss the more personal aspects of their experience of music. By resisting or restricting talk on certain topics, members maintain control of the threatening excess of language. At the same time, inhibiting detailed investigation preserves the 'mystery' of the scene and reinforces its transgressive potential. Rather than undermining transgression, mundane scenic practice ensures that transgressive practice is kept within safe limits, while nonetheless retaining its potency.

In chapters 6 and 7 we will explore in more detail how the complex interrelationship between these two logics provides a crucial dynamic that shapes practice within the scene. The next chapter will further examine the scene's mundane practices through a consideration of how power and capital are reproduced within the scene's infrastructure.

## The Scene and Power

In the previous chapter I argued that the experience of extreme metal is inseparable from the experience of the extreme metal scene. The scene is structured by a complex infrastructure through which members navigate on individual 'careers'. The scene's institutions and practices are embedded in webs of power both within and without the scene and an appreciation of the workings of power is therefore crucial for any understanding of the scene. Pierre Bourdieu's well-known concept of 'capital' is illuminating in this regard. In *Distinction* (1979), Bourdieu shows how power and prestige in society derives from the possession of forms of capital and that financial capital is only one of these forms. Different forms of capital circulate within different 'fields' (Bourdieu 1993) within which struggles to accrue and utilize capital take place. Possession of particular sorts of capital within particular sorts of fields endows agents with prestige and 'symbolic power' (Bourdieu 1991) over the development of those fields. Inequalities in the ownership of capital inevitably develop in fields but the possession of capital in one field does not guarantee possession within another. In fact, within the 'field of cultural production', ownership of economic capital is an impediment to ownership of 'cultural' capital (a concept that will be discussed further in Chapter 6). For Bourdieu, power is kaleidoscopic – fields 'refract' capital from other fields and from the overarching 'field of power'. So if we make an analogy between scene and field, we have a powerful tool to examine the multifarious ways in which power is reproduced through the extreme metal scene's infrastructure.

But while, as Bourdieu shows, the workings of power may be subtle, at times they are also direct. As I showed in Chapter 2, the scene has been subject to direct assaults. In the case of heavy metal in the 1980s, such attacks did not ultimately affect the music's popularity or commercial viability. Furthermore, the commercial popularity of heavy metal also ensured that the music industry was generally supportive of it. Attacks from leftist critics and from critics within the music press had a more subtle effect. Such 'gatekeepers' wield considerable cultural capital that is transferable within a number of music scenes and within youth culture in general. Heavy metal possessed virtually no such cultural capital. So while heavy metal thrived commercially through repeated attacks, it was also the subject of considerable ridicule.

Extreme metal inherited many of heavy metal's problems. Although, in many respects, extreme metal represents a departure from the scene that spawned it, those outside the scene rarely make the distinction. Consequently, heavy metal's low cultural capital and tendency to be attacked by powerful groups has to a certain extent been transferred to the extreme metal scene. At the same time, the scene's relative obscurity has meant that the scene has a measure of 'protection' from the more direct and forceful assaults from powerful forces. While obscurity provides protection from direct assaults on the scene, it does not of course provide protection from power per se. Bourdieu's work shows that capital and the power that derives from it is ubiquitous. Scene members are part of the same world as everyone is. The question is, how does the scene 'refract' the forms of power and capital that scene members are enmeshed in outside the scene?

## The Scene and Habitus

Bourdieu argues that members of fields possess particular kinds of 'habitus' (1989) that produce certain 'dispositions' – the sense of how to behave and what to expect in life. The habitus is both a product of capital and convertible into different forms of capital within different sorts of fields in different ways. The habitus that one brings into a field affects one's chances of 'success' and satisfaction within it. In other words, in the case of the extreme metal scene, the experience and backgrounds that members bring into the scene affects how members accrue capital within the scene. In most fields, particular kinds of habitus tend to dominate. A consideration of the dominant habitus in the scene thus requires a consideration of the characteristics of the scene's membership. In this section I will treat the scene as a global whole in examining what sorts of groups are dominant and which are marginal. In the next chapter I will focus on how such differences are enmeshed in differences between local, regional and national scenes within the global scene.

To start with, it is clear that the scene is not simply made up of young people. There are many members who have been involved since the beginning of the scene and are now in their late thirties. Hard evidence on the class background of scene members is hard to obtain. As I argued in Chapter 1, researchers have generally asserted that metal fans are predominantly young, white, working-class males. My own impression is that, in Europe at least, the more affluent working classes and lower middle classes tend to dominate. Certainly, with some exceptions, extreme metal does not seem to be the music of the 'underclass' in wealthy countries and there seems no shortage of scene members from relatively wealthy middle-class backgrounds. This situation may vary across the globe. Anecdotal evidence suggests that extreme metal scenes in some countries in South America *may* have members from extremely poor backgrounds (Ricardo Miranda, personal communication 25 March 1999). Conversely, in the Islamic Middle East and some parts of Asia, extreme metal scenes appear to be dominated by the wealthy. Generally speaking though, in most contexts extreme metal is neither the music of the poor and dispossessed, nor is it the music of the wealthy and privileged.

Those of black African descent are almost totally absent from the scene whether in the black diaspora, the Caribbean or sub-Saharan Africa. Ian Christie (2003: 206) lists a few exceptions in the UK and US metal scenes and there does appear to be a slightly greater number of black members in new wave of American heavy metal bands such as God Forbid and Chimera. Most of the few black people involved in the extreme metal scene are those with a close relationship with the hardcore punk scene, where black people are slightly more numerous. Those of Chinese descent constitute another notable absence, although not to the same extent as the absence of black people. Extreme metal scenes in mainland China, Hong Kong and Taiwan were slow to develop and remain marginal, particularly when compared to the much better-populated scenes elsewhere in East Asia. The marginality of people of Chinese descent also extends to countries where Chinese people form a substantial minority, such as in Malaysia and Indonesia. South Asians both within the subcontinent and in diaspora communities are also barely involved in extreme metal scenes.

The three most marginalized ethnic groups within the scene – blacks, Chinese and South Asians – remain marginal in countries where they are a majority or a minority. In most places scene members come from the ranks of majority groups (albeit perhaps members of majority groups that are disgruntled with their marginalization as Wallach (In Press) postulates). Where minority groups participate in the scene it is generally minority groups connected to thriving scenes in countries where they are a majority. So, for example, Hispanic Americans form a substantial minority in the US extreme metal scene. Within these limitations, the scene is exceptionally diverse. There are well-populated scenes in Japan, South America and South-East Asia as well as in Europe and the United States and a more detailed survey of extreme metal scenes across the globe will be presented in the next chapter.

Any observer at an extreme metal show anywhere in the world would immediately notice the numerical dominance of men within the scene. Female fans are most numerous for more melodic extreme metal subgenres such as power and gothic metal. Yet many women are active in the scene and some have reached prominent positions. Women run labels, fanzines and other scenic institutions. However, when they do become involved in the scene, women generally occupy ancillary, if important, roles. Many women work as press officers for record labels (a situation intriguingly similar to that in the music industry as a whole (Negus 1992)). In music making, very few all-female bands exist. Female musicians tend to be vocalists or, more rarely keyboard players or bass guitarists and tend to be more numerous in bands playing more melodic forms of extreme metal. Female backing vocals are a common means of adding musical colour in black and doom metal but in recent years bands fronted by female vocalists, such as Nightwish, Within Temptation and Lacuna Coil, have also become extremely popular (see Figure 8). Such bands tend to play more melodic, (sometimes called 'symphonic'), gothic-influenced forms of metal. Although the use of women to add a gothic-tinged glamour hardly revolutionizes the position of women

in the scene, it has possibly opened doors to less conventional forms of female participation: the Swedish death metal band Arch Enemy has achieved considerable success
with Angela Gossow's deep vocals.

The scene is also predominantly heterosexual. Openly gay scene members are

8: Within Temptation, a popular female-fronted band from the Netherlands. Reproduced with
the kind permission of Roadrunner Records.

extremely rare. The only well-known out gay man in the entirety of metal is Rob Halford, singer with Judas Priest. Although his image has always drawn heavily on gay S&M fashion, he only came out officially in the 1990s; perhaps a testimony to the need to be in an untouchable position before homosexuality can be openly alluded to. I have only met one openly gay scene member (in Israel) and he did not have a prominent role within the scene. While loose groupings of gay heavy metal fans occasionally emerge (such as the satirical glam metal act Pink Stëël), there has been absolutely no overt organization of gay and lesbians within the extreme metal scene. The only space where homosexuality is present within the scene is in the very occasional use of quasi-pornographic lesbian erotica in some promotional artwork. This use, of course, has very little to do with 'actual' lesbianism.

Can we explain the lack of certain kinds of scene members in terms of structural constraints or outright prejudice? Such factors play an important but not exclusive role and will be discussed further in the next chapter. In the case of sub-Saharan Africa there are music industries in even the poorest countries. As I have argued, the absence of blacks, South Asians and Chinese extends even to countries where they are in a majority. Furthermore, even in countries with structural conditions favourable to the development of extreme metal scenes, there is no easy explanation as to why one person will enter the scene and another will not. We have to accept the complexity of people's lives and dispositions. Only with regard to the very few scene members with whom I developed close relations could I even begin to suggest answers to such questions with any kind of confidence. Even in those cases, so idiosyncratic were the 'reasons' that members entered the scene that it would be unwise to attempt to draw firm conclusions from them.

What we can do is note that certain forms of habitus, engendered by certain backgrounds, seem to engender a *dislike* of extreme metal. Habitus generates the horizons of our expectations, guiding our attraction towards that which seems to be 'natural' for us. For instance, as John Shepherd (1991) shows, women often have a strong aversion to metal. For some reason, the sounds and aesthetics of extreme metal can only be incorporated into 'the feminine' with difficulty. Deena Weinstein argues that the absence of women within the scene is fundamental to metal, since the music's aesthetic is founded on notions of 'power' and 'power . . . is culturally coded as a masculine trait' (2000: 67). The habitus engendered by homosexuality and by certain ethnicities also appears to present difficulties in incorporating extreme metal. That is not to say that all such forms of habitus work to exclude extreme metal in the same ways for the same reasons. In fact, the reasons why extreme metal fits so badly into the habitus engendered by certain backgrounds are extremely unclear and would be better approached through an examination of those forms of habitus rather than through an examination of extreme metal.

It is also true that dislike of extreme metal is partly a consequence of practices of exclusion. Most of these practices are unspoken and subtle, ensuring that certain scenic minorities have difficulty in reaching high levels of involvement within the scene. But in part, this difficulty arises simply from the experience of being in a minority. We might reasonably assume that the experience of finding few people within the scene similar to themselves might dishearten prospective members. For example, Israeli scene members frequently express an acute sensitivity about their marginal position, both with regard to the global scene and to Israeli culture in general (something I explore in more detail in Kahn-Harris 2002). Take, for example, the following comment by an Israeli black metal musician:

> It's very, very, very frustrating. . . . you put more than a European band into what you are doing and you get a lot less response . . . it's like we're stuck in the edge of the world. (Shimon)

When Israeli scene members become aware of the apparently vibrant scenes in other places, the marginality of the Israeli scene leads some to disenchantment. In this way, the marginality of certain kinds of habitus can be self-reinforcing.

Explaining the marginality of women in the scene is a complicated matter. As Angela McRobbie (1991) has shown, female involvement in youth culture is more circumscribed than male involvement, as young women generally have less freedom to participate in the public sphere. However, involvement in the extreme metal scene does not depend on attendance in public at live shows and one can be an active member of the scene from one's home. Indeed, the scenic infrastructure of the feminist 'riot grrrl' scene is very similar to that of the extreme metal scene (Leonard 1998). Yet while the scene's infrastructure is theoretically ideally constructed to enable female participation, many women do not enter the scene alone. Those women who do enter the scene tend to do so with partners or groups of friends. From the start of their involvement in the scene, then, women often lack the autonomy of most male scene members. The marginality of female members is reinforced when women see few prominent female scene members and musicians, and have few role models to emulate. At gigs they see other women with their partners or female friends, often dressed glamorously, but they see few autonomous women who are not defined by their sexuality. Women who enter the scene with partners are often subtly marginalized in scenic interaction. On many occasions I have met male scene members with their female partners, but their partners were not introduced and remained silent. In the heavy metal scene, women were often treated merely as glamorous appendages of male scene members. The same is often true in the extreme metal scene, where women – if they are visible at all in the scene – tend to be visible as hyper-feminine or not at all. Images of women in the scene often verge on the pornographic (see Figure 9). The presence of female scene members in such roles is problematic as women are rarely present within the scene in roles not defined by their femininity. Women who wish to become involved in the scene are more limited than men in how they are able to define themselves.

9: A publicity photo for the British black metal band Cradle Of Filth's 2004 album *Nymphetamine*. Reproduced with the kind permission of Roadrunner Records.

Overt and sometimes crass sexism also excludes women. Some forms of heavy metal, notably glam metal, demonstrated a certain willingness to play with gender roles, but ultimately reinforced women's subordinate position (Denski & Sholle

1992). As Walser argues (1993), a key element of metal is the misogynist fantasy of a world without women. Metal masculinity is founded on notions of strength and power, embodied, as Weinstein shows, in the 'pumped up' torso that many scene members aspire to. These masculinist themes have been taken to their logical conclusion within some extreme metal texts, as we saw in Chapter 2 with the images of sexual violence in the lyrics of Cannibal Corpse. While the female scene members that I interviewed were eager to assert that they did not take such things 'seriously', we might fairly assume that such texts make identification with and attachment to the scene more difficult for prospective female members.

The practices of music making within the scene also reinforce the exclusion of women. As Mary Ann Clawson argues (1999), the practice of rock music making is implicated in practices of male socialization, practices to which women find it extremely difficult to contribute. As Mavis Bayton has shown (1989), women in music scenes are often assumed to be 'not serious', as one female death metal drummer told me: ' . . . when I play with other bands, it's like I don't know why but the drummers none of them talk to me' (Elaine).

Female scene members often strenuously attempt to prove that they are 'serious' about the scene, to the extent that they may echo sexist discourses:

> KKH: Why do you think there's so few women into metal?
> R:　 Because most women just fucking follow their boyfriends around, do you know what I mean? And just get into metal because their boyfriends are into it and, I don't know really, I don't, it's just one of those, one of life's mysteries I guess, no reason women can't be into metal but it's obviously their own personal choice. If they'd rather fuck around putting on make-up and talking about fucking shit in the toilets and pushing up their fucking wonderbras and PVC skirts, then you know it's up to them innit? (Zara)

As in the punk scenes studied by Lauraine LeBlanc (1999), women who enter the scene must abide by masculinist rules, undermining the generation of any kind of female solidarity. However, it does not necessarily follow that women in the extreme metal scene are totally cowed by the masculine domination of the scene. Rather, the minority of women in the scene are often quietly subversive of mainstream femininity – after all, they prefer aggressive music that 'nice girls' do not listen to. As Weinstein shows, women who are prepared to abide by the masculinist ethos of the scene can gain respect.

The absence of homosexuals from the scene can also be related to dominant constructions of masculinity. Scene members may frequently use such epithets as 'fag'. Homosexuality is associated with femininity and connotes weakness. Yet such insulting constructions of homosexuality seem to be no more prevalent here than in other scenes. The absence of gays cannot be totally explained by reference to homophobia. As is the case for women, there is at least the potential for gay scene members to reach high levels of involvement within the scene. It is possible that there are many more male homosexuals involved in the scene than are 'out', but this assertion remains unverifiable. Lesbians and female bisexuals have slightly greater visibility within the scene, if only through the occasional use of lesbian images by some bands that at least provide for the notional possibility of lesbian involvement within the scene.

The absence of certain ethnic groups is also linked to overt prejudice. Israeli scene members frequently complain about prejudice exhibited by scene members in other countries. Since the rise of the black metal scene and the concomitant flirtation with far-right discourses, Israelis have faced open hostility on occasions. Some northern European distros have refused to deal with Israeli bands, distros and labels, sometimes on the grounds that they are 'unreliable'. Some Israeli bands have received hate mail. The most extreme example of this was in 1991, when a prominent Israeli scene member received a letter bomb that is reputed to have been sent by Varg Vikernes. In scenic conflict, members outside Israel will occasionally make anti-Semitic comments in order to anger Israeli scene members. For example, one Israeli band received a bar of soap in the post with a note asking if they could 'find their ancestors in that'. However, such incidents occur infrequently and do not impede Israeli scene members to the extent that, say, sexism impedes female scene members. In general, racism is not as ubiquitous a force within the scene as sexism as it is almost exclusively confined to certain elements of the black metal scene. Nevertheless, for Israeli scene members such incidents are deeply hurtful. While Israeli members face active prejudice against them, the same is not true for black scene members, since they are almost totally absent. Given the presence of far-right views, we can assume that prejudice against such members would come from some quarters of the scene. However, the lack of black scene members has nothing to do with overt prejudice, since few have ever shown an interest in joining the scene. Again, self-exclusion plays a role. As Weinstein (2000) argues, the retrenchment of 'black' musics since the 1970s has served to create a powerful divide from 'white' musics.

The predominant habitus within the scene is reinforced through both subtle and overt practices of exclusion and self-exclusion. Young lower-middle-class and working-class males from a limited range of nationalities have a habitus that is predisposed to the possibilities of scenic involvement and those without this habitus, such as women and those from certain ethnic backgrounds, have to work harder to become involved in the scene. Only those with a habitus oriented towards a deep commitment can survive this process.

There is a limited synergy between the dominant habitus within the scene and dominant positions within the global field of power. Clearly members from developing nations find it more difficult to become involved within the scene and exclusions of women and homosexuals can coincide with power structures outside the scene. The fit is not absolute though, as dominant class positions do not translate into a dominant habitus. Within the context of Europe and North America at least, class brings relatively few advantages within the scene. The question of how power works within the scene is therefore not a simple one. Dominant scene members do not simply owe their position to the conversion of capital from outside the scene into capital within it. To understand how the scene refracts capital and how this translates into power within the scene we have to look more closely at the institutions of the scene.

### The Scene's Infrastructure

The institutions of the extreme metal scene provide the infrastructure through which members interact and through which capital flows and is accumulated. The key questions in assessing how the scene refracts power and capital are how far participation in the scene's institutions requires resources from outside the scene and how far capital accrued within scenic institutions is convertible into forms of capital outside the scene. The scene's principal institutions are described below.

### Writing and Trading

The scene was built in the early 1980s through the postal system as members and fans of early extreme metal bands began to contact one another by letter. The early scene grew out of the global punk scene, which developed at the end of the 1970s, facilitated by fanzines such as *Maximum Rock 'n' Roll*. Such fanzines were set up with a global focus and contained addresses of scene members throughout the world and adverts from people wanting to correspond. As the scene developed in that decade, the small global network of correspondents grew into a more established scene, with letter writing as its principal institution. Metal magazines such as *Kerrang!* and *Metal Hammer* published pen-pal adverts and, through such magazines, fans of mainstream heavy metal began to discover the nascent extreme metal scene. As more and more extreme metal bands began to release recordings, so more people began to write to those bands.

This worldwide network of correspondents was tied into networks of trading. For much of the 1980s there were few dedicated extreme metal record labels. Demo tapes, live tapes and rehearsal tapes were the predominant mode of transmission for extreme metal music. They were either traded for other tapes, or bands sold them directly at cost price. In the late 1980s some tapes would sell up to 2,000 copies, with tape trading resulting in an even wider circulation. Letter writers traded demo tapes, rehearsal tapes and live tapes with other traders (see Figure 10). Letters also generally included 'flyers' – small leaflets advertising particular bands or fanzines (see Figure 11). Flyers were and to an extent still are distributed in vast numbers and it is common to receive a handful of different ones with every letter or package. They provided a very efficient way of publicizing the existence of a demo or CD at a time when the scene was very dispersed.

*Source key: ST-studio recording/ RH-rehearsal recording/ AU-audience recording/ AD-audience recording on DAT recorder/ MX or SB-mixing desk-soundboard recording. For 7"Eps, V=vinyl copy, T=taped copy*

| Band | Town/Venue/Date /Title | Time | Source | F |
|---|---|---|---|---|
| 3D HOUSE OF BEEF (US) | London Red Eye 26/10/97 | 35 | AD | |
| 411 (US) | NY ABC No Rio 10/8/91 | 35 | AU | BA |
| 411 (US) | NY Holdbrook Civic Centre 3/6/92 | 45 | AU | BF |
| 5150 (US) | EP #2 1987 | 10 | ST | 40 |
| A PUBLIC HANGING (US) | Blunt objects vs sharp things demo | 50 | ST | B1 |
| A PUBLIC HANGING (US) | Snuff film soundtracks nos.1-5 demo 1992 | 45 | ST | M |
| A WAY OF LIFE (Fra) | 'Evilfest', London LA2 13/6/98 | 35 | AD | |
| A.R.G. ( ) | Demo 1988 | 30 | ST | 53 |
| ABHORER (Sing) | Rumpus of the undead demo | 20 | ST | 68 |
| ABHOTH (Swe) | Demo #2 1990 | 05 | ST | 32 |
| ABHOTH (Swe) | Eskilstuna 12/6/94 | 25 | AU | |
| ABHOTH (Swe) | Matter of splatter demo #1 1990 | 10 | ST | 32 |
| ABIGAIL (Jap) | Japan 11/8/92 | | AU | |
| ABIGAIL (Jap) | Nagoya, Japan 7/8/92 | | AU | |
| ABIGAIL (Jap) | Promo 1995 | 10 | ST | EK |
| ABIGOR (Aus) | Lux devictaest demo 1994 | 40 | ST | CD |
| ABLAZE MY SORROW (Swe) | Demo | 15 | ST | |
| ABOMINATION (US) | Chicago 12/10/88 | 35 | AU | 44 |
| ABOMINATION (US) | Demo #1 | 19 | ST | |
| ABOMINATION (US) | Demo #2 | 20 | ST | 46 |
| ABOMINATION (US) | New York City 14/12/88 | 20 | FM | 95 |
| ABSCESS (US) | Demo #1 1994 | 20 | ST | BG |
| ABSOLUTION (US) | NY CBGB 17/6/88 | 25 | AU | BV |
| ABSU (US) | Dallas, TX 22/8/91 | 25 | AU | BE |
| ABSU (US) | Marseille Mirabeau, France 26/4/97 | | AU | |
| ABSU (US) | Memphis Barrister's TN 19/7/95 | 45 | AU | CJ |
| ABSU (US) | Milwaukee Metal Mania 9, WI 29/7/95 | 25 | AU | |
| ABSU (US) | Montreal, Canada 25/7/95 | 45 | AU | DM |
| ABSU (US) | The temple of Offal studio rehearsal 1992 | 12 | ST | |
| ABSU (US) | Warrishofen 1/5/95 | 50 | AU | DM |
| ABSURD (Ger) | Thuringian pagan madness 7"EP (1995)/2002 | | V | |
| ABSURD CONCEPTION ( ) | Receptance of nonsense demo #1 1991 | 15 | ST | |
| ABSURD(Ger) | Thuringian pagan madness CSEP | | ST | |
| ABSURED (Swe) | Demo 1991 | 12 | ST | 20 |
| ABYSSIC HATE (Oz) | Cleansing of an ancient race demo 1994 | | ST | |
| AC/DC (Oz) | In concert 1976 | 30 | FM | |
| AC/DC (Oz) | Peel Session 3/6/76 | 15 | FM | |
| ACAO DIRETA (Bra) | Rehearsal 1988 | 15 | RH | 40 |
| ACCURSED (US) | Satanic ritual demo 1993 | 15 | ST | BE |
| ACCUSED (US) | Connecticut 5/11/87 | 40 | AU | 82 |
| ACCUSED (US) | Demo 1990 | 15 | ST | 34 |
| ACCUSED (US) | KCMU Seattle 8/85 | 45 | FM | 87 |
| ACCUSED (US) | Martha Splatterhead demo | 12 | ST | 96 |
| ACCUSED (US) | Mechanized death demo | 12 | ST | 51 |
| ACCUSED (US) | Promotional tape 1987 | 15 | ST | |
| ACCUSED (US) | Seattle 10/12/85 | 45 | AU | 49 |
| ACCUSED (US) | The archive tapes | 90 | ST | 53 |
| ACHERON (US) | Eternal suffering demo 1990 | 12 | ST | 31 |
| ACHERON GATES (Isr) | Forests of dark mayhem demo | 30 | ST | |
| ACID (Bel) | Enschede, Holland 7/10/84 | 45 | AU | DP |
| ACOUSTIC GRINDER (Bel) | Yper Vort'n'Vis, Belgium 21/7/91 | 30 | AU | CC |
| ACRIMONY (UK) | London Borderline 20/8/95 | 45 | AD | |
| ACRIMONY (UK) | London Bull & Gate 28/7/95 | 35 | AD | |
| ACRIMONY (UK) | London Dublin Castle 2/4/95 | 45 | AD | DM |
| ACRIMONY (UK) | London Falcon 17/8/97 | 60 | AD | EI |
| ACRIMONY (UK) | London Powerhaus 14/4/96 | 45 | AD | EC |
| ACROSTICHON (Hol) | Dehumanized demo | 20 | ST | 25 |
| AD INFERNOS (Nor) | Sinn demo 11/97 | | ST | |
| ADDICTION (Jap) | Demo 4/94 | 15 | ST | CC |
| ADORIOR (UK) | Beyond the distant blue demo 1996 | 30 | ST | |
| ADORIOR (UK) | London Red Eye 27/10/96 | 35 | AD | DI |
| ADORIOR (UK) | London Red Eye 29/6/97 | 40 | AD | |
| ADORIOR (UK) | London Standard 29/6/98 | 40 | AD | |
| ADORIOR (UK) | London Water Rats 25/8/96 | 30 | AD | |
| ADRAMELECH (Fin) | Human extermination rehearsal 1991 | 15 | RH | 24 |
| ADRENALIN OD (US) | Berkeley Gilman St. 19/7/87 | 45 | AU | DI |
| ADRENALIN OD (US) | Love song demo | 10 | ST | |
| ADRENALIN OD (US) | Mr.Rajah demo 1985 | 05 | ST | 50 |
| ADRENALIN OD (US) | New York CBGB 24/3/85 | 20 | MX | 67 |
| ADRENALIN OD (US) | Ottawa, Canada 21/5/88 | 50 | AU | 36 |
| ADRENALIN OD (US) | Radio show 15/5/86 | 25 | FM | 40 |
| ADVERSARY (Swe) | Remains of an art forgotten demo 1992 | 15 | ST | 20 |
| AES DANA (Fra) | Promo 1997 | | ST | |
| AETURNUS (Nor) | Walking path demo | 20 | ST | DM |
| AFFLICTED (Swe) | Advance demo 1991 | 15 | ST | 25 |
| AFFLICTED (Swe) | Stockholm, Sweden 1990 | 40 | MX | 33 |
| AFFLICTED CONVULSION ( | )Reh 31/5/89 | 10 | RH | 38 |
| AFI (US) | Green Bay 1022 Smith St., WI 15/7/95 | 25 | AU | CK |
| AFTERMATH (US) | Demo 1987 | 35 | ST | 91 |
| AFTERMATH (US) | Killing the future demo | 41 | ST | 67 |
| AGATHOCLES (Bel) | Aalast, Belgium 3/6/89 | 10 | MX | 86 |
| AGATHOCLES (Bel) | Beverlo, Belgium 30/7/93 | 45 | AU | BU |
| AGATHOCLES (Bel) | Caballic gnosticism demo 1988 | 10 | ST | 49 |

10: Part of an extensive tape trading list from 1999. Reproduced with the kind permission of Guy Strachan.

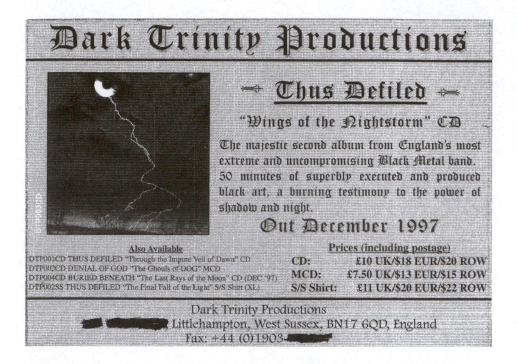

11. A flyer for the British black metal band Thus Defiled from 1997. Reproduced with the kind permission of Paul C. on behalf of Thus Defiled (http://www.thusdefiled.co.uk)

Tape trading and letter writing were most prevalent in the late 1980s and early 1990s. In that period the scene contained thousands of correspondents throughout the world. Since correspondence and trading requires relatively few resources, these practices facilitated an egalitarian scene. There was a strong ethic of reciprocity embodied in the ubiquitous maxim of 'include IRC [International reply coupon] or die!' Having said this, in some developing countries there are severe problems with the postal system. When ordering demo tapes, scene members generally enclose cash. While sending cash in the mail is less problematic in developed countries, some scene members refuse to order from, or send packages to, certain countries, such as Russia, where mail is often opened.

As I will discuss in more detail below, email has become the main method of scenic communication since the late 1990s. But email does not necessarily make for a more egalitarian scene, even if it costs nothing to send individual email messages. Email is less available to scene members with small amounts of money and remains, for the moment, less accessible to people in developing countries. Correspondence, through whatever medium, remains a widespread scenic activity, but has diminished in importance. Whereas, at one time, members needed to write to have any kind of sustained contact with the scene, outlets for extreme metal proliferated in the 1990s, making the scene easier to access. Correspondence is still important for the more involved scene members, but has become less and less necessary. It is an activity that is pleasurable and important to many scene members, even when not strictly necessary. It is common, for example when ordering a fanzine, to receive a friendly letter in response inviting correspondence.

### Distribution Networks

The formalized accumulation of capital within the scene began in the 1980s, when some traders set up 'distros', in order to distribute demos, fanzines and, later, records and CDs (see Figure 12). Initially, distros were little more than photocopied letters advertising a handful of items for sale at cost price or to be traded for similar items, but by the 1990s some of these distros had developed into highly profitable firms such as the UK's Plastic Head. As the scene developed, more and more labels were formed, resulting in increasing numbers of 'professional' recordings being made available for sale. Since many small labels were not distributed in shops, distros became the main point of sale for extreme metal recordings.

**Arte De Occulta presents:**

OCCULTA 001 - Setherial (SWE) - "För Dem Mitt Blod" 7" EP
"Two songs of FAST, VARIED & MELODIC
BLACK-METAL!"
Price: 30 KR/ 7 US$ or 10 DEM!

OCCULTA 002 - Sorhin (SWE) - "Skogsgriftens Rike" MLP
"4 songs of FAST & MELODIC unholy
BLACK-METAL!"
Price: 100 KR/ 16 US$ or 25 DEM!

OCCULTA 003 - Imperial (SWE) - "De Förbömdas Legion" CASS.CD
"5 songs of FAST & AGGRESSIVE
BLACK-METAL!"
Price: 30 KR/ 7 US$ or 10 DEM!

OCCULTA 004 - Haimad (SWE) - "The Horned Moon" CASS.CD
"3 songs of MELODIC & ATMOSPHERIC
BLACK-METAL!"
Price: 30 KR/ 7 US$ or 10 DEM!

-Special offer: buy OCCULTA 001+003+004 for only:
73 KR/ 15 US$ or 25 DEM!

- Send only wellhidden CASH (no imo/ reg.letters or coins)! No trades!
-For wholesales or promo, send 1 US$/ I.R.C./ FRIMÄRKE for info!
Arte De Occulta/ ▮▮▮▮▮▮▮/ ▮▮▮ GÖTEBORG/ SWEDEN

12: A flyer for a small Swedish black metal distro c. 1997.

Record shops began to sell extreme metal at the same time as the larger distros developed. Until the early 1990s extensive stocks of extreme metal were only available in a few small, 'independent' record shops, such as Shades in London. The larger distros that developed in the 1990s developed sophisticated networks for the distribution of extreme metal to record shops. Large chains now stock a wide variety of extreme metal CDs, including some very obscure labels. However, the mark-up on sales through some chain record shops is considerable. For example, in the UK CDs are commonly priced at £15+ by chain stores and at £12+ by distros and independent record shops. Extreme metal has become widely available through outlets that are much easier to access than the tape-trading networks of the 1980s. In the process, the scene has become enmeshed in capitalist processes through which transferable forms of capital are accumulated.

However, small distros that are less dependent on the accumulation of capital still exist. Given the quantity of recordings within the scene, members still need specialized distros that reduce choice and make obscure recordings more accessible. For example, UK distro Black Tears regularly produces a catalogue of fewer than 100 obscure doom metal recordings, each of which is carefully described. Distros such as Black Tears are not simply clearing houses for recordings, but institutions guided by a particular aesthetic. Nonetheless, even when distros are unprofitable, they use money as their main medium of exchange and they have eclipsed trading, an institution involving no transferable capital accumulation, as the main form of extreme metal distribution.

### Record Companies

The few extreme metal records released in the early to mid 1980s tended to be released on larger labels and sold large quantities. There was a substantial gulf between the small number of visible extreme metal bands, such as Slayer and Venom, and the large number of 'underground' bands. As the 1980s progressed, a few pioneering labels began to release new extreme metal recordings. For example, in the US Bryan Slagel's renowned 'Metal Massacre' compilations, featuring early work by Metallica amongst others, provided the basis for Metal Blade Records, now an important extreme metal label. By the end of the 1980s a number of punk labels, such as Earache in the UK and No Fashion in Sweden, began to release extreme metal recordings and some heavy metal labels, such as Germany's Nuclear Blast, also began to diversify into extreme metal. At the end of the 1980s there was a sudden proliferation of extreme metal recordings, as bands that had become established through tape trading began to release albums. At the same time, scene members began to finance extreme metal recordings and issue them on small, grass-roots labels.

The number of record companies within the scene grew exponentially in the 1990s. The largest, such as Nuclear Blast, now sell 100,000–200,000 copies of their top-selling extreme metal albums and have sub-labels and divisions based in other countries. Hundreds of small- and medium-sized companies sell a few hundred copies of each release. There was a brief period in the early 1990s when a few bands were signed to 'major' labels, such as Morbid Angel who were signed to Giant/Warner in the USA, and the British label Earache even had a short-lived licensing deal with the American giant Columbia. However, there was never any major commercial breakthrough and today only a small number of extreme metal bands such as Slayer are signed to major labels.

In the 1990s the proliferation of labels and of CDs financed by bands eroded the institutions of demo tapes and trading. Formerly, the release of a CD or record was a guarantee that a band had spent several years developing their sound through releasing demo tapes and trading them. Today, CDs may be released by very inexperienced bands. The proliferation of labels and CDs has had consequences for the circulation of capital within the scene. Before the early 1990s bands entered networks of capital circulation and accumulation very gradually, generally spending a considerable part of their early career trading their demos and building up a reputation. For example, the Swedish death metal band Entombed issued three demo tapes (two of which appeared under their former name, Nihilist) before the release of their debut album, *Left Hand Path* (1990). Today, with the erosion of tape trading and with bands selling their recordings from an early stage, scenic activity involves an earlier and greater engagement with capital. Bands and labels have adopted business practices drawn from the wider music industry. Larger labels generally behave like large independent labels in any other scene. Bands sign a contract for one or a number of albums and are either paid an advance, from which recording costs must be met, or have their recording costs paid for them in return for a lower royalty rate.

Nevertheless, despite the proliferation of record companies within the scene, less capital-dependent practices of exchange persist. The working methods of some smaller labels may resemble those of larger labels, but many others still operate very informal practices. In their relationships with bands, the smallest labels generally have no standard procedure but function through a plethora of individually negotiated agreements. Some of the smallest labels pay no royalties, providing bands with a given number of CDs to sell or trade. For example, the Israeli bands on the *Israheller* compilation (1997) each paid their own recording costs and in return received fifty copies of the CD. Moreover, the close relationships between labels and distros mean that even the larger labels often use practices of trading, distributing their product through exchange deals with other labels and distros worldwide. Many labels are involved in distribution to some degree, with the result that smaller labels/distros can operate virtually a cashless system, in which the only cash income comes from direct mail-order sales through their distro. For example, Israel's Raven Music has released a number of CDs subsidized by the label's attached distro. The distro then trades Raven Music CDs for releases by bands on other labels, to be sold by mail order. In this way, even releases by bands on small labels can be widely circulated without the need for a substantial financial commitment. So although the scene has become more formalized and 'business-like', informal trading procedures still persist, reducing the possibilities for capital accumulation.

The venerable scenic practice of correspondence also persists as a primary means by which bands are signed to labels. Owing to the global diffuseness of the scene and the relative rarity of live performances, bands are often signed to labels without ever meeting each other. Such is the volume of demos that most labels receive that bands are more likely to be signed if they have made some kind of name for themselves in the scene. Demo bands that have corresponded with other scene members may become known to label managers or to those who have influence on those managers. For example, the highly influential US death metal band Morbid Angel were signed in 1989 by the prominent UK label Earache on the basis of the personal recommendations of members of a number of bands already associated with the label.

### Bands and Musicians

The structure of extreme metal bands varies greatly. Some resemble the traditional stereotype of the rock band: a gang of close male friends playing together for years. More commonly, extreme metal bands are characterized by a great fluidity of personnel, with members continually dropping in and out. In contrast to Bennett's (1980) argument that the identity of rock musician is only possible inside a rock group, the identity of the extreme metal musician does not necessarily have to involve being in a group. Bands frequently have 'core' personnel, often the songwriters, around whom other members revolve. Extreme metal music is very difficult to improvise, owing to its dense sound and fast pace. Songs are generally built around successions of riffs, often worked out before rehearsal. Bands collaborate on arranging songs, concentrating on the order and setting of riffs. Extreme metal thus places certain difficulties on the nature of musical collaboration.

The reasons why band line-ups change vary. Sometimes, it is the result of personality clashes or musical disagreements. More commonly, it is simply that extreme metal musicians tend to orient their practice towards a wider scene than towards particular bands. This is particularly the case in locations with strong local scenes. Scandinavian bands, for example, are notorious for their constantly revolving line-ups. Scandinavian musicians are often associated with three or four bands simultaneously. For example, the Swedish guitarist Michael Aamodt used to play in the death metal bands Carcass and Carnage. He now plays in the death metal band Arch Enemy and the psychedelic doom metal band Spiritual Beggars. He has also played as a 'session' member of a number of other bands. Within the scene there is a strong culture of relocation. Many of the personnel in the bands that developed the influential death metal scene in Florida in the 1980s had moved from other parts of the country. International collaboration is also common (for example, Michael Aamodt's previous band, Carcass, was based in the UK). There are also a large number of one-person 'bands', with one songwriter/musician playing all instruments or drafting in session members according to need. Most famously, Varg Vikernes's band Burzum consisted only of himself.

While extreme metal bands are often fluid entities, in other respects they are frequently implicated in systematic, capital-intensive practices. Bands have always invested large sums of money in high-quality equipment (sometimes subsidized by endorsement deals with equipment manufacturers in the case of the bigger bands) and almost always hire properly equipped rehearsal rooms if possible. In Sweden, where studios are often subsidized, bands often rent a rehearsal space on a permanent basis, or share it with another band. Bands also invest in expensive recordings. Demos are often indistinguishable from 'proper' releases in terms of sound quality, and this was frequently true even in the 1980s. Bands generally pay for as much time as possible in the most expensive studio they can afford. Although the scene contains an aesthetic of fast and 'dirty' production, particularly within black metal, this aesthetic is fairly marginal. Extreme metal is a difficult music to record and, as a result, certain studios and producers have come to specialize in its production such as Fred Nordstrom's Studio Fredman in Gothenburg.

Despite the highly developed nature of band practices, musicians should not be seen as a separate class within the scene. Just as distros and record labels tend to merge, so musicians are frequently involved in numerous other scenic activities. For example, Yishai Schwartz of Israel plays in the doom metal band Moonskin, runs the label/distro Raven Music and also promotes gigs. Nonetheless, the increased formality and accumulation of capital within the scene in the 1990s has produced tension in the relationships between bands and other scenic institutions. When labels take over promotion and distribution from the bands themselves, disputes may arise over how effectively the label provides those services. Also, as elsewhere in the music industry, bands can be forced into inactivity owing to disputes with record companies. Such disputes can be all the more difficult when bands are signed to labels outside their home country as litigation may not be a realistic solution to disputes. For example, one Israeli band claimed that their foreign-based label continued to sell their CDs after telling the band that the title had sold out. The band attempted to litigate during the resulting dispute over royalties, but was ultimately defeated owing to the high costs and distances involved. The dispute prevented the band from releasing another CD for a number of years. The entry of capital into the scene thus increases the scope for conflict within the scene and raises the costs of unsuccessful scenic relationships.

Despite the increased amounts of capital circulating within the scene, most bands are unable to make a living from their music. The number of recordings that bands need to sell to make a living varies. However, most musicians I have spoken to generally agreed that bands needed to sell at the very least 60,000–100,000 CDs to make even a subsistence living and few bands are able to achieve this. Most band members are amateurs who have other jobs or survive through social security or student grants.

### Gigs and Gig Promotion

The extreme metal scene has always been globally dispersed, and in some locations there are barely enough scene members to make it worthwhile to stage gigs. Even in locations with strong local scenes, there are not necessarily many gigs. Live perform-ances are not a precondition for success within the scene and a number of prominent bands have never or rarely played live (e.g. Burzum, Bathory, Darkthrone). Most bands however do yearn to play live and some undertake long tours and try to play as often as they can. Touring is very difficult within the scene as few bands can guar-antee large audiences in a variety of locations. Bands often need record companies to support them in touring, but labels often have very limited resources available. Consequently, many tours are 'package' tours, with three or four bands collaborating to maximize their audience. Touring is generally only possible in areas where there are sizeable concentrations of scene members in close proximity, such as in Belgium, Germany, the Netherlands and Central Europe. Many tours do not visit Scandinavia or the UK, owing to the extra travel expenses involved. In areas marginal to the scene, the scarcity of live performances may ensure relatively large audiences. In Israel, for example, bands may attract crowds of 1,000–2,000 or more – more or less the size of the entire domestic scene.

Since the 1990s, festivals featuring or devoted to extreme metal have become increasingly common. Festivals that began in the 1980s including the Milwaukee Metal Fest and the Dynamo Festival (Netherlands) have now become important parts of the metal calendar. Big summer outdoor European festivals such as Wacken (Germany), Fury Fest (France) and Graspop (Belgium) bring fans from across Europe in their tens of thousands. Their line-ups also tend to contain heavy metal, nu metal and sometimes punk bands as well, but extreme metal tends to dominate the running order, even if the headliners are from more popular genres. There are also smaller, specialist indoor festivals, modelled on punk 'all-dayers', such as Norway's Inferno, that tend to be dominated by one or other particular metal genre. By concentrating a large number of bands in one site for a short period, festivals allow scene members to overcome some of the problems with touring. Bands that usually play to crowds of a few hundred may play to crowds in the tens of thousands.

### Magazines, Fanzines and Promotion

In the 1980s, coverage of the most popular extreme metal bands in mainstream metal magazines, such as *Metal Hammer* and *Kerrang!*, brought the scene to the attention of many potential members. However, these publications did not (and still do not) deal exclusively with the extreme metal scene. Moreover, in most countries radio and television have only covered extreme metal in a very limited way if at all. Fanzines developed to compensate for this lack of coverage and are still a crucial institution of the scene (see Figure 13). As a medium of communication, fanzines produce a kind of dialogic intimacy between reader and writer (Atton 2002; Duncombe 1997), which facilitates the formation of the scene as an 'imagined community' (Anderson 1991). Most fanzines have circulations of a few hundred and often last no longer than three or four issues. They involve a considerable amount of work, although desktop publishing has eased this burden somewhat and, consequently, fanzines are now produced more regularly and have more pages. Most fanzines are written in English and are circulated worldwide, but a considerable number are written in other languages and concentrate on local scenes. Some fanzines concentrate on particular extreme metal subgenres or on particular aspects of the scene (such as *Endemoniada*, which focuses on women in the scene). Most fanzines consist of reviews and postal interviews, making production cheaper and allowing for a global focus.

There have been certain changes in fanzine production since the 1980s. Early

13: A page from *Mutilated Mag* (issue 2, 1991), a long defunct Welsh death metal fanzine.

fanzines such as Bryan Slagel's *New Heavy Metal Revue* were primarily concerned with mapping and celebrating the scene. On the whole, they were highly supportive of bands and encouraged the growing production of extreme metal and provided information on access points to other scenic institutions. In the 1990s fanzines began to

14:  The Cover of *Isten 100*, 1999 (a black and white photo of a silk screen print on a denim vest). Reproduced with the kind permission of Isten.

develop more complex critical languages. Some prominent fanzines that developed in the 1990s, such as Finland's *Isten* (see Figure 14) and Norway's *Nordic Vision* became as likely to criticize bands as they are to encourage them. In this way, fanzines have come to resemble the wider music press (Toynbee 1993).

15: The cover of *Terrorizer* 128 2005. Reproduced with the kind permission of Dark Arts Ltd.

The increasing number of high-circulation fanzines that resemble fully-fledged magazines, such as the USA's *Grimoire Of Exalted Deeds*, has served to facilitate the entry of capital into the scene in the 1990s. There are increasing numbers of magazines that cover extreme metal such the Netherlands' *Aardschok*, the UK's *Terrorizer* (see Figure 15) and Sweden's *Close Up*. Magazines differ from fanzines in that they use telephone or face-to-face interviews, have paid staff and are available from a wide selection of outlets. Magazines such as *Terrorizer* also tap into global networks of distribution and are available throughout the world from chains such as Tower Records. As with the growth of distros, this development has made it easier for members to access the scene and has also provided opportunities for capital to be accumulated. The wide circulation of magazines gives them considerable influence over the musical content of the scene and in determining which bands become successful. Whereas fanzines allow for a profusion of opinions, magazines tend to concentrate critical power.

The importance of magazines has obliged labels and bands to utilize increasingly complex promotional strategies. In the 1980s bands became known through correspondence, tape trading and interviews with small fanzines. While these practices remain important, now even the smallest record labels issue press releases and promotional photographs. In addition, CD releases are accompanied by huge mail shots of promotional CDs to fanzines, magazines and the few radio stations that play extreme metal. The profusion of releases has also forced labels to be ever more proactive in their promotional strategies. Some labels have set up promotional offices and employed publicity companies to ensure that releases are promoted effectively in as many countries as possible. Advertisements are increasingly common, even in low-circulation fanzines. Record companies have released low-price compilation 'samplers', in order to publicize their bands. Indeed, some compilations are given away free with fanzines. Capital ownership has become increasingly important in the promotion of bands. Larger labels can consolidate their position through their greater resources and smaller labels have to work increasingly hard to get noticed. Nonetheless, the persistence of small fanzines ensures that it is still possible for bands to become known through word-of-mouth reputation.

One promotional strategy that is slowly growing in importance is videos. For a long time, most extreme metal bands never made videos. This may have been partly an ideological decision (despite their popularity Metallica never made a video until 'One' in 1988) but there were few outlets for extreme metal on television until the 1990s. Until its cancellation in 1995, MTV's 'Headbanger's Ball' did show some extreme metal videos, live shows and interviews (particularly on its 'Into The Pit' feature). With the proliferation of digital and cable TV channels across the world, so outlets for diverse styles of music have mushroomed, offering opportunities for extreme metal bands. The introduction of 'enhanced' CDs featuring videos also offers exposure to bands' videos. The Internet has also allowed bands to show streaming or downloadable videos from their own sites. It is also increasingly common for even relatively obscure bands to release DVD compilations featuring live or video footage.

### The Impact of the Internet

The scene has developed from a set of informal, loose-knit networks into a complex and highly sophisticated infrastructure. The scene's 'subcultural substance' (Hodkinson 2002) would seem to ensure its continued existence. However, the development of the Internet in the 1990s has at least the potential to disrupt and transform the scene's well-established practices. Extreme metal aficionados, like other music fans, were quick to explore the possibilities of online bulletin boards and Usenet groups as they developed in the late 1980s and early 1990s. As the Internet developed in the 1990s the use of websites and email grew exponentially.[1]

In assessing the impact of these developments it is tempting to suggest that the Internet threatens to make existing scenic institutions obsolete through replicating their functions in a more efficient manner. It is clear that *some* scenic institutions have been or are in the process of being replaced or replicated by online equivalents. Email has greatly eroded the practice of letter writing. Online bulletin boards, e-groups and online discussion have also greatly increased the speed and scope of correspondence. However, what is interesting is how long it has taken for online communication to supersede postal communication. Some of the scene members I have had dealings with did not adopt email until as late as 2000 and even then some still preferred to write letters, revealing a reluctance to abandon this much-loved practice. Letter writing has an aesthetic value for some scene members and has not been entirely abandoned.

One institution that *has* all but been replaced is the demo tape, which has been eroded both by the cheapness of CD production and by the newer practice of posting sound files on bands' own or other music websites (such as *myspace*). Tape trading and distros have however only been partly transformed by the Internet. It is true that the ease of obtaining demo and other recordings has, strictly speaking, lessened the need for distros and trading lists. However, many rarities from the heyday of tape trading in the 1980s and 1990s have as yet not been transferred in their entirety from analogue tape to digital formats and, given that transferring is only being done piecemeal when individual trades are made, it is likely that the process will take a while. The Internet facilitates and improves the experience of trading through sites linking to individual traders (e.g. *Metal Trade*) and sites identifying unreliable traders (e.g. *Anus.com*'s list of 'People Accused of Being Bad Traders'). Tape-trading lists may be placed online but many of the actual artefacts remain outside the digital world.

Distros have not become obsolete as, given the large amount of recordings available, there is still a need for respected sources that can guide peoples' choices of what to buy. Some distros such as the UK's *Plastic Head* have created large online stores and other online stores such as *blackmetal.com* have been started from scratch. Many small distros such as *Black Tears* have now made their catalogues available on the web, even if online ordering is not always possible. Most record companies and distros now have a presence on the web, with most having online stores of some kind (e.g. *Relapse Records*) with some smaller ones persisting in receiving payment through the mail (e.g. *Northern Heritage*), although online payment systems such as PayPal have made ordering much easier from such sites.

A major question is whether the Internet threatens to make CDs and other formats obsolete in favour of downloaded sound files. Certainly CDs continue to be sold and as yet there are few signs of the imminent economic collapse of the scene, although some vaguely contend that 'sales are down'. Furthermore, there is a strong collector's ethos within the scene, which has manifested itself in the increased popularity of vinyl recordings and specialist reissue labels such as Nuclear War Now. Album artwork and lyric sheets are important to extreme metal fans and are as yet only poorly or inconveniently replicable in online form. Record labels have also begun to offer 'extras' in CDs such as videos, rare tracks and extra information that help to keep CDs an attractive purchase. We should also not forget that in some parts of the world, such as parts of South America and South-East Asia, tapes (often bootlegged) rather than CDs remain important and there is a long way to go before computers will be ubiquitous in those areas. Aside from the continued attractiveness and advantages of existing recording formats, extreme metal labels have yet to develop an efficient and industry-wide system for easy online purchase of downloads. Some extreme metal labels sell downloads whereas others do not. Online music stores such as *iTunes* and *Napster* have erratic collections of extreme metal and generally do not stock items from smaller labels.

Even if sales of downloaded music have as yet not replaced sales of CDs and other formats, online file sharing systems such as *Soulseek* contain a vast array of extreme metal recordings, including notable rarities and demos. This represents a more serious challenge to existing scenic institutions than online sales do. However attractive vinyl is aesthetically and how many extra features CDs might now offer, it is hard to resist the temptation of free music. Some band members and label owners have argued that fans try out albums for free before buying the original copy, but it is hard to tell – whether or not this is true – whether the resulting volume of such sales will be equivalent to previous volumes of sales. There certainly does not seem to be the same worry about file sharing within the extreme metal scene as in the mainstream music industry, partly because so few bands and labels are profitable. While industry lawsuits and new laws may restrict file sharing in the future, the relative lack of capital in the extreme metal industry will probably ensure that extreme metal will be one of the last forms of music to disappear from such services. It was of course a lawsuit from Metallica against *Napster* that began the process of cracking down on file sharing. The hypocrisy of this action, from a band for whom tape trading provided such a central element in their early popularity, has often been noted.

The Internet has not replaced fanzines or magazines either. Since the mid 1990s a large number of 'webzines' have developed, such as *Chronicles Of Chaos*. They largely replicate paper-based fanzines in that they are focused on reviews and interviews. While some update continuously, others are updated as 'issues'. The lack of restrictions on size that the web affords means that long-standing webzines can have quite substantial databases of reviews. It is true that the comparative ease of setting up a webzine together with the lack of difficulty in distribution compared to fanzines has meant that there are fewer small circulation fanzines than previously. As with the continued existence of vinyl, fanzines are increasingly aestheticized as objects and that will probably ensure their continued existence on a small scale. Some fanzines, particularly well-established ones such as *Isten*, set up websites to archive previous issues and have thereafter continued on the web. Others such as *Grimoire Of Exalted Deeds* use the Internet for publicity, publishing occasional 'tasters' of the paper copy. The development of webzines does not seem to have affected the continued rise of extreme metal magazines. Magazines continue to thrive and new magazines, such as the USA's *Decibel* are set up all the time. Most magazines also have a web presence, some being little more than tools for publicity (e.g. *Terrorizer*) whereas others replicate a substantial part of their paper content (e.g. *Aardschok*).

While the development of the Internet has not resulted in the simple replacement of existing scenic institutions, it has inspired the development of new institutions and resources. Bulletin boards and online discussion groups have been around in one form or another since the late 1980s. While the extreme metal scene has always had sophisticated communication networks, the speed of discussion in online forums arguably facilitates new forms of sociality. Not only does it facilitate conversations between dispersed scene members, for those who have access to a computer in the workplace it also allows for the continuance of scenic communication in hitherto inaccessible times. Online discussion also has the potential to make participation in scenic discourse easier for those who are currently marginal to the scene, such as women. Certainly it allows for the development of new interest groups and alliances. As yet, however, such potential does not appear to have been realized (for example, the Usenet group *alt.homosexuality.death-metal* contains only spam).

The development of websites devoted to extreme metal has been dramatic. There are now very few bands that do not have their own website. For new bands, websites fulfil a vital publicity function and often contain sound files to download. More established bands may have a number of sites – an 'official' site, a mini-site on their record label's homepage, a *myspace* page and possibly some fan sites. Information about artists that was previously only available to committed correspondents is now available to all. Furthermore, the ease of updating websites means that news can be circulated quickly and efficiently either on the news pages of band websites or through specialized news sites such as *Blabbermouth* or *Metal Underground*. Band websites do of course vary in quality and in the amount of information given. Some such as *Burzum.com* offer essays and interviews whereas others offer little more than a brief biography and some pictures. Although most record labels today have their own website, they have made varying use of the possibilities that the web affords. Some of the bigger labels such as Relapse offer multiple features such as downloading of sample tracks, interviews and biographies. It seems likely that the importance of label and band websites will only increase as the need to respond to illegal downloading becomes ever more urgent.

The Internet also provides for the development of new and esoteric interests. It is the ideal location for humorous projects such as the parody webzine *Infernal Combustion* and the *Unholy Black Metal Songtitle-O-Matic* song title generator. Other websites feature such metal ephemera as guitar tabs (e.g. *MetalTabs.com*), fonts and desktop themes (e.g. *Windows 666*). There are many gateways and guides to scene resources on the web, such as *Mega's Metal Asylum,* containing links to large numbers of bands. Sites such as the *British Northern Metal Web* provide guides to particular local and regional scenes. Cataloguing scenes is a popular online project of sites such as the *Metal Travel Guide*. Some websites have developed into complex and idiosyncratic guides to a host of metal and non-metal resources, containing links, articles and bulletin boards, such as the voluminous *American Nihilist Underground Society*. However, while the web is ideal for the publishing of highly personal accounts of extreme metal, as yet there have been fewer weblogs devoted to the scene than one might expect, perhaps because webzines have long provided an outlet for personal expression within the scene.

The most novel development that the Internet has provided is online radio stations. Extreme metal shows and radio stations have always been thin on the ground due to the low density of fans in most areas, together with the complex technical and legal requirements inherent in broadcasting. Online stations such as *Snake Net* offer easy access to extreme metal music throughout the world. While online television has been slower to develop, stations such as *Metal Injection* are surely likely to become more common.

The impact of the Internet on the scene has not been straightforward. It has produced new institutions and practices, rendered some scenic institutions virtually obsolete, transformed others and left others (such as live concerts) untouched. It may be that the Internet is more important for younger and newer scene members than for older, more experienced ones. Whereas at one time prospective members were obliged to search hard to find the scene, the Internet makes the scene easier to access, quicker to become part of and easier to stay in touch with. Correspondence that once took weeks may now take hours. Information that was once hidden is now instantaneously broadcast. Minority interests can be effectively nurtured and isolated members can find each other easily.

We cannot assume though that the impact of the Internet is straightforwardly beneficial. The slowness and obscurity of a scene based around the postal service did at least make for effective 'filters' to information. The Internet facilitates a huge flood of information, but makes discrimination harder. While the Internet might be thought to democratize access to audiences for newer bands, it may simply bury them under an avalanche of information or conversely expose them unfairly early. Furthermore, despite the possibilities of the Internet for generating new kinds of community, these possibilities remain unactualized for minorities such as homosexuals and women who remain (with exceptions) marginalized even online.

It is possible that the Internet may provide a potent antidote to the accumulation of capital within the scene by making it difficult for institutions to accumulate capital and facilitating access to the scene for marginal members. It is also possible that existing capital-rich institutions may use the Internet to consolidate their position in as yet unknown ways. However, at the time of writing, the Internet does not appear to have made the scene either a more egalitarian or inegalitarian space.

### The Scene and the Accumulation of Capital

There has been a historical shift in the way capital circulates through the institutions of the scene. In the 1980s the scene was small, fluid and informal. Participation in the scene demanded little capital derived from outside the scene and in turn produced little capital that could be circulated outside it. In the 1990s and onward, the scene became more formalized and capital accumulated within it, resulting in a greater need for scene members to draw on capital from outside the scene.

Despite this accumulation of capital, the scene has remained relatively small and obscure throughout its existence, ensuring that the total amount of capital in circulation has remained modest compared to larger scenes. Nevertheless, there was a period in the 1980s when the scene might have become less obscure and more popular. In the 1980s a few extreme metal bands such as Slayer achieved success within the burgeoning heavy metal scene. The extreme metal scene could have grown rapidly in popularity, assisted by the institutions of the heavy metal scene. One reason that the scene did not grow in this way was the antipathy that scene members showed to some of the most popular forms of heavy metal (particularly glam metal) and the close relationship that the scene had with the punk scene. Instead, in the late 1980s, when the scene was on the cusp of a great surge in popularity, the divide from the heavy metal scene was reinforced so as to develop a distinct extreme metal scene. The informal networks and institutions of the scene became highly formalized, ensuring the efficient circulation of extreme metal almost exclusively within the extreme metal scene alone. While the scene remained obscure, the access points into the scene multiplied for those willing to find them, and producing and obtaining music within the scene became easier. Although scene members made use of capital-accumulation practices derived from outside the scene, these practices were rarely used to market extreme metal outside the scene. Instead, the penetration of the scene by networks for capital accumulation was a by-product of the formalization of scenic practice undertaken to ensure the scene's integrity.

Once networks of capital accumulation emerged in the early 1990s, they began to redirect scenic practices in certain directions. Once institutions have a cash income, they need to adopt conventional money-management procedures such as keeping accounts and paying taxes. Once institutions make profit, allowing their owners and staff to be paid, such institutions must continue to make profit and orient their practices accordingly. The profit motive may come to dominate such institutions. Profitable bands may no longer have time to correspond with scene members. Profitable record labels may not be able to afford to sign and support bands that have little chance of providing some return on their investment. Profitable distros may not offer favourable terms for exchange or sale. Inevitably, power relations and hierarchies within the scene begin to emerge. Wealthier, more successful scenic institutions are able to promote their product more widely and so influence the overall direction of the scene. In the 1990s, with a huge number of recordings produced within the scene, members needed to find ways to discriminate, making promotion and marketing even more important and giving greater power to gatekeepers within the scene. Those distros, labels and fanzines with the greatest amounts of financial capital have had the greatest chance of ensuring that certain recordings will be heard. As a result of all of these changes, in the 1990s an increasing split has emerged within the scene between the 'underground', which continues to operate on the basis of informal networks of reciprocity, and those larger scenic institutions that have to accumulate capital in order to survive.

This determination, at least among a subset of the scene, to maintain a space separate from profit-making considerations, together with the relatively modest profits available within the scene, ensure that the extreme metal scene retains a degree of insulation from global flows of capital. This degree of insulation also gives the scene a measure of safety from direct external threats, such as moral panics. Furthermore, while the scene does have a dominant habitus, the advantages accrued from possession of that habitus are relatively modest. In Bourdieu's terms then, the extreme metal scene possesses a reasonable degree of autonomy from the field of power. This is not the end of the story though. Even if scenic hierarchies deriving from external sources of capital are manageable and relatively muted, there are still complex differences, hierarchies and tensions within the scene. The next two chapters delve further into these differences, hierarchies and tensions.

## Cores and Peripheries

The early extreme metal scene was globally dispersed, decentralized and capital poor. While the scene was initially largely confined to Western Europe and the English-speaking developed world, it quickly spread around the world by the end of the 1980s, engendering a complex process of multidirectional global flows within the scene (Weinstein In Press). But while flows of music, texts and personnel began to spread in all directions by the early 1990s, 'cores' and 'peripheries' were simultaneously entrenched within the scene.

While the scene has a high degree of autonomy and the total 'stock' of capital within the scene is limited, global inequalities in the possession of capital can lead to inequalities in capital within the scene. Those in developing countries and those from poorer backgrounds within developed countries have fewer resources to obtain musical instruments, recording time and CDs. In countries that have compulsory military service, members may be removed from the scene for considerable periods of time. Conversely, in some parts of the world, scene members are able to utilize resources from outside the scene, such as the social security system, very effectively.

It is inevitable that global inequalities in the distribution of capital will facilitate or hamper involvement in the scene. The question is, how far? How far do these global inequalities create hierarchies within the scene? How far are inequalities on entry into the scene alleviated through participation within it? Given the relative autonomy ensured by the scene's infrastructure, we cannot simply map global hierarchies onto scenic hierarchies. This chapter examines how global inequalities in the distribution of various kinds of capital are enmeshed in, and to some extent mitigated by, the complex processes through which the scene produces a plurality of scenes from within itself.

That the scene does not simply replicate the inequalities inherent in global capitalism can be seen in an examination of the scene's cores and peripheries. The core markets, where the greatest numbers of CDs are sold, are Germany and parts of northern Europe. Yet these core markets do not necessarily produce the greatest number of successful bands and influential institutions. Conversely, the core areas for the production and dissemination of extreme metal do not necessarily coincide with the core markets. The Scandinavian countries, for example, produce an enormous number of successful bands, but are less lucrative markets compared to Germany, Belgium or the Netherlands.

The multiple cores within the scene mean that the concentration of capital in the scene is to some extent mitigated. Furthermore, the cores of the scene do not necessarily coincide with the strongest cores of the global capitalist system. The scene tends to be strongest in locations that are slightly 'off centre'. The scene is less strong in locations that are highly marginal to global flows of capital, such as developing countries. Although in certain such countries, such as Argentina and Indonesia, extreme metal may be very popular, the prevalence of bootleg recordings and the paucity of bands succeeding internationally mean that in global terms such scenes remain peripheral. Few bands from such locations become known throughout the global scene. At the same time, the scene is not at its most productive or strong in market terms in places central to global flows of capital and power, such as metropolises like London. Nor is it strong in disadvantaged areas within such locations – extreme metal is, for the most part, not the music of the deprived inner city. The scene is strongest in places that are close to, but slightly removed from concentrations of global power. Extreme metal tends to be most popular and productive in provincial areas within powerful countries. In the UK, extreme metal has always been much more important in the Midlands and South Yorkshire than in London. Similarly, in the USA, the most important extreme metal scene has been in Tampa, Florida, rather than Los Angeles. Globally, extreme metal is similarly important in countries that are close but not too close to global centres of power; so Norway and Sweden are superpowers in extreme metal terms.

These 'off centre' cores are all locations in which scene members have sufficient wealth and other resources to be able to participate effectively within the scene, but the presence of such resources does not in itself explain why this pattern has emerged. One possible reason is that in such locations few other activities are available. Provincial towns and suburbs have been described as anomic and boring, producing disaffected youth attracted to the aggression of metal (Gaines 1990). However, too many counterfactuals exist for us to accept this explanation wholeheartedly. Some core locations, such as Norway and Sweden, have thriving, state-supported networks of participation in a wide variety of youth-cultural activities, even in the smallest towns.

There is no simple, reductive reason why some areas have become cores and others peripheries. Rather, cores become iteratively self-reinforcing. Gothenburg, for example, was marginal to the extreme metal scene until the early 1990s. The pioneering death metal band Grotesque stimulated the formation of a tight-knit clique of musicians. The shop Dolores also provided a point around which the scene coalesced (as have other stores such as Helvete in Oslo in the early 1990s). Bolstered by the support given to musicians in the city, bands began to form in a highly conducive environment and supportive scenic institutions proliferated. The result was a highly creative local scene. Chance and charisma are as important in the development of the scene's cores and peripheries as global flows of power and capital.

Since the early 1980s, a fairly unified scene (albeit one largely confined to certain areas of the world) has developed into a constantly shifting complex of scenes across the world. As I asserted in Chapter 1, the scene contains other scenes that have varying degrees of autonomy from each other. As more people became interested in extreme metal, so local concentrations of scene members emerged and particular institutions developed around them. The more those local scenes generated their own infrastructures, the less crucial global infrastructures became, although they remained important.

Scenes tend to entrench capital within them, but while capital differences can become institutionalized within scenes, the quasi-autonomous relation of scenes to each other means that individual scene members are never entirely bound by their location in one particular scene. Networks of international collaboration ensure that individual differences between scene members are easier to bridge than differences in capital between scenes. Members produce extreme metal music and practice within a complexity of overlapping scenes within scenes, which allows – potentially at least – for movement. So how do we understand and 'map' this complexity?

Scenes are both discursively and institutionally reproduced along two different kinds of scale. The first are place-based scales. Scenes are reproduced globally, regionally, nationally and locally. This superficially appears like a series of Russian dolls: the global scene, the European scene, the Swedish scene and the Gothenburg scene. But the situation is more complicated than this. For one thing, not every scene on every level discursively and institutionally replicates the other. The European scene has a much more allusive existence than the Swedish scene, for example. Furthermore, scenes cross-cut and overlap each other. One might talk of a Scandinavian scene or a Nordic scene as well as a Swedish scene. Finally, not every possible scenic configuration exists. There are Jerusalem, Tel Aviv and Haifa scenes, but no Eilat scene.

Scenes are also reproduced on a genre-based scale. Different forms of extreme metal have dedicated institutions and scene members who may be more interested in those forms than others. One can talk then of separate death metal, black metal and doom metal scenes. Within them are a constantly shifting set of other scenes such as gore metal, gothic metal and so on. Also related to these generic scenes are the Christian and Nazi extreme metal scenes.

Generic and place-based scenes cross cut and coincide in complex ways. The global extreme metal scene itself represents a scene that is both generically and geographically located. The same is true for some local scenes that have a particular generic speciality such as the Norwegian black metal scene. Indeed, since the early 1990s there has been an increased tendency to 'localize' extreme metal sounds. Scene members talk of the distinctiveness of the Gothenburg death metal sound, for example. Artists, particularly in black metal bands have increasingly sung in non-English languages and some have incorporated 'folk' music into their sounds. The scene's generic and geographic fragmentation has thus reinforced each other.

Over and above the development of place-based and genre-based scenes, the fragmentation of the extreme metal scene has resulted in many different kinds of scene. I want to briefly outline a number of factors that differentiate scenes from each other along two dimensions of what I call 'structure' and 'construction':

### Construction

By construction, I mean the ways in which scenes are discursively and aesthetically constructed through talk and a range of other practices. Three principal forms of construction can be identified.

*Internal Discursive Construction*    This refers to the extent to which people inside a scene discursively construct that scene as a distinctive space, whether or not the term scene is actually used. Through processes of internal discursive construction scenes become 'visible' and 'recognizable' to members.

*External Discursive Construction*    Processes of discursive construction may occur externally to scenes themselves. Indeed, processes through which scenes are identified as distinctive spaces those outside those scenes may in fact be more significant than internal processes. Scenes that are famous the world over, such as the Tampa death metal scene, may be much more vaguely constructed within those scenes themselves.

*Aesthetic Construction*    Scenes are constructed through the development of particular aesthetics, musical and otherwise, that become both internally and externally visible. Sometimes this process occurs in a highly self-conscious way, as in the self-mythologization of Norwegian black metallers in the 1990s. More usually, aesthetics become attached to scenes in much more contingent ways as some forms of extreme metal become more popular than others.

### Structure

By structure, I mean those aspects of scenes that are implicated in the reproduction of specific institutional and other practices. A number of principal structural factors can be identified.

*Infrastructure*    Scenes vary in the extent to which they reproduce their own distinctive infrastructure – institutions such as record labels, distros, gigs, etc. Some scenes may have a proliferation of distinctive institutions shared by no other scene, whereas others are much more weakly institutionalized. Institutional 'thickness' is correlated with the degree of autonomy that scenes have.

*Stability*    Scenes vary widely in the extent to which they are stable entities. Some scenes have lasted for well over two decades and have produced long-lasting institutions. Other scenes emerge briefly and tentatively before either being subsumed into other scenes or disappearing altogether.

*Relation to Other Scenes*   Some scenes, generally scenes reproduced at the larger end of the scale, contain a multiplicity of other scenes, whereas other scenes are discrete, non-proliferating entities. Scenes also differ in the closeness and quality of their relation to other non-metal scenes. In particular, some scenes have a much closer relation to punk than other scenes. In some scenes there may be a wary relation between punk and metal scenes. In others, the two scenes may cross-fertilize considerably. The same is true with the relation to more mainstream forms of metal and with the relation to the wider music industry.

*Capital*   Members of some scenes may possess more non-scenic capital than members of other scenes. In the process, scenes themselves become repositories of capital, leading to wide variation between scenes. Furthermore, the global extreme metal scene itself produces its own forms of 'cultural capital', which will be discussed in the next chapter, and these forms of capital also become entrenched in particular scenes.

*Production and Consumption*   Scenes vary in the amount and quality of the extreme metal texts and discourses they produce. They also vary in the extent to which they export and import scenic materials to other scenes. Some scenes may be highly productive and export consistently to other scenes without themselves providing large markets for other extreme metal products. The reverse is also true.

The term scene is rarely applied to a particular space unless there is a substantial degree of both scenic structure and construction. The term scene is meaningful to members when it describes a space that is both institutionally distinctive to some degree and has some degree of self-consciousness. Scene is most frequently and unanimously used in cases where geographical boundedness (embodied in civic institutions such as cities or in nation states), institutional and aesthetic distinctiveness, and scenic discourses coincide.

There are a number of models for the ways in which scenes, individual members and institutions 'fit' together into one another. The 'neatest' one is the Russian dolls model described earlier in this section. A Gothenburg band such as The Haunted has contributed to the reproduction of a distinct local scene, and at the same time to distinct Swedish, European and global scenes. Yet not all institutions are 'shared' in this way. The significance of some local metal pubs to a particular local scene is usually greater than their contribution to larger-scale scenes. Conversely, some institutions have barely any local relevance at all. Plastic Head Distribution, probably the UK's most important distributor, is situated in the small Oxfordshire town of Wallingford, but has not noticeably contributed to extreme metal activity in the area.

The same is true for individuals. Some are important contributors to local scenic activity with little relationship to the global scene. Others may know few scene members locally but are important figures in the global scene. Most practices within the global scene simultaneously contribute to a number of scenes, but the degree of contribution to each scene varies considerably.

### Comparing Extreme Metal Scenes

The multiplicity and variety of scenes makes investigating how global flows of capital do or do not contribute to hierarchies and inequalities in the scene a complicated business. Such issues are not reducible to simply looking at global flows in capital, or even in tracing the cores and peripheries of the scene. Rather, capital is embodied in scenes that relate to each other in highly complex ways.

In order to illustrate the relationship between scenes, capital and scene members' location, I will in this section describe a number of scenes across the world. I will look first at scenes in the USA, Sweden, the UK and Israel. In being coterminous with national differences in capital, national scenes have a certain degree of primacy over more locally based scenes as nation states remain crucial in structuring local conditions of music making (Cloonan 1999). I will also look more briefly at how scenes vary across sub/continents. These brief descriptions will draw on some of the factors of scenic differentiation described above.

### The USA

Perhaps more than in any other country, metal is an entrenched part of American popular culture. In the 1970s and 1980s, heavy metal was one of the most popular musics in the country and American bands were popular worldwide. Metal was part of a rock culture that continues to be a crucial part of the popular cultures of America's Midwestern heartlands (Klosterman 2001). While its centres of popularity may have been in the Midwest, Los Angeles and Southern California were very much the heart of the American, and indeed the global, metal industry. American metal was situated at the very epicentre of both American and global popular cultural production. It is perhaps this centrality that explains both the attractiveness of metal as a target for campaigns by the Christian right and also its massive lack of cool from more cosmopolitan cultural elites.

Extreme metal in America has its roots in this metal culture. Indeed, America was one of the locations where extreme metal first developed. Of particular importance was the 'Bay Area' thrash metal scene, centred around San Francisco and Oakland, that nurtured bands such as Exodus, Violence, Megadeth, Testament, Death Angel and – most important of all – Metallica (although Metallica were originally formed in Los Angeles). These bands, together with Los Angeles's Slayer, were crucial in the development of extreme metal. Influenced both by the early 1980s 'new wave of British heavy metal' and by early 1980s Southern Californian punk bands such as

Black Flag, Bay Area bands were instrumental in developing the blueprint for thrash metal. American thrash metal rapidly developed through the 1980s into an integral and important part of the American metal scene. By the late 1980s some of the first thrash bands had signed to major labels, and Metallica became one of America's biggest bands with Megadeth also selling large numbers of records. In the process, any sense of the Bay Area scene as an autonomous phenomenon was lost. Although bands have continued to emerge sporadically from the Bay Area, the scene has lost its productive, genre-defining edge. In truth though, the Bay Area scene was a product of a set of bands and live shows and lacked enduring and globally extensive institutions such as fanzines, distros and record labels. Furthermore, music scenes in California, particularly Southern California, are so close to the centre of the global music industry that maintaining an autonomous scenic structure is difficult.

American bands also played a central role in the development of death metal in the 1980s. In particular, the scene in Tampa, Florida became world renowned as a centre for death metal production. In 1986 the band Death, led by Tampa's Chuck Schuldiner released what is considered one of the first death metal releases *Scream Bloody Gore*. Although Tampa's scene preceded the formation of Death (the band Nasty Savage had already had some success), Schuldiner's personal patronage and efforts led to its expansion. Following Schuldiner's lead, bands from Tampa and elsewhere in Florida (or who had relocated there) such as Obituary, Deicide and Morbid Angel released some of death metal's foundational albums by the end of the 1980s. An important part of the Tampa scene was the bands' use of Morrissound Studios and the engineers Tom Morris and Scott Burns. Albums produced at this studio by Morris and (particularly) by Burns had a highly distinctive sound – highly 'produced', clean and 'middle range' with crisp, drum sounds and an almost inaudible bass. The prestige of the Tampa bands gave impetus to another generation of Tampa and Florida bands, such as Malevolent Creation and Cannibal Corpse, which were quickly signed to record labels. Further, Morrissound Studios attracted bands from across the world and in doing so helped to standardize death metal in the late 1980s and early 1990s.

Yet the Tampa scene was not all that it appeared. While the city and its environs and indeed the rest of Florida did produce a considerable number of bands, it does not necessarily follow that there were any more bands than anywhere else in the USA or the world. The great attention given to Tampa in the late 1980s and early 1990s resulted in a greater number of bands from the area being signed to labels and although this may have acted as a stimulus to local musical production, it was not necessarily a sign that the Tampa scene was any more popular or more vibrant than anywhere else. Indeed, gigs appear to have been no more frequent in Tampa than anywhere else in the USA. But more importantly, the Tampa scene was not especially institutionally productive. No long-standing or influential fanzines, labels or distros came out of it and even Morrissound was never primarily a metal studio. Since the mid 1990s, Tampa and Florida have become scenes like any other, the only difference being that some of the members of the original Tampa bands continue to live there.

The history of the Tampa scene illuminates the coexistence of vibrant musical creativity with weak institutional creativity that characterizes most American extreme metal scenes. There has been no shortage of important and popular American extreme metal bands and at times these bands have been concentrated in particular local scenes. But the development of key scenic institutions has been much more erratic. Important American fanzines such as *Grimoire of Exalted Deeds* and important labels such as Relapse, have largely developed completely unconnected from any kind of local scenic anchor. American scenes often produce thriving live music scenes – the Akron scene described by Berger (1999b) being a typical example – but they are less good at developing a broader institutional base. An exception is the New York scene, which has historically benefited from the city's strong punk and hardcore scenes to develop a productive and long-lasting extreme metal scene, based largely around death metal. The New York scene is also an exception to the rule that global metropolises are relatively unimportant in extreme metal.

Despite being situated in the world's most powerful country with a globally dominant music industry, the American extreme metal scene is weaker than might be imagined. The huge size of the country that makes touring difficult, the unevenness of institutional entrepreneurship, the huge commercial importance of metal and allied genres such as grunge, all make the American extreme metal scene a curiously fragmented phenomenon. America's weak welfare system and massive divides between the rich and the poor make it more difficult than in some other countries for members to find the time and resources to devote to the scene. The history of persecution of American youth cultures, including metal, and the relative disenfranchisement of American youth (high drinking ages, youth curfews, etc.) only reinforce this difficulty.

The global importance of the American scene has also been variable. In the 1980s, despite the importance of underground methods of production such as tape trading, much extreme metal was released on the larger metal labels such as Metal Blade or on major labels. A band such as Metallica could be of seminal importance in the development of extreme metal while still a highly successful global act. This close relationship to the music industry, or at the very least the metal industry, was of more benefit to American bands than anyone else and also inhibited the development of an autonomous extreme metal infrastructure in the country. In the early 1990s, a number of musicians and bands, which might elsewhere have gone on to develop careers in extreme metal, went on to form highly successful bands, such as Slipknot and Machine Head that were important to the development of nu metal. Although nu metal, which will be discussed further in the next chapter, does draw on elements of extreme metal, it is not part of the extreme metal scene. Indeed, given the nu metal scene's domination by American bands, it represents a turning away from the global scenic infrastructure and 'a reclamation by the United States of rock and roll as an exclusively North American form' (Udo 2002: 24).

In the 1990s, with the development of a plurality of extreme metal infrastructures throughout the world, America became increasingly 'just another country' in extreme metal terms. Meanwhile, American extreme metal became increasingly underground and spread between autonomous nodes throughout the country, barely connected to local scenes. The American scene remained musically conservative, tied to death metal until the end of the 1990s, only slowly and erratically adopting black metal. Black metal emphasizes austerity, self-control and solipsism whereas American metal culture emphasizes partying and live performance. Black metal emphasizes ethnicity and national identity. American metal culture is so much at the heart of global music culture that it has found it hard to see itself as 'different' in any way. Interestingly, two of the American bands that have been most interested in drawing on ideas of ethnicity and difference have drawn on heritages entirely alien to them: Absu, who have drawn on a bizarre mixture of Scottish and Mesopotamian mythology, and Nile, who draw on Egyptian mythology.

Since the turn of the century, the American scene has produced a new distinctive subgenre sometimes called the new wave of American heavy metal. Bands such as Killswitch Engage and God Forbid have drawn on metalcore (a cross between metal and hardcore) and Swedish death metal to create a music that is becoming increasingly popular worldwide. Yet it is unlikely to become globally dominant in the way that nu metal or 1980s American metal was. Rather, the new wave of American heavy metal perhaps represents the American scene coming to terms with its position as just another scene and concentrating on producing interesting new takes on extreme metal rather than dominating the global scene.

The American extreme metal scene is full of paradoxes. It stems from and is to some extent a part of a globally dominant and capital-rich industry. Yet this closeness has inhibited its development and autonomy. It is historically important but increasingly 'just another' scene. It is situated in a rich and powerful country but is marginal and at times persecuted. There is no better illustration of the complexity of the relationship between global flows of capital and extreme metal scenes.

### Sweden

Extreme metal in Sweden has a long history. Bathory was one of the first extreme metal acts anywhere, releasing their eponymous debut album in 1984. Bathory pioneered the black metal sound that was to become massively influential in the 1990s. The band (effectively just the vocalist/guitarist Quorthon) drew on Viking anti-Christian themes, particular on the pioneering album *Blood, Fire, Death* (1988). As the 1980s progressed, so increased numbers of death metal acts emerged in Sweden. By the late 1980s, a small scene had coalesced in Stockholm. A number of Stockholm bands, such as Entombed and Dismember, developed a highly distinctive death metal sound, produced in Thomas Skogsberg's Sunlight Studios. This sound was much more distorted, less complex and more punk-influenced than the Tampa death metal sound that emerged at the same time. For a time, the Stockholm and Tampa sounds were the two poles around which death metal developed. While the Stockholm scene soon faded, the city has retained a highly productive scene, constantly enriched by bands moving from elsewhere in Sweden. This productivity is both musical and institutional, with a number of labels, distros and magazines based in the city.

In the early 1990s a number of bands in Gothenburg emerged playing a highly distinctive form of death metal featuring noticeably melodic rhythm guitar patterns. From the mid 1990s a number of these bands, particularly In Flames, Dark Tranquillity and At The Gates, rose to global prominence. The 'Gothenburg sound' became famous in the extreme metal scene and has influenced bands across the world. It was and still is most assiduously practised in Gothenburg where a host of other bands continue to play this style of music. This is not the only style of extreme metal played in the city (in fact Dissection, one of the key Gothenburg bands, are musically closer to black metal than death metal), but the success of the death metal bands acted as a stimulus for further bands to form. The reputation of the Gothenburg scene was such that bands from the city found it easier to get signed to record labels than bands from elsewhere. The notoriety of the Gothenburg scene was such that bands and musicians from elsewhere in Sweden moved to the city. The net result was that the Gothenburg scene developed an extraordinarily accomplished pool of musicians. Gothenburg also developed a vibrant infrastructure. Many of the early death metal bands had congregated around the record shop Dolores. The shop eventually started a label and distribution company, Black Sun, which ensured that more Gothenburg bands could have their music released and globally circulated. At the same time, many of the Gothenburg bands recorded their music with the producer Fred Nordstrom at his Studio Fredman. This studio became a magnet for other bands from Sweden and across the world, further increasing the scene's fame.

The Swedish scene is respected and even revered across the world, partly due to its developing new forms of extreme metal. Swedish scene members also have pride in their scene. In the early 1990s some black metallers from Sweden even had a running feud with members of the Norwegian scene. That said, Swedish extreme metal and black metal in particular shares with other Scandinavian forms of extreme metal a tendency to draw on notions of Viking heritage. Bands such as Unleashed and Amon Amarth are often described as 'Viking metal' (see Figure 16). This sense of heritage is rarely Sweden-specific although there are exceptions, such as the folk metal band Otyg who sing in an archaic Swedish regional dialect. There is a strong sense in the Swedish scene that there is something particularly apt and fitting about playing extreme metal in Sweden.

16: Viking metal: The Swedish band Amon Amarth pose in front of a longship. Reproduced with the kind permission of Metal Blade Records.

One of the most noteworthy features of the Swedish scene is its remarkable productivity. This productivity extends to record labels, distros and fanzines, but it applies particularly to musicians. Musicians start young and release album after album. Bands often go through frequent changes in their personnel with new bands forming, morphing and dissolving all the time. Musicians will often play in several bands at once, playing different forms of music in each. One example of this is Peter Tägtgren who plays in the death metal band Hypocrisy and the industrial metal band Pain. He has also appeared in a number of one-off projects such as the black metal group War and is the owner and producer of the Abyss studios where many black metal bands have recorded. While some bands do have stable line-ups, for the majority of Swedish extreme metal musicians membership of the scene is more salient than membership of one particular band. The Swedish scene is superficially constantly in flux but its membership remains stable and enduring.

The productivity and stability of the Swedish scene stems in part from the strength of the Swedish music industry and of Swedish civil society in general. For a country on the fringes of Europe with a population of less than 10 million, Sweden has a remarkable global musical profile. As Robert Burnett argues, Sweden's music industry is a 'substantial earner of foreign exchange for the Swedish economy' (2001: 16) and 'this makes Sweden one of the largest net exporters of popular music, after the US and the UK' (2001: 18). Part of the reason for the strength of the Swedish music industry is the country's high level of support for musicians. Music education, both in schools and municipal music schools is strongly supported financially by the state. Estimates from the 1980s suggested that 200,000 young were studying music in schools at any one time,[1] and Burnett states that 400,000 people sing in choirs. The *Folkbildning* system of non-state organizations supports music making through *Folkhögskola* ('folk high schools') and *Studieförbund* ('study circles'). The latter are particularly important in allowing bands to benefit from subsidised rehearsal space, musical instruments and courses. In addition, Sweden's relatively generous welfare and education system provide for some an effective subsidy for music making. The result of all these institutions is an exceptionally musically literate population with many opportunities for musicians to develop to a professional standard. These institutions benefit the extreme metal scene no less than any other kind of music. Further, the proliferation of musical resources in a country with a widely dispersed population ensures that strong local and regional scenes feed into a strong national scene.

The Swedish scene also benefits from being closer to the cultural mainstream of the country than is the case in many other countries. Extreme metal is still a small scene, but rock and metal generally are important in the country's cultural life. Unlike in the UK, for example, metal bands are often found on national television and bands with extreme metal roots such as In Flames have been nominated for Swedish Grammie awards. Indeed, metal can come close to being part of the Swedish establishment – in 2006 the popular power metal band Hammerfall recorded a video with the Swedish women's Olympic curling team! While the more difficult forms of extreme metal are much less visible, there are many exceptions to this. For example, in 1998 the black metal band Dark Funeral played the large annual Hultsfred music festival.

The Swedish extreme metal scene is one of the most capital-rich of any national scene. Although its relatively small population means that its market size is relatively modest, it is extremely important in developing and disseminating a constant stream of new sounds and acts. The prestige and influence that the Swedish scene has in global terms is substantial.

### The United Kingdom

The UK has been of pivotal importance in the development of metal. Bands such as Led Zeppelin, Black Sabbath and Deep Purple were crucial in the foundation of heavy metal in the 1960s and 1970s. In the early 1980s, bands such as Iron Maiden, Def Leppard and other members of the new wave of British heavy metal were important in further developing heavy metal. The UK has also been important in the development of extreme metal, particularly in the mid to late 1980s with the formation of grindcore. Bands such as Napalm Death, Carcass and Bolt Thrower combined punk and early death metal to develop an extreme sound that has been widely influential. The Nottingham-based record label Earache was also important at the time in providing exposure both to these bands and to other emerging death metal bands, such as America's Morbid Angel.

Part of the distinctiveness of the British scene lies in the paradoxical importance of London. London's cosmopolitanism and huge population make it a hub in the global extreme metal scene. There are concerts most nights of the week in some venue or other and a number of important scenic institutions are based in the city. The London scene is bolstered by tourists and travellers visiting the city and contributing to the scene in various ways. Yet the London scene has never had a distinct musical identity nor, given the size of the city, have many London bands achieved global status in the scene (Iron Maiden being the most notable exception). The size of London has always meant that extreme metallers have always been a near invisible minority in most places except in the centre and areas such as Camden where they congregate for concerts.

The odd position of London is illustrated by the case of the small scene that emerged in the mid 1990s in the West London satellite town of Uxbridge. None of the bands ever achieved any success, although some recorded demos and albums on small labels. However, the existence at the time of the weekly clubs the Devil's Church in Kings Cross and the Braindead club in Walthamstow, both of which were attended by a number of Uxbridge metallers, helped to reinforce a sense of cohesion amongst them. Furthermore, in the mid 1990s an annual day-long festival for underground punk and metal bands called the Ux-Fest was initiated in an Uxbridge youth centre. All this meant that some Uxbridge metallers began to talk of an Uxbridge scene. Yet like many other parts of London, Uxbridge fades imperceptibly into other suburbs and lacks a distinct social and cultural life. The result is an extreme metal scene with a weak identity and shaky autonomy.

As in many other countries, extreme metal is most popular in provincial contexts. The West Midlands spawned Black Sabbath and was at the centre of the late 1980s grindcore scene, with the Birmingham pub The Mermaid being a particularly important venue. The West Midlands remain an important metal centre. South Yorkshire has also been an important base for metal bands and labels of global significance, such as the doom band My Dying Bride and the label Peaceville. In these locations at least, the extreme metal scene has a much stronger self-identity and is less 'submerged' than the London scene is. Elsewhere in the country though, the extreme metal scene remains widely dispersed with small scenic concentrations in sometimes surprising places. For example, members of the popular black metal act Cradle of Filth live in rural Suffolk and for a number of years the influential black metal label Misanthropy was also based there.

While the UK's place in extreme metal history is assured, the situation of the scene since the early 1990s is less clear. The UK continues to produce bands of worldwide significance and popularity, such as Cradle of Filth. It is also the location for a number of extremely significant scenic institutions such as Earache and Peaceville Records. The British metal media remains important, with magazines such as *Terrorizer* having a worldwide reputation. More generally, scene members continue to emerge throughout the country. The scene is clearly active and vital. At the same time, the global significance of the UK scene has declined since the early 1990s, regardless of the subsequent productivity of the scene. In recent years the scene has produced fewer bands of global import than it used to. Since the 1990s British extreme metal has become increasingly out of step with global trends in extreme metal, and particularly European trends. Although Britain has developed some important black metal bands, black metal has never had the popularity in Britain that it has elsewhere, nor are more gothic-influenced forms of doom metal and power metal as popular in the UK as in Europe.

In part, the UK's difference from other scenes derives from one distinctive element of the scene; that is, what is seen as over-seriousness is viewed with some suspicion in the scene. Further, humour and irony have always had a very important place within the scene. Some 'serious' UK bands such as Carcass and Gorerotted have had a markedly tongue-in-cheek attitude to some of the more outrageous aspects of extreme metal. Parodic and comic acts such as Lawnmower Deth have also been popular in the UK. Black metal's 'no fun' slogan was always out of step with UK metal culture and UK black metal bands such as Cradle of Filth have emphasized irony and an earthy normality in interviews. The same reticence also applied to the resurgence of traditional heavy metal and power metal in the late 1990s. Whereas much of Europe embraced the return of traditional metal aesthetics, the British scene was much warier for a long period until British bands such as Dragonforce emerged to give the music a distinctly light-hearted spin.

The UK scene faces a certain kind of isolation. Its emphasis on avoiding overt seriousness renders it distinct from much of European and American metal culture. At the same time, metal and extreme metal has generally been marginalized in the wider British music culture. Metal bands are rarely covered in the mainstream media and almost never appear on television. There have also been a few instances of harassment from the authorities (Cloonan 1996). At the same time, historically the UK scene has generally benefited from its location. No less than in any other music scene, British extreme metal musicians were able to play music while supported by the welfare system or student grants, although in recent years this has become more difficult. The British scene also benefits from the UK, and London in particular, being a global hub in the music industry. While this is still the case to a certain extent, the decline of the dominance of British music worldwide (Frith 2004) has also affected the British extreme metal scene. The gradual decline in capital of the UK extreme metal scene has increasingly rendered it, like America, as 'just another scene'. While its history will always be celebrated, the special privileges this confers are likely to decline.

Israel

Israel's complicated history and geopolitical situation has had important consequences for its popular music culture. The Israeli music industry is extremely productive and was an important element in the development of Hebrew culture after independence (Regev & Seroussi 2004). Until relatively recently though, Israeli popular music was very isolated, with little direct contact with overseas music scenes. Israeli metal[2] has become increasingly globalized, just as Israeli popular culture has become increasingly globalized.

In the 1980s, Israeli metal was highly marginal both within and outside the country with few bands active and little infrastructure. The pioneering work of the band Salem (see Figure 17) helped to change this through releasing a number of demos in the late 1980s. While crude, these demos circulated widely in the underground and helped the nascent Israeli scene to develop global connections. In the 1990s, the Israeli scene mushroomed and scenic institutions started to develop. Israeli bands released demos and albums, labels and distros were formed and foreign bands visited the country. Some bands were signed to foreign labels. The most successful were Salem (signed to Germany's Morbid and later SPV labels) and Orphaned Land (signed to France's Holy Records and later Germany's Century Media), both of whom received some success. In particular, Orphaned Land (see Figure 18) has been critically acclaimed for its unique fusion of metal and Middle Eastern sounds.

17:  Zeev Tannenbaum, vocalist of Salem at the 2004 Metalist festival, Tel Aviv. Reproduced with the kind permission of Muir Vidler (http://www.muirvidler.com)

Salem and Orphaned Land were for a long time exceptional. Until recently few Israeli bands have made much impact outside the country and few have been signed to foreign labels. Part of the problem with the Israeli scene is that it has tended to grow and contract in fits and starts. Military service means that committed members are often lost to the scene. The febrile economic situation and minimal social security make devoting time to the scene a difficult business. The wider political situation also has an effect. Much of the growth of the Israeli scene occurred at a time of relative political optimism post-Gulf War I. The outbreak of the second intifada in 2000 meant that foreign bands stopped coming to the country for a time.

Until very recently (and arguably even now) Israeli extreme metal has had a kind of novelty value within the global scene. The supposed 'unlikeliness' of the Israeli scene makes the scene highly recognizable both within and outside the country. While this has guaranteed a certain amount of attention to the scene, some of this attention has been unwelcome. As might be expected in a country with a wide religious–secular divide and strong conservative political forces, there have been moral panic-type exposés in the media (particularly over Israeli black metal) and occasional criticisms from political figures. As we saw in the previous chapter, Israeli scene members have also faced racist abuse.

18: Orphaned Land in 2004. Reproduced with the kind permission of Kobi Farhi (Photograph: Itamar Gero).

Such attention, while unwelcome and upsetting, has the side effect of further increasing the visibility and coherence of the Israeli scene. Some scene members are highly resentful of this visibility and have sought to resist it as much as possible through downplaying or even hiding their Israeli location in scenic interaction.

Others, such as Orphaned Land, have used their location as a resource to create a unique form of extreme metal. Increasingly though, Israeli scene members have come to realize that the most successful way of interacting within the global scene is to work hard at making the scene productive and its products of international standard. In recent years a number of bands have come to be signed to non-Israeli labels, such as Rabies Caste who signed to Earache and Betzefer who signed to Roadrunner. Other accomplished scenic institutions such as the label/distro Raven Music (see Figure 19) and the *Metalist* website (which also organizes an annual metal festival)

19: A 2001 flyer from the Israeli scene advertising a release party in Tel Aviv for the new Raven Music catalogue, featuring performances by the Jerusalem-based black Metal band Arallu and other Israeli bands. Reproduced with the kind permission of Raven Music.

also attest to the narrowing of the gap between the Israeli scene and other global scenes. The increased globalization of Israeli culture has also facilitated global interaction on a more equal level.

The Israeli scene's small size means that all the significant players know each other, and this is an advantage in creating a productive scene. As in countries such as Sweden, there is a tendency for bands to form, release CDs and then to split up, only for the musicians to form other bands. While the national scene has a strong coherence and unity, there are distinctive local scenes in Tel Aviv, Jerusalem and (to a lesser extent) Haifa. The Jerusalem scene in particular has thrived off the seeming contradiction of its location within a 'holy' city, producing amongst other things, the black metal band Arallu's iconoclastic *Satanic War in Jerusalem* (2002). In contrast, the Tel Aviv scene benefits from its location in the heart of secular Israel in a city with a vibrant alternative music culture.

While the Israeli scene lacks capital in all sorts of ways, the gap between it and other global scenes has narrowed somewhat. Unlike in the UK and America, for Israel to become 'just another scene' would in many respects be an achievement rather than a demotion in its status.

## Europe

All the countries in Western Europe have substantial scenes with a diverse range of institutions and bands. The Nordic countries are at the heart of the global extreme metal scene. The Norwegian scene barely needs any introduction, given the notoriety of its black metal scene. The scene thrives to this day and, like the Swedish scene, features a bewildering range of musicians and bands. While the scene is best known for black metal, the scene produces the full range of extreme metal genres. Furthermore, Norwegian 'post-black metal' acts such as Ulver and Arcturus have pioneered some of the most challenging and avant-garde forms of extreme metal. In contrast, the Finnish scene has become noteworthy for specializing in highly commercial forms of metal that have grown out of extreme metal. Like the Norwegian and Swedish scenes, the Finnish scene thrives and has in recent years become an important global scene. Acts such as Nightwish and Children Of Bodom have become extremely popular, particularly in Europe, but the scene is also known for more extreme acts such as Impaled Nazarene. In contrast to the three other Nordic scenes, the Danish scene has struggled to develop a global profile to the same degree, although the scene is productive and produced the pioneering satanic band Mercyful Fate. Perhaps surprisingly given its 'Viking' roots, the Icelandic scene is fairly marginal in global terms.

As I have mentioned before, Northern Europe is at the heart of the global extreme metal market. The high population density and short distance between cities mean that it is relatively easy and lucrative for bands to tour Germany, the Benelux countries and some Central European countries. The high living standard and strong social security systems in most Western European countries make devoting time to the scene relatively easy.

The German scene in particular is globally important as the biggest single market for most forms of extreme metal. While a number of important labels and other institutions are based in the country, the global visibility of bands from the German scene is somewhat more erratic. In the 1980s, German thrash bands such as Kreator and Sodom produced a highly distinctive and influential sound. Similarly, German power metal bands such as Helloween and Blind Guardian continue to be well regarded. But while a large number of German bands make a significant contribution to the global scene, there is little that is musically distinctive about German extreme metal today.

Southern European countries have generally been less conducive environments for scenic activity. Spain, Portugal and Italy remain, with some important exceptions, somewhat insular in global terms. The Greek scene is somewhat larger and more productive. There is some evidence of loose networks on pan-Balkan and pan-Mediterranean cooperation. For example, in January–February 2005 Orphaned Land played Greece, Turkey and Bulgaria on their 'Flooding the Balkans' tour.

Extreme metal in Eastern Europe and Russia developed well before the end of the Soviet Union and its client states. Bands such as Hungary's Tormentor and the Czech Republic's Krabathor released demos that were circulated globally through tape trading. Extreme metal in Eastern Europe is extremely popular, although its global commercial importance is somewhat hidden by the prevalence of bootlegging. Poland in particular is increasingly reaching Scandinavian levels of prominence with frequent tours by Western bands and the substantial global popularity of bands such as Behemoth and Vader.

### South America

The popularity of extreme metal in South and Central America is hidden somewhat by the prevalence of bootlegging. Furthermore, until recently few bands from outside the continent toured there and only a small number of bands from these countries have become globally popular. Many South American countries contain extremes of poverty, which makes scenic involvement difficult or confines production (although not necessarily consumption) to the small middle and upper classes. The result is that most of the South and Central American countries lack capital in the global scene and are relatively invisible in global terms.

The major exception to this marginality is the Brazilian scene. The enormous 'Rock in Rio' festivals have featured a number of metal bands and are world famous. The global prominence of Brazilian music and culture has benefited the extreme metal scene. In the 1980s, bands such as Sarcofago and Sepultura and others were important in the development of thrash, death and black metal across the world. Sepultura went on to become the biggest extreme metal band in the world in the early to mid 1990s, although the rise in their popularity was partly the result of moving out of the country (Harris 2000). Their popularity has faded substantially since the departure of singer Max Cavalera in 1996. While Brazilian bands such as Angra and Krisiun continue to have some global prominence, the same cannot be said for bands from the rest of the South American scene.

### South-East Asia

Extreme metal scenes in South-East Asia share many of the characteristics of South American scenes. Metal is very popular in a number of South-East Asian countries, particularly Malaysia, Singapore, and Indonesia, with active scenes producing the full range of musics and institutions. Indeed, Jeremy Wallach (In Press) argues that Indonesian, Singaporean and Malaysian scenes are some of the largest in the world, with considerable interconnections between them. Until recently, few Western bands toured in this region, but when they do, crowds in the tens of thousands are common. Yet even more than in South America, these scenes are isolated from the rest of the global scene. Again, the popularity of extreme metal is hidden somewhat by the prevalence of bootleg recordings. Few bands from this region have ever made more than a minimal impression on the global scene (Singapore's Impiety and Indonesia's Kekal being rare exceptions).

Scenes in South-East Asia have faced political difficulties. In Malaysia, the dominance of Islam has resulted in periodic campaigns against metal and Satanism. In February 2006 for example, the Norwegian black metal band Mayhem was scheduled to give a performance in Kuala Lumpur, but following objections from members of the country's parliament, the concert was banned. In Indonesia, the oppressiveness of the Suharto government was a theme in the metal produced in that country (Wallach 2003). More generally, in a part of the world undergoing extremely rapid changes, metal provides a vibrant means of protest.

### Other Scenes

Japan has long provided a lucrative market for some bands and has also produced a number of influential bands such as S.O.B., Sigh and Loudness. Japan also has a strong experimental music tradition and is perhaps best known for its groundbreaking 'noise' acts such as Merzbow who have proved influential on and been influenced by extreme metal. Elsewhere in the Pacific Rim, there is a strong Australian and a less strong New Zealand scene. While the Australian scene is fairly isolated from the global scene, it is an increasingly popular tour destination and has produced a few bands who have made a modest international impact. The Australian scene has in common with the British scene an emphasis on humour, often coupled with a down-to-earth vulgarity. Australia's best-known band Sadistik Execution developed a reputation based on their tongue-in-cheek provocation of outrage. Elsewhere in the Pacific and Oceania, metal is virtually non-existent.

While there appear to be sizeable numbers of metal fans in the Islamic Middle East and North Africa, scenic infrastructure is limited. Only in the more liberal Islamic countries, such as Egypt and Morocco, or those with a strong secular counter-culture, such as Iran and Turkey, is there much scenic activity. Scattered bands from countries such as Saudi Arabia do operate despite considerable difficulties. Even in more liberal environments, the danger of persecution is acute, as I discussed in the case of Egypt and Syria in Chapter 2. Metal in many Islamic countries is so underground that it is largely disconnected from the global scene save via the Internet. Interestingly, Orphaned Land has been a catalyst for Middle Eastern scenic development. After a show in Turkey (3 July 2004) they posted the following message on their website:

> Orphaned Land finished the show in RTN Festival successfully. We thanks [*sic*] to all the people from Turkey, Greece, Israel, Jordan, Syria, Saudi Arabia and other countries who contributed to the great atmosphere of this show.

Elsewhere in the world, scattered groups of extreme metal and metal fans gather and cooperate in shifting alliances. Scenic activity is developing in China, India and Nepal (Greene 2001) and other Asian countries. As I noted in the previous chapter, Sub-Saharan Africa (with the exception of white South Africa and Namibia) and the black Caribbean appear to be metal-free. In countries with tiny or non-existent scenes, members either participate with the global scene directly or interact with other fans in small peer groups.

### Conclusion – Resisting and Taking Advantage of Location

The production and consumption of extreme metal within a complex of scenes has two contradictory effects. Scenes entrench capital (and indeed, lack of capital) through the workings of their infrastructure. At the same time, the location of extreme metal practice within scenes also ensures that they have a degree of autonomy from global flows of capital. While there are capital differences between scenes, scenes nonetheless ensure that the inequalities and differences in capital within the global scene as a whole are not simply reducible to wider global inequalities. It is true of course that capital differences between scenes follow the basic contours of global flows of capital – so scenes in South-East Asia and South America are much 'weaker' in global terms than scenes in Europe and the USA. There are fundamental asymmetries within the scene that enable European and American bands to penetrate other global markets more effectively than the reverse. At the same time, there are also differences and fissures between scenes that are not simply explainable by global differences in capital. There is a significant difference between the structure of the US scene and most European scenes. The richness and productiveness of the latter's infrastructure and the ease with which they take advantage of and contribute to the wider society are contrasted with the persecution that the US extreme metal scene has suffered from at times.

The embedding of extreme metal music and practice within scenes is something of a mixed blessing. Those who are located in weaker, less promising scenes sometimes seek to 'resist' their location. Most dramatically, some scene members have left their native countries in order to relocate in more promising locations (Sepultura being the most famous example). Less happily, some Israeli scene members have tried to take their bands elsewhere with no appreciable success. More generally, some scene members in marginal locations resist being defined by their location. Some scene members I interviewed in Israel in the late 1990s were keen to emphasize their hatred for the country (Kahn-Harris 2002). As Pierre Hecker argues (2005), metal in the Middle East tends to be anti-nationalistic in contrast to the national pride shown in Scandinavia. Indeed, as Emma Baulch (2003) notes in the case of Bali, in some locations the faithful copying of 'foreign' extreme metal styles is a source of prestige and authenticity. For those in difficult locations, extreme metal scenes can provide a way of 'transgressing all limits of the local', as Paul Greene puts it in the case of Nepal (Greene In Press).

Increasingly though, pride in even the most marginal and unpromising location has started to become the norm. For example, bands in Indonesia have started to sing in non-English languages with greater frequency (Wallach 2003). In Brazil, the later career of Sepultura shows how the nation, initially rejected, became 'rediscovered' as a source both of pride and of musical inspiration (Avelar 2003). The rise of 'folk' themes in extreme metal has given scene members from across the world the ability to find a way to positively reconcile themselves with their location. The increasing musical heterogeneity of the global scene will be further discussed in the next chapter, in which I look more closely at how 'subcultural capital' creates hierarchies of prestige within the scene that cut across the scenic hierarchies and inequalities discussed in this and the previous chapter.

## 6 EXTREME METAL AND SUBCULTURAL CAPITAL

### From Cultural Capital to Subcultural Capital

The previous two chapters have argued that the scene has a degree of autonomy from global flows of power and capital. While the relative power of the scene's constituent local scenes broadly follows the contours of global power relations, there are multiple exceptions. Within the extreme metal scene, being born into the right sex, ethnic group or nationality is not destiny, although it certainly helps. However, over and above the forms of difference that structure social life in all its power-fullness, the scene creates its own, indigenous, sources of difference and capital.

As in Bourdieu's model of the field, the scene is a space of conflict, constituted through struggles over capital. The principal such struggle is over the 'cultural capital' accumulated through displaying competence in the scene's cultural practices (Bourdieu 1979, 1993). In adapting Bourdieu's ideas to the analysis of cultural capital in dance-music cultures in the United Kingdom, Sarah Thornton introduced the concept of 'subcultural capital'. Subcultural capital is 'objectified' ' . . . in the form of fashionable haircuts and well assembled record collections' (1995: 11) and 'embodied' 'in the form of being "in the know", using (but not over-using) current slang and looking as if you were born to perform the latest dance styles' (1995: 11–12). Members of the dance-music scenes Thornton examined are obsessed with making distinctions and producing hierarchies of status that translate into hierarchies of power. As in dance-music scenes, subcultural capital is accrued in the extreme metal scene by constructing and performing various forms of discourse and identity. Subcultural capital is both endowed by other scene members in the form of prestige and power and claimed by scene members for themselves in the ways they perform their identities. To possess subcultural capital, whether by claiming it for oneself or having it endowed by others, is to gain self-esteem and a rewarding experience of the scene. In this chapter I will describe the two principal forms of subcultural capital that circulate within the scene: what I call mundane subcultural capital and transgressive subcultural capital. My argument is that the experiences of transgression and mundanity I discussed in chapters 2 and 3 are struggled over and contested by scene members in their attempts to gain power, status and capital within the scene.

Mundane Subcultural Capital

> Every one of us has heard the call
> Brothers of true Metal, loud and standing tall
> We know the power within us has brought us to this hall
> There's magic in the Metal, there's magic in us all

(From 'Metal Warriors' by Manowar, from the album *The Triumph of Steel* (1992))

Manowar are a power metal band, straddling the extreme metal and wider metal scenes. Power metal lyrics have a tradition of self-celebration that other extreme metal lyrics lack. The lyrics of 'Metal Warriors' do, however, express a widespread attitude in the extreme metal scene. The lyrics, together with their triumphalist musical backing, celebrate the 'we' of the scene, all bound together by the 'magic' of metal, all proud of their belonging. The song celebrates the scene as a space of collective power, a space of what Michel Maffesoli (1996) calls 'puissance' – a power almost beyond words that emerges when people of similar interests gather together, reproduced in the elusive 'atmosphere' of collective praxis.

'Metal Warriors' effectively encapsulates the potential of mundane subcultural capital. Of course at first sight, there appears to be little that is mundane about this celebration of puissance. Puissance seems to have little to do with the mundane, simple pleasures we discussed in Chapter 4 and, in particular, with mundanity's solipsistic features. Paradoxically though, solipsistic mundane practices are nonetheless oriented towards producing effects within the collective space of the scene. In celebrating the scene as a collective space, one can read 'Metal Warriors' as a celebration of the mundane, individual practice that constructs and maintains that space.

Mundane subcultural capital is oriented towards the possibilities of the collective puissance that is produced as a collective result of the mundane efforts of the totality of scene members. It is a form of capital accrued through a sustained investment in the myriad practices through which the scene is reproduced. It is accrued through self-sacrifice, commitment and hard work. Just as the practice of transgression is in reality nearly always limited practice that nonetheless implies the threatening possibilities of excess, so mundane subcultural capital may in practice be produced solipsistically and even boringly, but it nonetheless implies the possibilities and joys of collective activity.

As with all forms of cultural capital, the demonstration of *savoir faire* within the scene is crucial for the accumulation of mundane subcultural capital. Scene members claim subcultural capital by knowing the complex histories of the scene and by having heard the music of its vast number of bands. We saw in Chapter 3 how the process of developing scenic knowledge is one of the key pleasures of becoming involved within the scene and this knowledge is eagerly displayed. In interviews, scene members often emphasize the depth of their knowledge of the scene, as in the following extract from an interview with an Israeli scene member:

> . . . I wanted first to know very well the music that I listened to, and then come to more heavier stuff. . . . I wanted to know the heavy metal scene better and then to come into more areas. (Yoav)

Yoav claims subcultural capital by demonstrating the care he has taken to acquire a profound knowledge of extreme metal and its roots in heavy metal. Knowledge of the historical development of extreme metal canons is extremely important to scene members. These canons are the result of the making of complex 'distinctions' (Bourdieu 1979) within the scene. Practices of distinction are displayed through demonstrations of appropriately detailed scenic knowledge. A large number of generic and subgeneric terms assist in this process. Within death metal, for example, subgeneric distinctions such as 'technical death metal', 'Swedish death metal' and 'black/death metal' provide useful ways of identifying the music of particular bands.

Generic terms are imprecise and subcultural capital is displayed through precision and knowledge. Subcultural capital is most effectively displayed through knowledge of individual bands and albums. As I have argued elsewhere (Harris 1997), a band's music tends to be described by reference to other bands. Take, for example, this extract from a review of a demo by the US death metal band Incantation, taken from the Welsh fanzine *Mutilated Mag* (Issue 2, 1991), that appears in Figure 13 (see p. 87):

> After leaving <u>*REVENANT*</u>, guitarist John McEntee joined up with Sal Seijo on guitar, Ronny Deo on bass, Peter Barnevic on drums and Will Rahmer of <u>*MORTICIAN*</u> on vocals, to form none other than <u>INCANTATION</u>. Formed in '89, they finally release a demo, and from what started as just a slight murmur, has evolved into some of the best grinding Death Metal to hail from New York, New Jersey area in a long time. Featuring four tracks, extreme stuff, in the vein of <u>REVENANT</u>, <u>*MORBID ANGEL*</u>, <u>*DERKETA*</u> and <u>*MASSACRE*</u>. Starting off with "Profination" through to "Devoured Death" which takes us onto side two for "Entrantment of Evil" and "Eternal Torture". Recorded in May 1990 at Stardust Studios with Ed Lotwis engineering (Of <u>*REVENANT*</u> fame!). A very clean and crisp production, bar the bass drum, which could have been a bit louder.

The importance of bands is emphasized by capitalizing and underlining. Incantation is first situated in the context of the history of other bands and scene personnel and then placed within a fairly non-specific genre of 'grinding Death Metal'. Subcultural capital is claimed through the ability to place Incantation within a highly specific history of 'grinding Death Metal' in the New York/New Jersey area. The only description of the music that does not rely on bands or generic names is located in the final sentence describing the production. Without a detailed knowledge of death metal, the reader would have little idea of Incantation's sound. Even with this knowledge, the review gives little clue as to the musical merits or otherwise of Incantation. The review functions to display the writer's impressive subcultural capital in navigating a complex set of distinctions. The reader, should they also know them, is given a chance to be complicit in the knowledge of distinctions. If the reader does not understand these distinctions, the review gives them the chance to develop this knowledge. Indeed, by reading enough reviews of this kind, anyone could, in theory, develop a detailed knowledge of the scene without ever hearing any music!

Subcultural capital can also be acquired through a detailed knowledge of the institutions and practices of the scene. This knowledge is considerably more difficult to acquire than a detailed knowledge of extreme metal music, since it requires an active experience of the scene. In many ways, a detailed knowledge of scenic practice seems to produce more mundane subcultural capital than a detailed knowledge of the scene's music. The statements we saw in Chapter 3 that emphasize the work and seriousness that scene membership involves are claims of mundane subcultural capital. Mundane subcultural capital is produced through a commitment to work hard *for* the scene, as an almost altruistic commitment to the collective. Indeed, commitment to the collective sometimes also crosses over into more conventional forms of altruism. Benefits for scene members in distress are not unknown. For example, there was considerable support for Chuck Schuldiner, founder of Death, in his fight against cancer before his death in 2001. More often though, it is through more mundane activities that altruism towards the scene is demonstrated. In the first of the following extracts Nathan describes how he set up his own label and in the second, Lars describes the aims of his scenic involvement:

> . . . sat around with [name] who's my partner in [name of label], we were round my house one night, and we just got talking about the way the metal scene was going. We decided that, you know, we could we could do something for the scene as such, the bands we believed in. (Nathan)

> The only thing I'm aiming for is to survive actually, it's that's all I want. I want to survive and to do the things that I think is right for the scene. (Lars)

A professed altruistic commitment to the scene is part of a scenic ethic, adherence to which is itself a powerful source of subcultural capital. Here, Tony explains the ethical principles behind his distro (part of this extract was quoted in Chapter 3):

> I think [name of distro] has always been based around honesty and that was always my aim was to provide quality music with a fast reliable service which is what I wanted from a distro. If I ordered from someone I wanted stuff to come back straight away and not people sending out alternatives because stuff was not

in stock so they just send you anything that they think you will like, that was never what [name of distro] was about. (Tony)

Given the geographical dispersion of the scene, much of the ethics of the scene revolve around being a reliable correspondent. Since disputes are hard to resolve over long distances, reliability and honesty are crucial in avoiding intra-scenic conflict. Considerable discussion occurs within the scene over which institutions are most reliable in their transactions. Those that have a good reputation are rewarded with considerable subcultural capital and tend to grow and to last. Those that have a reputation for 'rip offs' are loudly disparaged (see Figure 20).

The increased entry of external forms of capital into the scene since the 1990s has made the ethics of the scene considerably more complicated. Altruistic ethics are threatened when there is the potential for some scene members to make a profit and when money changes hands, the potential for disagreement increases. However, making money from the scene does not automatically preclude the generation of mundane subcultural capital, as is the case in, say, the punk scene. While scene members are frequently poor, the metal scene does not have the 'aesthetic of poverty' that is present in the global punk scene (O'Conner 2000). Other than within some subsections of the black metal and grindcore scene, the scene has no rigidly policed ideological opposition to commerce, as commonly exists in other popular-music cultures (Frith 1983). Profit and commerce are tolerated *provided* that they are by-

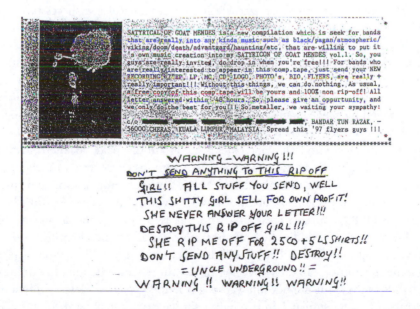

20: Anonymous flyer warning about an alleged 'rip off girl' from Malaysia c. 1997.

products of scenic practice, rather than ends in themselves. As long as the scene 'comes first' and an element of altruism is sustained, commercial imperatives are not necessarily problematic. Indeed, some argue that the introduction of the profit motive within the scene guarantees ethical practice. Tony continues:

> I've never seen the point in non-profit motives [laughs]. I mean what is the point? If you want to do something you might as well do it well. I can't see that you could provide a quality service with a on a non-profit basis. (Tony)

Profit may in fact be seen as a just reward for the accumulation of subcultural capital, as in the following extract from an interview with Trey Azagthoth, a member of the band Morbid Angel, in the Finnish fanzine *Isten 100* (1999):

> Do you earn money out of Morbid Angel? Can you live *alone* on it?
> 'Yeah. I can live alone on it. I've lived alone on it ever since '89. But I don't live like, not, you know, rich as far as financially . . .'
> Oh I didn't mean that, but do you make ends meet?
> 'Yeah, I do make ends meet. It has a lot to do with managing my money, a lot of *hard* work, you know, whatever.'
> That's amazing.
> 'Oh yeah!'

Making money from the scene involves certain obligations that must be met if members are to maintain subcultural capital. Successful members need to retain an unselfish commitment to those who are less successful. All the successful owners of scenic institutions that I have interviewed emphasized that they paid themselves less than they could, preferring to plough profits into signing and releasing records by new bands. Owners of successful labels may be criticized for making money, but on the grounds that they have not continued to act ethically and altruistically within the scene. Commerce is rarely opposed in principle, but is frequently opposed in practice.

Long-standing scene members who have a reputation for ethical dealing and a commitment to the scene gain subcultural capital in the form of respect and fame. Respect translates into sales and increased attention paid to their institutions. Mundane subcultural capital is also acquired by musicians, but in a slightly more complicated way. Mundane subcultural capital is about contributing and sustaining the scene and not, principally, about innovating within the scene. As Ruth Finnegan points out (1989), musical creativity is not necessarily the same as musical innovation. Innovation is an individual practice more suited to the claiming of the transgressive subcultural capital that we will discuss in the next section. Musicians accrue mundane subcultural capital by developing existing styles. The majority of musicians and bands in the scene are not innovators but refiners. Nonetheless, within a musical landscape of many similar bands refining similar styles, it is hard for musicians to accrue mundane subcultural capital by musical means alone. Those bands that accrue the greatest amounts of mundane subcultural capital are generally those that are most adept at working within scenic institutions. They are the bands that are the most skilled at forming relationships with a wide range of scene members. Accruing mundane subcultural capital by these means maximizes a band's chances of having their music released by a prominent label with a high standard of production. In this indirect way, success within the scene allows mundane subcultural capital to be convertible to other forms of capital through increased sales.

### Transgressive Subcultural Capital

Mundane subcultural capital is accrued through a commitment to the collective. In contrast, transgressive subcultural capital is claimed through a radical individualism, through displaying uniqueness and a lack of attachment to the scene. Indeed, transgressive subcultural capital can be claimed through a critique of the scene itself and, by implication, of mundane subcultural capital.

One of the most powerful of such critiques can be found in the above-quoted Finnish fanzine *Isten 100*[1] (see Figure 14, p. 88). *Isten* first appeared in the 1980s and each issue is individually named and themed. Published in 1999, *Isten 100* presented an extended critique of the scene and of what it calls 'scene metal'. The authors argued that the contemporary scene is so supportive as a community that it is killing 'art'. They defined scene metal as follows:

> 1) Music that exists merely because its makers think it's important for them to be a part of metal and the underground scene, and to make the relationship official as quickly as possible.
> 2) Music that is played by people who are really quite fascinated by the idea of making some music of their own, but have yet to find an emotion or an idea to express.

The writers of *Isten 100* complained that there is no proper criticism of 'boring', uncreative bands and that as a consequence the scene is undiscriminating, homogeneous and bland:

> Look at you!
> You are cardboard people propped up in a scenery of a thousand years of greatness. Controlled by an industry that's only barely profitable but so deeply in love with itself it sups off its own excrement. You write, release and listen to songs about total war, but only brawl like a bunch of four-year-olds at best. And deep down inside, you're all in agreement, whatever you say.
> Which is exactly why you love 'metal', probably. Friend Metal. Life Metal. Scene Metal.
> Consensus Metal. [. . .]
> Yes-man Metal. Objective Metal. No Metal At All.

Unlike most fanzines, *Isten* 100 contains no reviews and only a few select interviews. The lack of reviews means that the huge numbers of mediocre metal releases are simply ignored. The interviews are largely with innovative, idiosyncratic characters that have pioneered new sounds. Implicit in *Isten 100* is a 'great man' theory of art, which treats the best art as coming from 'geniuses' who have strived for autonomy from the conformist influences of their times. This is an unashamedly elitist viewpoint and, indeed, transgressive subcultural capital *is* elitist. Transgressive subcultural capital involves a desire to be different, to challenge and transgress accepted norms within and outside the scene.

Black metallers have been most enthusiastic in claiming transgressive subcultural capital, in particular, the members of the early 1990s Norwegian scene. Norwegian black metal bands strove to transgress boundaries within the extreme metal scene itself. Early black metal bands scorned other bands and scenic institutions in order to establish a tiny, 'true' 'elite'. As in *Isten 100*, there was an assumption that the majority of people in the scene are mediocrities, with only a select few able to join the elite. Black metal bands continue to be far more vigorous in claiming transgressive subcultural capital than mundane subcultural capital. Norwegian scene members were rewarded with considerable notoriety and subcultural capital. The activities and personalities of the early 1990s scene remain a source of fascination to this day. Characters like Varg Vikernes and Euronymous are still revered for their total commitment to transgression. Similarly, those who are seen as musical innovators within the scene are endowed with transgressive subcultural capital. Bands that pioneered new styles, particular those who did so in the 1980s such as Bathory and Venom, are widely admired.

As we saw, scenic discourse produces mundane subcultural capital through critical languages that are primarily concerned with placing bands within systems of distinction. In contrast, transgressive subcultural capital is claimed through scenic discourses that involve a far more 'personal' engagement with music. In the 1990s the scene developed critical languages that came to resemble the 'auteur' forms of criticism that developed within rock discourse in the 1970s (Frith 1983). These forms of criticism concentrate on how music makes the writer feel, as with the following example taken from a review of the album *High on Blood* by the band Deranged, from the Swedish fanzine *Davthvs* (Issue 2, 1998):

> Shit shit shit shit shit this is fucking something that Dying Foetus here below could only dream of. Sorry Jason but 'High On Blood' beats you in your own sport because here we are not talking about HATE I mentioned in your review, here we are talking about H A T E in its most unadulterated, pure, beatufiul [*sic*] form! . . . see, I am so upset I cannot even spell 'beautiful'!
>
> Holy hell and her grandmother, I knew Deranged had potential and 'Rated – X' ruled the shit out of any Swedish brutal death ensemble but "High On

Blood" just has the kind of ferocity its leaves me speechless I lick the record.
I'm in love.

In using the band Dying Foetus and the subgenre of Swedish brutal death metal as musical reference points for Deranged, the review contains elements of the mundane scenic discourses examined in the previous section. However, the focus of the review is on how the music makes the reviewer feel. The review is highly personal, drawing on odd private jokes and strange constructions.

This review is typical of the efflorescence of critical writing within the scene in the 1990s. As transgressive subcultural capital became a more common form of currency within the scene, members began to treat the scene as a forum for producing idiosyncratic forms of art. Bands began to experiment with incorporating a wide variety of musical influences into extreme metal. Writers began to draw on critical languages pioneered outside the scene. In this way, transgressive subcultural capital has more in common with forms of cultural capital circulating in other artistic fields than mundane subcultural capital does. Transgressive subcultural capital constructs art and individuality as the predominant ways of gaining capital. Potentially, at least, 'great art' produces forms of capital that can be transferable into and from other scenes. To a certain extent, transgressive subcultural capital is not subcultural at all. It is rather a particular version of a form of capital that exists wherever artists and other individuals seek to attack taboos and 'the mainstream'. While transgressive subcultural capital circulates within the extreme metal scene, its attachment to the scene is contingent and pragmatic – to possess transgressive subcultural capital is to be *part of* the scene but not *of* the scene.

### Transgressive and Mundane Subcultural Capital

We might think that gaining one form of subcultural capital precludes gaining the other. Indeed, some scene members who are committed to transgressive subcultural capital would argue precisely this. Similarly, those committed to mundanity may strongly disapprove of those elements of transgressive practice that threaten the scene. Mundane subcultural capital is far easier to claim than transgressive, but while scene members must work harder to claim transgressive subcultural capital, its rewards may be greater. The most revered scene members are those who have committed themselves to transgressive individualism in some way. Those who are respected for their mundane commitment to the scene, such as label managers, never quite achieve the same level of adulation. While mundane subcultural capital translates far more easily into forms of capital deriving from fields of power, it does not, unlike transgressive subcultural capital, have the potential to be translated into cultural capital circulating in other fields and scenes.

But both forms of subcultural capital are necessary to the scene. Transgressive subcultural capital requires an audience. That audience is most readily available within a well-ordered scene and the scene can only be properly ordered with a system

that awards mundane commitment. Conversely, although scene members may be
content to commit themselves to the mundanity of the scene they must still, as we
saw in Chapter 3, occasionally experience the pleasures of transgression in order to
maintain a commitment to the scene. Both forms of subcultural capital tacitly affirm
the necessity of the other.

Furthermore, it is possible for members to claim mundane and transgressive
subcultural capital simultaneously. As Thornton shows, subcultural capital is claimed
through *not* doing certain things. She argues that, 'Nothing depletes capital more
than the sight of someone trying too hard. For example, fledgling clubbers of fifteen
or sixteen wishing to get into what they perceive as a sophisticated dance club will
often reveal their inexperience by over-dressing or confusing "coolness" with an exaggerated cold blank stare' (1995: 12). The same is true within the extreme metal scene.
New (generally young) members entering the scene are frequently disparaged. For
example, Yoav told me how he had met one young fan who was under the impression that the band Metallica had released a black metal album (in fact, the album in
question was informally entitled *The Black Album* due to its all-black sleeve):

> . . . it's very frustrating the actual situation of the scene, because you are dealing
> with people who don't know what metal is, you know people who think that
> Metallica released a black metal album. It's ridiculous. (Yoav)

New members are seen not only as ignorant – precluding them from mundane
capital – but also as slaves to 'trends' – precluding them from transgressive capital.
'Trend' is a word with entirely negative connotations within the scene. As another
Israeli scene member, Motti, explains:

> . . . people in Israel they just jump on trends, I don't know there was a punk
> thing in Israel like in, the late nineties er the late eighties [. . .] the early nineties
> and then the metal scene started, and then they progressed to trance I don't
> know how it happened.

'Trend-followers' cannot claim either form of subcultural capital. They are both ignorant and conformist. Scene members try to gain both transgressive and mundane
subcultural capital by displaying both knowledge and individuality. The incursion of
new members or new spaces onto the scene is something that scene members actively
try to prevent. To enter the scene with any kind of capital, new members must work
hard to achieve the required scenic knowledge. Moreover, they have to show themselves to be 'true' individuals rather than members of a group. Yet they must not, as
Sarah Thornton points out, 'try too hard'. New scene members who try too hard to
be transgressive are often ridiculed, as in the following anecdote:

> . . . I met a guy in a nightclub, he plays in a band round here [. . .] well he's just
> a little boy who doesn't know what he's doing and he came up and he said 'oh

aren't you [name]?', I said yeah so we got talking about music and beer and all that innocuous sort of stuff and he says 'oh I'm into Satanism me', I said 'oh really?' and he goes 'yeah yeah yeah' and he went on and on, he goes 'I've got the book of spells back at my house do you want to come and see?', I said 'yeah go on then we'll have a look'. So we went back to his place and no word of a lie he got this book out and it was a Penguin book of poetry and on the front it had a quote saying all poetry is magic and he honestly believed it was the book of spells. (Nathan)

The 'boy's' attempt to impress this prominent black metal musician and claim transgressive subcultural capital is met with ridicule. I have heard many similar stories of the desperate attempts of new members to impress established ones. Such stories provide ways for more established scene members to claim both mundane and transgressive subcultural capital. New members provide a convenient 'other', against whom capital can be claimed.

The disparaging of new members reveals certain fundamental anxieties about the scene and the nature of appropriate scenic behaviour. There is continual anxiety over how far the scene should welcome heterogeneity and change. 'Trends' represent the prospect of change and of greater heterogeneity within the scene. Change and heterogeneity weaken the mechanisms through which mundane subcultural capital is claimed. Those who invest most in mundane subcultural capital are most fearful of change and difference. In contrast, transgressive subcultural capital rewards individuality, unpredictability and innovation. In theory, then, those most committed to transgressive subcultural capital should welcome change and heterogeneity.

As we have seen, however, individual scene members orient themselves towards both transgressive and mundane subcultural capital in varying degrees, provoking an ambiguous response to the prospect of change and heterogeneity. As Keith Negus (1999) points out, in all musical genres there are tensions between genre as 'routine' and genre as 'transformative'. Genres are sites both of innovation and of stable creativity within strict limits. Within the extreme metal scene these very different views of creativity and innovation are negotiated in the context of the tension between the instability rewarded by transgressive subcultural capital and the homogeneity rewarded by mundane subcultural capital. In order to examine this tension more closely, I want to present a brief musical and discursive history of the extreme metal scene since the early 1990s.

### The Development of the Scene Since the Early 1990s

The 1980s were a time of great innovation in extreme metal. Not only were thrash, doom and death metal created, but other experiments in extreme metal brought surprising new influences into the scene. For example, Celtic Frost's *Into The Pandemonium* (1987) dabbled with gothic, classical and pop influences. Yet by the early 1990s much of this creativity had petered out, as mundane subcultural capital had become the predominant form of capital circulating within the scene. The death metal music that dominated the scene had become extraordinarily uniform and other forms of extreme metal had been pushed to the margins of the scene. At that time, scene members emphasized their 'normality', wearing casual clothes (see Figure 1, p. 3) and spending most of their time in correspondence with other scene members. Strict limits were placed on the circulation of transgressive subcultural capital. While death metal bands generally frequently wrote lyrics on transgressive themes and the music avoided all trace of melody, by that time such transgression had become routine. The production of such transgressive material had become a precondition for participation in the scene and, therefore, had almost ceased to be transgressive. At the same time, the scene was effectively insulated from the world, making difficult the public transgression of any non-scenic boundary.

Yet while the scene was musically and discursively at its most mundane, homogeneous and static, in other respects the scene was able to incorporate difference and change. The early 1990s were the time of the scene's greatest growth. Coinciding with the decline of heavy metal, there was a rapid influx of new scene members, helped by the high profile of a few bands on the border of the extreme metal and heavy metal scenes. For example, many UK scene members date their entry into the scene to the 1990 'Clash Of The Titans' world tour, featuring Slayer and Megadeth. The scene grew throughout the world, extending to places where extreme metal had previously been unknown, with the influx of new members particularly marked in 'marginal' countries, such as Israel.

The black metal scene that developed in Norway and elsewhere in the early 1990s was principally oriented towards the development of transgressive subcultural capital. Although the precise details of the violent events within the Norwegian black metal scene described in Chapter 2 remain unclear, it seems likely that scene members were engaged in a process of one-upmanship, in which each attempted to be more transgressive than the other. Within the highly cohesive Norwegian scene, transgressive subcultural capital became amplified and presented as an alternative to the prevailing logic of mundane subcultural capital.

The black metal scene produced dramatic musical and discursive innovations. Criminality, racism and associations with the far right were new phenomena in metal. The black metal scene challenged the extreme metal scene, previously committed to mundane stability, to incorporate new sounds and practices that were highly disruptive and potentially dangerous. At the same time, black metal scene members were themselves fearful of change and difference, even as they introduced considerable disruption and diversity to the scene. Like many revolutionary movements, the black metal scene looked backwards as much as it looked forwards. Black metallers such as Euronymous and Varg Vikernes were not only critical of the early 1990s scene for not being sufficiently transgressive, but also for having 'betrayed' metal. The black metal scene looked backwards to early 1980s British metal and German thrash metal. The 1980s were seen as a 'golden age', during which metal was clearly identifiable and dangerous. Black metal thus attempted to redefine mundane subcultural capital by criticizing change, diversity and tolerance.

The early 1990s black metal scene developed a logic of subcultural capital accumulation that has survived to this day. Whereas transgressive subcultural capital was formerly of lesser importance than mundane, the black metal scene ensured that the two now have equal importance. Although individual scene members do not necessarily have an equal commitment to both forms of subcultural capital, neither form of capital has come to dominate the scene.

Since the early 1990s the scene has evolved as a space both of difference and experimentation, and of nostalgia and stasis. The logic of mundane subcultural capital ensures that all existing extreme metal genres have been refined incrementally by scene members. However, there has also been a quite startling amount of radical experimentation within extreme metal. At the forefront of this experimental tendency have been some of the members of the early 1990s Norwegian black metal scene. Bands such as Ulver and Arcturus (see Figure 21) have incorporated classical music, 'trip hop', sampling, operatic singing, and drum and bass into their music. In addition, stimulated by black metal's preoccupation with myths of nationality, a variety of bands from all extreme metal genres have incorporated 'folk' musics. Such bands span the globe including Sepultura from Brazil (Harris 2000), Orphaned Land from Israel, Otyg from Sweden, Skyforger from Latvia, Finntroll from Finland and many more. It is also more common now for bands to sing in non-English languages.

Some extreme metal bands have also refined their sound in less esoteric ways, coming close to producing a new form of 'alternative rock'. For example, the UK's Anathema were originally a doom metal band, but went on to develop a form of music with strong similarities to Pink Floyd and Radiohead. The Gathering from the Netherlands, also previously a doom/death metal band, now play a form of psychedelic/gothic rock. Some bands with roots in the extreme metal scene such as Opeth have created ambitious modern forms of progressive rock and others such as Neurosis and Isis have also drawn on the extended song-lengths and tempo changes of progressive music. Other bands such as Sunn0))) or Blut Aus Nord play music at the fringes of the avant-garde. The music of such bands still circulates almost exclusively within the extreme metal scene. The scene's music has diversified to such an extent that some of its output cannot realistically be termed extreme and some cannot be easily termed metal.

At the same time, the contemporary extreme metal scene has reacted with great hostility to the incorporation of other kinds of difference. In the mid 1990s nu metal bands developed a sound drawing on grunge, hardcore, death metal, rap and funk musics, with bands such as Korn, The Deftones and Limp Bizkit (see Figure 22) mixing downtuned guitars and metal riffs with alternately rapped, screamed and sung

21: Extreme metal becomes experimental: the Norwegian band Arcturus in 2005.
Reproduced with the kind permission of Season Of Mist Records.

lyrics focusing on the dysfunction of the singer (Udo 2002). Nu metal bands and fans wear baggy clothes, often made by sportswear manufacturers, and generally have short hair and a proliferation of body piercings and tattoos. By the late 1990s nu metal had become almost as popular as heavy metal had been in the 1980s, with a huge worldwide following, which included many female fans. Nu metal is dominated by bands from the USA, particularly from southern California.

The majority of extreme metal scene members are extraordinarily vehement in their denunciation of nu metal. Nu metal has become an 'other' against which subcultural capital can be claimed:

22: Nu metal: Limp Bizkit in 2003. Reproduced with the kind permission of Universal Records.

. . . we haven't got some kind of ego or image or nothing like that do you know
what I mean? Well we don't give a fuck what we look like yeah? We ain't gonna
go, I dunno, 'yeah yeah let's go and all get our nose pierced and fucking get some
eyebrow rings and wear some baggy shit' and you know what I mean? [. . .]
We're trying to stay totally clear from the fucking Korn, Limp Bizkit, new wave
or er, arse metal that has been introduced [. . .] just don't want to be associated
with trendy metal man. (Richard)

One reason for nu metal's pariah status is its perceived 'trendiness', particularly
regarding its emphasis on visual image. Another extract from a British interview is
also revealing:

[Talking about Korn] . . . I don't like their, the way they portray themselves and
the way they are and the way their music is it's just too, weak [. . .] it's like I don't
get any feeling to it. It's like with death metal bands I can see, someone got a
good feeling in there you know they've got their hearts into it and shit you can
hear it in the music and whatever (Pauline)

In this extract Korn are, in some ill-defined way, 'weak', superficial and depthless by
comparison with death metal's seriousness and commitment.

It is also argued that nu metal bands lack an engagement with the history of metal.
As the Editor's reply to a letter in *Terrorizer* (February 1999) puts it:

In 1990, for example, Obituary were probably just as popular as Coal Chamber
are now . . . but they also covered 'Circle Of The Tyrants' [a song by Celtic Frost]
and talked about Mercyful Fate and Slayer a lot in interviews. Ultimately,
everyone has to be given a chance to find out about the past as well as the underground . . . and some of the options in today's market don't really allow that. . . .
Frankly, it's harder to talk to a West Coast metal band who have virtually no
memory of anything before 'Chaos AD' [1993 album by Sepultura] than it is to
natter with veterans like Voivod or Bruce Dickinson, even if these legends are
ten to twenty years older than the writers on this mag. (65)

Not only are nu metal bands perceived to have removed themselves musically from
extreme and heavy metal music, but they have also refused to ally themselves discursively with the history of these scenes. Even if the scene has become musically diverse
in the 1990s, that diversity is still founded on members paying due respect to the
history of the scene. Since the display of historical knowledge is a crucial way of
gaining mundane subcultural capital, nu metal bands have effectively excluded themselves from gaining capital within the extreme metal scene.

Nu metal is also precluded from gaining transgressive subcultural capital as the music
draws on two musical/discursive sources that are 'abjectified' within the scene. Nu
metal attends extensively to gender, drawing on grunge music to discuss ambivalence

towards sexuality, masculinity and femininity. For example, self-loathing provoked by sexual anxiety is a common theme found in Korn's lyrics. The song 'A.D.I.D.A.S.', from the album *Life is Peachy* (1996), contains the chorus, 'All day I dream about sex/All day I dream about fucking'. Such a preoccupation with sexuality is absolutely antithetical to the forms of transgression practised within the extreme metal scene. Within the scene sexuality is something to be ignored, or conquered with an excessive masculinity. The fact that nu metal bands often conceal a rampant misogyny and fear of femininity behind their anxiety does not matter – the presence of femininity in any shape or form cannot be tolerated within the extreme metal scene. In this context, the large number of female nu metal fans serves to confirm the music's abjectification. Nu metal also welcomes musical and other influences from black cultures. Nu metal bands draw on rap and funk music, and the scene's 'sportswear' style is very similar to that found in rap culture. Such influences cannot be tolerated within extreme metal. They are never explicitly criticized on racial grounds but, like femininity, 'blackness' is something that must be totally removed and ignored.[2] Extreme metal is the apotheosis of a process through which the pivotal influence of black musics (particularly the blues) on the development of metal has progressively been erased. This is exemplified by the minimal attention that scene members give to Jimi Hendrix's importance in metal history (Wells 1997).

However much extreme metal has incorporated musical difference in recent years, nu metal transgresses the acceptable boundaries of difference within the scene and must therefore be excluded from the scene. The scene thus reproduces a classic 'symbolic boundary', which defines nu metal as 'impure' (Douglas 1984). Partly in response to the rise of nu metal, the extreme metal scene has, since the mid 1990s, begun to (re-)incorporate elements of traditional heavy metal. As we saw, black metal emphasized the imagined glorious past of traditional metal. This nostalgic tendency was consolidated by subsequent revivals of thrash and power metal. By the late 1990s, power and heavy metal bands such as Iced Earth, Nevermore and Hammerfall had achieved great popularity within the scene and some 1980s bands that had lost popularity in the 1990s, such as Manowar, became popular again. In some parts of the world, including Germany, Greece and South America, such bands became as popular as nu metal bands. These bands unapologetically stress 'metal' as a signifier and assert the power of mundane subcultural capital (as in Manowar's 'Metal Warriors'). They stress the importance of long hair, leather and an 'us and them' attitude to the non-metal world. The return of traditional metal has had the effect of 'purifying' the scene. Since the turn of the century there are signs that this process has had an effect outside of the extreme metal scene, with new wave of American heavy metal bands that have a much firmer background in extreme metal beginning to challenge the commercial popularity of nu metal within the wider metal scene.

What is remarkable about the contemporary extreme metal scene is the way in which reactionary and radical versions of extreme metal coexist. The scene has become a space that is both conservative and at the same time a space within which metal forms the basis of wide-ranging musical explorations. That is not to say that all scene members embrace all styles of metal, and there is a certain amount of suspicion between the most traditionalist and the most experimental members. Nevertheless, musical coexistence is made possible by the equal weight given to mundane and transgressive subcultural capital within the scene. Although the possibilities for earning capital were formerly limited to a fairly narrow range of strategies, in the contemporary scene members can accrue capital by a variety of musical and discursive means. The scene maintains a delicate balance that ensures that both transgressive and mundane subcultural capital have currency in the scene. The scene manages to maintain an equilibrium between its transgressive 'forces of fragmentation' and its mundane 'forces of unification' (Roccor 2000).

### Capital, Power and Politics

Subcultural capital is not easily convertible into capital within other fields or scenes. Moreover, subcultural capital does not work as a resource in the same, concrete way as the forms of capital we discussed in the previous chapter – it cannot, for example, be used to buy more advertising space or to record more albums. Subcultural capital becomes problematic when it builds on other divisions in capital. Those who possess subcultural capital may go on to gain other forms of capital through, for example, selling more records. Conversely, for those for whom participation in the scene is already difficult, such as women and those from certain marginal locations and ethnicities, subcultural capital may be particularly difficult to claim. Mundane subcultural capital, for example, requires so much in-depth knowledge that those from marginal countries or poorer backgrounds may find it difficult to accrue it. Subcultural capital can therefore become concentrated in the hands of those who possess other kinds of capital.

At the same time, the economy of subcultural capital is always complicated by the way it can be claimed for oneself, ensuring that at least potentially, the struggle for subcultural capital is a 'level playing field'. Furthermore, the very nature of both transgressive and mundane subcultural capital helps to attenuate inequalities in other forms of capital. Mundane subcultural capital engenders an ethic of collective support that helps to support marginal scene members. Transgressive subcultural capital's rewarding of individuality and idiosyncrasy is also potentially more accessible to those with low amounts of other kinds of capital, since it does not require detailed scenic knowledge. In and of itself then, subcultural capital is more accessible than other kinds of capital.

This chapter and the last two chapters have shown just how complicated the question of capital is. In Chapter 4 I argued that while the scene has a relatively high degree of autonomy, it nonetheless allows members to accumulate forms of capital that are transferable into other scenes and to utilize capital from outside the scene as a resource within it. In Chapter 5 I showed how capital, difference and hierarchy are embedded within the complexities of scenic structures. In this chapter I have shown how the scene has developed its own forms of capital and how the logics for accumulation of these forms of capital produce both change and stability.

Just as the logics of transgressive and mundane subcultural capital ensure a balance is maintained between change and innovation, so the scene simultaneously allows for capital accumulation while attenuating the worst of its effects. But just as the delicate balance between the transgressive and the mundane constantly threatens to be upset, so the logic of capital accumulation always threatens to overwhelm the scene. There is an ever-present danger of the scene's inequalities deepening and collapsing into wider, global inequalities. To understand how this process does or does not take place, we need to look more closely at how power and capital is negotiated within members' everyday experience of the scene. The next chapter investigates the politics of the scene through an analysis of how 'reflexivity' works within it, focusing particularly on the important role that music plays in the negotiation of the political.

## The Reflexivity of the Scene

If the scene can be compared to a game or contest, as Bourdieu's work implies, then 'at stake' in participation in the scene is the possession of subcultural capital and its rewards of prestige, self-esteem, community and identity. The corollary of the possession of subcultural capital is the possibility of ignominy, loneliness and ridicule. Yet most of those who enter the scene seem to 'play the game' fairly effectively, or at least without undue stress. Most scene members manage to accrue sufficient subcultural capital to be comfortable within the scene. In Chapter 3 I argued that a pleasurable experience of the scene was dependent on members developing 'reflexively managed scenic careers' that allowed them to negotiate the complex balancing act between scene and everyday life.

This chapter will look more closely at how members reflexively manage their scenic careers. Anthony Giddens describes reflexivity as 'the continuous monitoring of action which human beings display' (1984: 8). While this is a process that occurs on the 'micro' level of the individual, it is tied into 'macro' processes of 'structuration'. Giddens argues that 'structures' ('rules and resources recursively implicated in social reproduction' (1984: xxxi)) are reproduced within the fine detail of everyday interaction. Actors continually reproduce and manipulate structures through their reflexive management of everyday life. Giddens argues that the very nature of reflexivity has changed in modernity:

> The reflexivity of modern social life consists in the fact that social practices are constantly examined and reformed in the light of incoming information about those very practices, thus constitutively altering their character . . . We are abroad in a world which is thoroughly constituted through reflexively applied knowledge, but where at the same time we can never be sure that any given element of that knowledge will not be revised. (1990: 28–9)

In modernity, reflexivity ensures that all structural principles are continually subject to question. Interaction in modernity is based on the tacit acknowledgement that the world is changeable and that no certainties exist regarding the consequences of human action. Scott Lash (1994) similarly suggests that 'reflexive modernization' involves the 'empowerment of subjects' as agents are able to reformulate the rules and resources that constitute structure. Crucially for Lash, reflexivity is more present in certain areas of modern societies than others. The reflexivity he describes is, in fact, reflexivity about reflexivity, a kind of 'higher order' of reflexivity. For Lash, as for Giddens, reflexivity becomes a potential as well as something that is ever present. The critical social theory that Giddens, Lash and others have formulated aims to add to the overall process of reflexive modernization through identifying those areas where reflexivity is most strongly present or where it should be nurtured.

Lash argues that one place in which reflexivity is extensively practised is within those 'reflexive communities' that are 'vastly different from traditional communities' and 'offer possibilities of even more intensified reflexivity' (1994: 167). Lash specifically associates reflexive community with subcultures and other communities formed around shared practices. He also associates reflexive communities with Bourdieu's 'fields'. He defines reflexive community in four ways:

> first, one is not born or 'thrown', but 'throws oneself' into them; second, they may be widely stretched over 'abstract' space, and also perhaps over time; third, they consciously pose themselves the problem of their own creation, and constant re-invention far more than do traditional communities; fourth, their 'tool's and products tend to be not material ones but abstract and cultural. (1994: 161)

Reflexive communities are continually active and self-aware. They are founded on the breakdown of certainty that modernity engenders, but they nonetheless avoid the atomization of individuals. They offer the empowerment of reflexivity, without its concomitant insecurity.

The extreme metal scene seems to perfectly fit the definition of reflexive community: scene members 'throw themselves' into the scene; the scene is 'stretched' over time and space; scene members constantly debate what sort of space the scene should be; the scene's products are purely cultural; scene members seem to practise 'intensified reflexivity'. As we saw in Chapter 4, the scene has highly sophisticated networks for communication and information. Practice is continually reformulated in the light of information, in order to produce a safe balance between transgression and mundanity. As we saw in Chapter 6, the cultural products of the scene, particularly in the 1990s, demonstrate a sophisticated engagement with a variety of musical forms.

### The Unreflexivity of the Scene

The problem with applying the concept of reflexive community to the extreme metal scene is in accounting for cases where the practice of reflexivity appears to be only partial and selective. In fact, within the scene there seem to be multiple incidents of what one might call '*un*reflexivity'. Consider the following extract from an interview with the Danish black metal musician Peter Mesnickow, who also worked for the record label Euphonious, which appeared in the Norwegian fanzine *Imhotep* in 1997 (Issue 3):

> As some have probably noticed we (Euphonious Records/Voices of Wonder DK
> where I work) have placed an anti-nazi logo on our releases. This doesn't mean
> we are nigger-lovers or something like that. But since Voices of Wonder have
> been accused of being a nazi-label several times we just had enough!! (38)

The temptation would be to rely on an easy explanation for this quotation – that
Peter Mesnickow is a complete idiot. To put this in more sociological terms, in not
attending to the obvious contradiction between printing anti-Nazi logos and using
the term 'nigger lovers', Mesnickow appears to be demonstrating a failure to be fully
reflexive. At the same time, however, by printing an anti-Nazi logo on their releases,
thereby recognizing and attempting to forestall the criticisms of anti-racists, he and
the company for which he works are deploying reflexive awareness of the consequences of their actions. In this extract, however, Mesnickow is also reflexively fore-
stalling the potential criticisms of racists that the label's staff are 'nigger lovers'. In the
final analysis though, given his implicit assumption that one can satisfy both racists
and anti-racists at the same time, Mesnickow's practice appears to be unreflexive.

Below is another, less dramatic example of apparent unreflexivity from an interview with a Swedish label owner:

KKH: From what I read in fanzines, a lot of Swedish people in the metal scene
are very unhappy about immigrants in Sweden. What's your attitude to
that?

R: Immigrants in Sweden? Well um

KKH: Do you have a problem with that?

R: No. I don't care where people live in on the whole globe, you know. I don't
care. Of course I can always ask myself why just Sweden had to be, to have
all the immigrants but I don't care actually because I want to go wherever
I want to go and I hope that people would respect me and treat me as a
human being. . . . so I'm definitely not Nazi or anything like that. (Lars)

As in the previous extract, but in a much more limited way, the interviewee simultaneously draws on the language of racism and the language of anti-racism. He draws
on 'liberal' discourses to explain why he 'doesn't care' about the presence of immigrants in Sweden while at the same time asserting that Sweden has taken more than
its share of immigrants. His disavowal of racism is made ambiguous through his
unwillingness to follow through the implications of discourses.

In my research into the extreme metal scene I have encountered many apparently
baffling instances of unreflexivity in which the practice of reflexivity seemed to be
absent or limited. For example, I met an ex-punk scene member who claims to be
committed to anti-fascism who also told me that 'Enoch Powell was right'. There is
the strange case of the prominent Norwegian black metal musician who has made
many racist comments, but is, in fact, of Moroccan descent. There are other strange

cases of black metal bands and Christian bands cooperating with and playing on each others' albums. Contradiction may be an essential part of human discourse (Potter & Wetherell 1987), but the exercise of reflexivity is designed to knit together contradictions into coherent narratives. Yet in these cases and many others within the scene, contradiction is not attended to, leaving only baffling silences.

Such silences are part of a wider (and again, apparently unreflexive) phenomenon in which difficult issues are simply ignored. A British scene member once showed me a piece of his artwork depicting a stereotypical African 'tribesman' spanking a white woman. I mentioned that some might find the illustration racist. He replied 'they might do, but it isn't' and would brook no further discussion. Similarly, in the following extract, Elaine demonstrates a refusal to attend to issues of sexism:

> [Responding to a question about whether misogynist lyrics in death metal might put women off] Could do but I don't see it, as the way they're seeing it, so I don't know . . . I think they just kick up a fuss just to kick up a fuss. (Elaine)

Elaine is reluctant to engage with the issues being discussed and any attempt to attend to sexist lyrics as 'kicking up a fuss'.

This wariness at 'kicking up a fuss' is shown most dramatically in the ways that the violence of the black metal scene is often dealt with in scenic discourse. An examination of stories about bands and individuals caught up in violent acts in *Terrorizer*[1] magazine reveals a remarkable coyness. The January 1995 issue contained a feature on the Norwegian black metal band Emperor that mentioned the imprisonment of the band's drummer Faust for murder, but contained no explanation or discussion of this apparently extraordinary episode. More extraordinarily, an interview conducted in prison with Varg Vikernes in March 1996 (and illustrated with the picture shown in Figure 7, p. 47) did not mention the cause of his imprisonment nor his racist views, focusing instead on his music. The same was true of an interview conducted in February 2005 with Jon Nödtveit of Dissection, recently paroled from a sentence for accessory to murder, which did not discuss his crime. Interviews with various bands of which Faust became a member following his parole have also failed to mention the murder for which he was convicted. An intriguing comparison with the rap scene can be made here. Whereas the extreme metal scene effaces imprisonment, it is openly discussed and even celebrated in rap (Lynskey 2005).

### Reflexive Anti-Reflexivity

The examples quoted above apparently show scene members as at the very least wilfully ignorant, lacking in self-awareness and politically naive. While this conclusion would certainly conform to the common stereotypes of metallers as moronic, how do we understand the apparent coexistence of determinedly reflexive and unreflexive practices within the scene? This question is all the more puzzling when we consider that *Terrorizer* magazine is a publication that has pioneered some of the most sophisticated critical writing in the scene.

Yet if we look again at these apparently unreflexive practices, the picture becomes more complicated. Unreflexive practice is ignorant practice, practice that 'does not know better'. Unreflexive practice is defenceless against the flows of signs and capital that constitute the processes of reflexive modernization described by Lash and Giddens. The above examples should not be seen as instances of members' inability to be reflexive; in fact, they seem to be the result of members' active *suppression* of reflexivity, of *anti-reflexive* practice. Whereas unreflexivity derives from a failure, anti-reflexivity is an active achievement in holding the reflexivity of modernity at bay. Whereas unreflexive practices leave members defenceless against processes of reflexive modernization, anti-reflexive practices simply refuse to admit that such processes exist. If reflexivity is founded on an appreciation of the contingent, ambiguous, unintended character of practice, anti-reflexivity is founded on the illusion that the world is simple and obvious. The above examples show members stubbornly taking statements at 'face value' and ignoring contradiction. Anti-reflexivity produces a simplistic world in which nothing need be examined and everything is just as it appears.

If the scene is a reflexive community, then it is difficult to separate apparently anti-reflexive practices from this wider reflexivity. Anti-reflexive practices must always at some level be implicated in reflexive practices. It is more appropriate, therefore, to refer to the practices we discussed in the previous section as *reflexively anti-reflexive*. If unreflexivity is 'not knowing better' and anti-reflexivity is 'not wanting to know', then reflexive anti-reflexivity is 'knowing better but deciding not to know'. Reflexive anti-reflexivity can therefore be defined as anti-reflexivity practised by members who are capable of producing reflexive practice within the reflexive space of the scene. In fact, given the intense reflexivity of the scene and the intense reflexivity required to become involved in it, unreflexivity and anti-reflexivity are relatively rare within the scene.

Reflexive anti-reflexivity is analogous to Lawrence Grossberg's concept of 'authentic inauthenticity' (1992). Grossberg argues that in postmodernity authenticity remains an important value in rock – as it is in extreme metal where to be 'true' and not 'trendy' is paramount – but an authenticity that acknowledges the impossibility of differentiating between the authentic and inauthentic. In postmodernity, to claim allegiance to a particular rock style is never to fully engage with the consequences of that allegiance. As Grossberg argues, 'If every identity is equally fake, a pose taken, then authentic inauthenticity celebrates the possibilities of poses without denying that that is all they are' (226).

I want to draw on a number of examples to show how reflexive anti-reflexivity offers a distinct way of experiencing the scene. In 1999 the (now defunct) Norwegian black metal band Immortal posed for publicity pictures that were later reproduced in the sleeve of their album *At The Heart Of Winter* (1999). Some of the pictures are shown in Figure 23. The two core members of the band, Abbath and Horgh (the bigger built one), are dressed in leather trousers and adorned with spikes, both common elements of metal clothing. They are also wearing 'corpse paint', a style of face painting pioneered by black metal bands but drawing inspiration from the face painting of Kiss and earlier glam rock bands.

One possible 'preferred reading' (Hall 1993) of these pictures is that the band look stupid. There is a certain comic hubris in a black metal band apparently attempting

23:  The Norwegian black metal band Immortal. From the inlay sleeve of *At The Heart Of Winter* (1999). Reproduced with the kind permission of Osmose Productions.

to look 'evil' and warlike, but ending up looking ridiculous. One might also read these pictures as 'camp'. Susan Sontag defined camp as the 'love of the unnatural: of artifice and exaggeration' (1982: 105), as 'art that proposes itself seriously, but cannot be taken altogether seriously because it is "too much"' (1982: 112). The apparently exaggerated seriousness of the Immortal photographs almost begs to be read as camp.

Given the close association between camp and homosexuality, it is hard to imagine that Immortal wanted their photographs to be read as such. Moreover, given the importance that seriousness and 'trueness' has in black metal, it is equally hard to imagine the band welcoming comic readings. It would, therefore, be very easy to read the pictures as revealing an unreflexive lack of awareness of possible readings of the pictures.

We cannot assume, however, that either the band or their audience are oblivious to the connotations of these images. In fact, a highly developed appreciation of the comic can be found within the scene. The important point about the comic within the scene is that it generally does not undermine the scene, its music or its personnel. Rather, it is founded on a love of 'cheese', a celebration of lack of taste and lack of hipness that, unlike camp, does not uphold the categories of good and bad taste (Oakes 2004). Take, for example, this extract from a review by Nick Terry of *At The Heart Of Winter*, which appeared in *Terrorizer* (April 1999) alongside two of the pictures:

> If our long-suffering designer Dave Tonkin has picked it right, above this review will be possibly the best (or worst, depending on your aesthetic sensibilities or lack of same) photograph you will see in Terrorizer this year, let alone last or next. You will agree, I am sure, that this photo is truly magnificent. Picked yourself off the floor yet? Stifled that belly-laugh? Are you sitting comfortably? Then I'll begin. (48)

The review treats laughter as the inevitable response to the pictures and the magazine further reinforced this response by including a poster montage of the pictures two issues later.

In my research I came across dozens of examples of members revelling in the humorous possibilities of the scene. Humour appears to be a perfectly appropriate response to black metal in particular:

> I always had a tongue in cheek attitude towards it [black metal]. When it first started out I just couldn't believe these things that these people were saying and that other people actually thought that they really seriously meant what they were saying half the time, like Euronymous saying I wouldn't care if all my friends died and they just didn't, they just made me laugh, these sort of things. I didn't take them seriously. (Tony)

> [Describing a visit by a black metal band] . . . and they came to the office and

this was the middle of summer and I was wearing a pair of shorts and T-shirt and it was boiling, sweltering at eleven o'clock in the morning, they were all stood there going [makes devil sign] and they were all like covered in black with all these great big leather coats and I said 'aren't you fucking boiling?' [laugh] 'you wankers' [laugh]. But of course they were all like you know [makes serious face] and I just, I was ripping the piss out of them in the office and he was going 'no, no'. (Will)

It was very amusing, it was hilarious. Like when you, when I for the first time heard a black metal song sung in Norwegian on one of their early Darkthrone records, it was it was hilarious. (Lars)

Black metal has been a common object of satire within the scene. For example, the Swedish fanzine *Pure Passion* (Issue 1, 1997) printed a cartoon depicting 'A day in the life of a true Satanist' and a revised version (by the artist Aurora Walderhaug) is shown in Figure 24. The panels (depicting a man in corpse paint) were captioned as follows: 'Slaughtering Christian morons', 'Conference with Satan', 'Ritual sex orgies', 'Going to the shops milk' and 'Washing the car'. The Norwegian fanzine *Mimmes Brun* (Issue 1, 1997) printed a fake interview with an imaginary band, 'Moon Rites', satirising many of the conventions of interviews with black metal bands:

> **Ok, you and Moon Rites play Black Metal and . . .**
> Actually not, we play Dark Forest Metal.
> **Dark Forest Metal . . .? So you play the same style as Under The Fog.**
> No. Under The Fog plays Forest Fog Metal, which is something else.
> **I suppose Under The Fog is not as Dark as you then?**
> Well, they are Dark, but not like us. More Foggy I think.
> **Your other band, Storm Funeral then, what kind of music do you play with them?**
> We play Neo-Tormented Storm Metal exclusively.

Metal parody bands such as Insidiöus Törment, Pink Stëël and Nanowar, generally parody the conventions of mainstream heavy metal (such as the 'heavy metal Umlaut' in the case of the first two bands – see the Wikipedia entry of the same name). There have also been musical parodies of black metal such as Death Kristjan [*sic*], who, according to *The Oficial Homme Page Of Death Kristjan*,[2] claim to play 'Treu Not Nice Black Metal' and are supposedly from Dagestan SSR. Another black metal parody, Impaled Northern Moon Forest, a side project of the grindcore band Anal Cunt, play songs with titles such as 'Gazing At The Blasphemous Moon While Perched Atop A Very Very Very Very Very Very Very Forsaken Crest Of The Northern Mountain'. More generally, the Internet features satire sites such as *Hell's Laughter* and *Infernal Combustion*. Affectionate celebrations of metal idiocy can also be found such as *Where Is Mitch Hale?*, a site attempting to trace a rather gormless participant

24: A day in the life of a true Satanist. Illustration by Aurora Walderhaug. Reproduced by permission.

in a British TV documentary on metal. 'Viral' emails featuring extreme metal parodies, doctored photos and animations also circulate widely through the scene.

Extreme metal has, from the beginning, contained camp and comic elements. Venom, generally considered to have 'started' black metal with the album *Welcome to Hell* (1981), used satanic imagery to an unprecedented degree, but within the scene there was, and is, a clear consensus that the band were not 'really' Satanists and that their attitude to Satanism was tongue-in-cheek. Norwegian black metal bands are sometimes contrasted with Venom in this regard:

> All the black metal bands in the 1980s, they used to sing a lot of the things that these Norwegian bands sing about, but you knew deep down that they never meant it. It was alright you know, it was safe. It was all, you know, you just knew Venom weren't Satanists, they were a rock and roll band, with these Norwegian bands, they were, I thought they were completely and utterly crazy and they were for real. (Tom)

So highly developed is the practice of reading elements of extreme metal as comic that some scene members initially had difficulty in reading Norwegian black metal as serious. For example, Digby Pearson, manager of the British label Earache, initially could not believe on meeting him that Varg Vikernes was a Nazi as he claimed to be, only realizing that he was sincere when his activities in Norway were later revealed (Mudrian 2004).

The early 1990s black metal bands attempted to make metal 'real' again and remove its mundanity. At the same time though, these bands were generally fervent fans of Venom, reinterpreting the band as 'serious' and problematizing humour in the process. In the early 1990s Norwegian scene, black metal was seen as the opposite of 'fun' and some bands claimed never to laugh, an attitude that has persisted among some black metallers. That these bands felt the need to actively oppose laughter is ample testimony to the multiple possibilities of comic and camp readings of black metal. As we have seen, however, the bands did not entirely succeed and humour remains important within the scene. Any black metal imagery of the type used by Immortal risks being read as camp and comic. Why then do bands such as Immortal continue to draw on it?

Crucially, we should not assume that humour and camp are incompatible with transgression. As Gavin Baddeley shows (1999), some strains of Satanism, particular Anton LaVey's Church Of Satan, have a deep appreciation of the comic. Furthermore, we should not assume that humour within the scene undermines the serious, as the serious and the humorous are closely intertwined. In the interviews quoted towards the start of this section, the interviewees, having ridiculed black metal, went on to show that laughter did not stop them becoming more seriously attracted to the scene. Taking pleasure from humorous anecdotes does not undermine members' commitment to the scene. Similarly, a humorous reading of the Immortal publicity pictures does not necessarily undermine Immortal's credibility. The *Terrorizer* review of *At The Heart Of Winter* went on to praise the album without reservations. The band's ludicrous imagery served, in fact, to inspire affection towards Immortal. Of course, it is not necessarily the case that the band wanted to be seen as humorous in any way. However, the costs of being seen as humorous were minimal and, therefore, did not need to be attended to. The band's apparent anti-reflexivity was based on a reflexive evaluation of the minimal risks that possible comic readings of the photos might produce.

Reflexive anti-reflexivity practice ensures that laughter is never overwhelming and the humorous never undermines the serious. Although, as we have seen, elements of the extreme metal scene, and the black metal scene in particular, are often seen as ludicrous, the full implications of humorous readings are left unexplored. Quite *why* the Immortal photos might be seen as amusing is left unsaid. The delight in camp never leads to a wholehearted reading of the scene as camp. Scene members still read the scene seriously, even as they acknowledge its comic aspects. In some cases this acknowledgement is explicit, as in the *Terrorizer* review of Immortal. In other cases this acknowledgement is implicitly made through a reflexively anti-reflexive suppression of humour. This suppression of humour can be seen in a *Terrorizer* article (May 1999) on the band Manowar by Greg Whalen:

> . . . Manowar is more than just a band. It's a need, a calling, a way of life . . . a fucking *legend*.
>
> Some people don't understand this. They look at the furry loincloths, the leather waistcoats and the swords, and they laugh. But to mock is to miss the point completely: Manowar is not there to be scrutinised or studied. Manowar just is. (34)

Whalen does not deny that Manowar could be construed as amusing. However, he argues that to understand Manowar 'properly' one needs to remove humour from one's critical vocabulary. Reflexive anti-reflexivity allows scene members to tactically marginalize that which they 'don't want to know'. Members can 'play' in serious ways with imagery that might otherwise be ridiculed. They can enjoy the *frisson* of humour, without ever undermining their profound commitment to the scene. Reflexive anti-reflexivity can therefore be a 'playful' form of practice. In play signifiers are manipulated so as to destabilize fixed and unitary meanings (Derrida 1990). To play is to enjoy discourses not for their intrinsic 'meanings', but for their unstable and polysemic qualities. Play is acutely, gleefully reflexive in celebrating the ability to manipulate discourse for one's own contingent and fleeting ends.

But while reflexive anti-reflexivity may be playful, it is not necessarily benign. Reflexive anti-reflexivity allows members to draw on almost any image or discourse within the scene, however offensive it may be to some members, while at the same time allowing them to 'back away' from the full implications of their actions. It may be that much of the racist, sexist and homophobic discourse within the scene is not entirely 'serious', yet this does not lessen the pain it might cause to members. In an earlier publication (Kahn-Harris 2004a), I examined an incident from the late 1990s in which one Israeli musician, Balzamon of Bishop Of Hexen, got caught up in a dispute with Melankol X, editor of the prominent Norwegian fanzine *Nordic Vision*.

The dispute culminated with Melankol X insulting Balzamon, saying 'you are from Israel and that alone is enough to hate you forever'. Balzamon complained loudly about his racist treatment in a variety of scenic publications, yet received little support. In fact, Melankol X has acted in unproblematic ways with other Israeli scene members. Balzamon was therefore caught up in an impossible dilemma – to accept the abuse as 'not serious' or to give voice to the hurt he felt and risk ridicule. The problem is that just as anti-reflexive practice, produced by otherwise reflexive individuals can be characterized as reflexively anti-reflexive, so Balzamon's apparently reflexive attempts to defend himself from racist abuse can, within the reflexively anti-reflexive space of the scene, be characterized as unreflexive.

### Music and the Politics of the Scene

The prevalence of play has important implications for the politics of the scene. The notion of politics is antithetical to many scene members. One incident that demonstrates this has been described in detail by Moynihan and Søderlind (1998) and by myself (2004a). In 1994 Fenriz of the Norwegian black metal band Darkthrone asked their British label Peaceville to include a statement in the sleeve-notes of their album *Transylvanian Hunger* that included the words, 'If any man should attempt to criticise this LP, he should be thoroughly patronised for his obvious Jewish behaviour'. As a consequence of the resultant furore in the metal and non-metal media, Darkthrone quickly capitulated and the album was issued without the offending statement. Darkthrone issued a statement in which the band denied they had fascist or racist sympathies. The statement explained the use of the word 'Jewish' in the following way:

> . . . Darkthrone can only apologize for this tragic choice of words, but PLEASE let us explain this. You see in Norway, the word 'Jew' is used all the time to mean something that is out of order, if something breaks down, if something is stupid etc. It's always been like this, we don't know why, it's just a coincidence in our slang language. . . .

It is almost impossible to believe that Darkthrone had no idea that the pejorative use of the word 'Jew' could possibly be construed as offensive. Furthermore, as Moynihan and Søderlind point out, the denial that the band had racist or fascist sympathies was disingenuous, considering that Fenriz had previously made a number of apparently fascist statements in fanzines. Moreover, when *Transylvanian Hunger* was finally issued, the phrase 'Norsk Arisk Black Metal' ('Norwegian Aryan Black Metal') was printed prominently on the sleeve (see Figure 25).

At the same time, other interviews with Fenriz seem to indicate a more playful attitude to racism and fascism and incidents have been reported to me of Fenriz interacting with Israeli scene members without problems. I would argue therefore that Darkthrone were cynically utilizing reflexive anti-reflexivity in order to maximize the transgressive potential of racist discourse, without becoming irrevocably enmeshed in

25: The back cover of Darkthrone's *Transylvanian Hunger* (1994). Reproduced with the kind permission of Peaceville Records/Snapper Music.

outright fascist activity. Yet why attempt to avoid controversy at all? Why *not* embrace fascism and racism? If Darkthrone had gone down this route, the band would have become enmeshed in public controversy within and outside the extreme metal scene. Moreover, their 'attitudes' would have been foregrounded at the expense of their music and this is anathema to most extreme metal musicians. As Darkthrone put it in their statement:

> Darkthrone is *absolutely not* a political band and we never were. [Emphasis in original]

Within the extreme metal scene the denial of political intent is a common defence used by those who have drawn on fascist and racist discourses. As one black metal musician told me, in response to an interview pointing out the similarity between his satanic views and fascism:

> I'm very much against all forms of politics. We don't take no part in any political values. I've never been interested in politics at all, so I don't really know what fascism really is about, so I don't know. (Eric)

Other scene members have used disparaging definitions of politics more aggressively, in order to deflect criticism. The album *The Fire and the Wind* (1999), by the (now defunct) British/New Zealand band Demoniac, featured a song entitled 'Myths of Metal' that contained the chorus:

> Hitler Metal want to bang my fucking head
> And fist the living dead in the middle of the night alright
> I really want to bang my head and fist the living dead in the
>    middle of the night my sign
> The Metal's in my blood and the power is here and now for you!
> HITLER METAL! SIEG HEIL!

Faced with the threat of the record being banned in Germany, the band released an apologetic statement explaining that the song was a tongue-in-cheek tribute to 1980s German thrash metal. Yet on their website (http://www.demoniac.com, accessed 1 April 2000) they were far less apologetic, printing the following statement under the lyrics to the song:

> For the NERDS . . . No this song is NOT about Hitler or any of your politics bullshit! If you don't get the joke, fuck off. This song is about banging to heavy fucking metal and having a good laugh. We don't give a fuck about Hitler. Fuck off if you don't have a sense of humour.

Politics is constructed here both as humourless and as entirely compatible with metal culture.

The use of the term 'politics' within the scene is restricted to interventions in the public sphere that are consciously intended to have an impact on social institutions. From this perspective, virtually nothing within the scene is political. This definition of politics upholds an 'autonomous' view of music, which sees it as ideally removed from social forces. Such a view is part of a long tradition of idealist musical discourse that has obscured the connections between music and society (Chanan 1994). Music is seen as non-verbal and hence unknowable and abstract (Durant 1984; Fornäs 1997). Anything 'political' is seen to sully the purity of music. As Bettina Roccor puts it: 'The message of heavy metal is . . . not more and not less than the music called heavy metal' (2000: 84). Indeed, music has a more paramount place in the extreme metal scene than is the case in other scenes such as the goth or punk scenes, where other practices such as fashion and activism are just as important.

For extreme metal scene members, music connotes the scene and politics connotes that which is outside the scene. Discourses that emerge from spaces outside the scene are seen as threatening and members attempt to keep them at bay. Any attempt to draw on discourses from outside the scene must be subordinate to the music:

> If you're gonna be a racist and if you're gonna be a fascist and if you're gonna make metal, just make sure your metal's good, before your mouth and before your ideas. Don't use your ideas to sell your album. (Zara)

Scene members are often strongly criticized if their commitment to music is perceived to be subordinate to their commitment to politics. As the reviewer of an album by the Christian band Mortification acidly puts it in the British fanzine *The Crypt* (Issue 2, early 1990s): 'I very much doubt that the primary motivation behind this band has anything at all to do with the love of music'. With a very few exceptions, overt Christian bands and overt Nazi bands tend to be confined to their own, largely autonomous scenes.

Of course, music and the scene can never be detached from flows of power and capital and hence a non-political scene is an impossibility. As I have argued in previous chapters, the scene is enmeshed in relations of power and capital, despite its relative autonomy as a field. For members to pay attention to forms of power and capital is to raise the spectre of politics, making any challenge or even discussion of such aspects of the scene extremely difficult. As a result, members may flirt with racism and sexism and make use of forms of capital drawn from fields of power, confident in the knowledge that most challenges can be dismissed as political. So a sinister effect of reflexive anti-reflexivity is its highly efficient protection of the workings of power. This protection is all the more problematic given that the practice of reflexive anti-reflexivity is not shared equally throughout the scene. It is practised less in more marginal locations within the scene and less by newer scene members.

Those who have challenged power within the scene most effectively have generally been those with a close connection to the more explicitly political hardcore punk scene and thus have a degree of protection from ostracism. The punk scene provides an effective resource for those wishing to challenge the accumulation of capital within scenic institutions and for those wishing to challenge racism. However, the punk scene is a less than effective resource for those wishing to challenge sexism and homophobia. There have been few attempts to deal with sexism and homophobia within the extreme metal scene. Those few initiatives that have taken place have received little support, such as the *Awakenings: Females In Extreme Music* compilation (1997), which was the subject of extremely mediocre reviews. There is simply no available haven or resource for people with strong views on these subjects who nevertheless enjoy extreme metal. Moreover, despite the influence of the punk scene, those who resist the exercise of forms of power within the scene must generally do so within the scene's own terms, which is a difficult task. Individuals or groups that cannot or will not practise reflexive anti-reflexivity have become marginalized. Scenic minorities either have to accept that they cannot reflexively attend to difference or they have to leave the scene.

At the same time, even if challenges to forms of power are difficult within the scene, reflexively anti-reflexive opposition to politics also ensures that the scene has not become a bastion of the far right. The relationship to racist and fascist discourses and practices has remained a playful, rather than a committed one. We should not mitigate the real hurt caused to those who suffer racist abuse. However, such incidents remain isolated and are not translated into concerted campaigns. The opposition to politics is at least even-handed. In opposing anti-racist activity the scene also opposes racist activity. Members with the most overtly fascist and racist views have been pushed to the furthest margins of the extreme metal scene, into a closer accommodation with the Nazi music scene. Indeed, in the Norwegian documentary film *Satan Rides the Media* (1998), Varg Vikernes claims that after his activities and views became exposed in the media he became unpopular in the scene, as it forced members to choose whether to be serious or not. It is also note-worthy how (thus far) scene members' hatred of religion has generally been confined to Christianity and, to a much lesser extent, Judaism. Islam tends to be criticized in rare, brief, 'throw away' anti-immigrant comments in interviews with European scene members, rather than in lyrics. To attack Islam would be to risk considerable attention and danger. Transgression remains focused on targets where dangers are known and can be reflexively managed.

### Conclusion

Reflexive anti-reflexivity is not a practice shared unanimously by all scene members, nor has it been equally important in all periods of the scene's history. However, in recent years reflexively anti-reflexive practice has tended to marginalize other forms of reflexive practice. To slip briefly into a functionalist explanation, reflexive anti-reflexivity has come to dominate the scene because it fulfils a certain kind of 'defensive' function very effectively. We saw in previous chapters how the scene maintains a balance between the practices of transgression and mundanity. The reflexively anti-reflexive construction of music provides the mechanism through which this balance is achieved.

As well as a mechanism that ensures the survival of the scene, reflexive anti-reflexivity is also the source of some of the most important pleasures that the scene offers. Within the scene, members can draw on the most transgressive discourses present within Western culture – including racism – with negligible 'risk'. They can say the things that could less easily be said outside the scene while still preserving the comforts of mundanity. Members can 'have it all'. The scene is predicated on the illusion that the world is a simple one in which nothing dangerous has consequences. True, maintaining this illusion requires constant reflexively anti-reflexive work, yet this work can itself be a source of playful pleasures. Members can laugh or be serious within the scene, safe in the knowledge that they are never irrevocably committed to any one practice or discourse.

In the final chapter of this book I want to examine further *why* reflexive anti-reflexivity is pleasurable through situating the practice within the pleasures and pains of modernity. I will then go on to look at how far the extreme metal scene needs to change and what those outside the scene can learn from it.

## Modernity, Transgression, Community

The last few chapters have shown how the scene allows members to experience the pleasures of transgression and mundanity in a relatively safe, secure and autonomous environment. Indeed, reflexive anti-reflexivity allows members to maintain the illusion that this safe environment is immune from the complexities and problems of the world. From what are scene members seeking to escape?

Some previous studies have located the attraction of metal in its providing a form of fantasy escape from the meaninglessness of post-industrial society (e.g. Berger 1999b; Harrell 1994; Petrov 1995). Deena Weinstein (In Press) has argued that 'metal has globalized effectively because it responds to the psycho-structural needs of an audience that remains much the same in its structural situation throughout the world'. This ambitious claim is to some extent challenged by studies of metal in the developing world. Drawing on the case of Nepal, Paul Greene (In Press) points out that the conditions to which metal responds have distinctly individual, local manifestations. Jeremy Wallach (In Press) similarly notes that in South-East Asia, metal is a response to industrialization rather than deindustrialization. Given the attraction of extreme metal in a diverse range of contexts, I would argue that the scene provides various locally specific forms of escape from a wider, all-encompassing 'modernity', rather than from any one of modernity's specific manifestations.

From the nineteenth century onwards, the social sciences have been preoccupied with understanding modernity and diagnosing its pathologies. For all the differences between them, most thinkers from the 'classic' period of the social sciences associate modernity with a particular kind of fraught experience. Different thinkers have diagnosed this fraughtness differently. For Marxists, the experience of 'alienation' (Marx 1976) is one of profound disempowerment. Workers are unable to control their labour power or (in some versions of Marxism) even to be reflexive at all (Althusser 1992). Durkheim's concept of 'anomie' (1984) refers to the experience of alienation from one's fellows produced by modernity's increasingly complex division of labour. Max Weber (1964) also diagnosed an experience similar to alienation in his analysis of bureaucracy. He showed how modern processes of 'rationalization' construct an 'iron cage' of bureaucracy, in which humans become dominated by bureaucratic systems not of their own making (Weber 1976). More recently Jürgen Habermas (1989b) has argued that 'systemic' imperatives within modern society are 'colonizing' the 'lifeworld' of free communication, making it increasingly difficult to maintain control of the structures within which members of society move. Similarly, the 'Frankfurt School' argued that capitalist rationality had become so dominating that it had ossified historical movement and criticality (Adorno & Horkheimer 1997). Social theorists have also argued that the experience of modernity is one of 'fragmentation' (Frisby 1985) in which individuals, particularly in urban centres, spend their time in fleeting, transitory relationships (Simmel 1971). In general then, social theories of modernity have been dystopian. Only in postmodernity have theorists come close to celebrating the experience of modernity and even then they generally do so ambiguously (Baudrillard 1988).

The modern world certainly offers excitement and an almost unlimited supply of new experiences and challenges. However, it is an exhausting world that, as we saw in the previous chapter, requires the constant exercise of reflexivity to navigate. The world is moving ever faster (Virilio 1986) and becoming more overloaded with flows of information, necessitating constant decisions from endless options. The constant practice of reflexivity in modernity means that nothing can ever be taken for granted. Selfhood in modernity is 'condemned' (Jervis 1999: 69) to practise a reflexivity so insistent and all-embracing that it can reduce individuals to madness.

Transgression is one way of surviving the fraught experience of modernity. It is one of the few sources of almost unrestricted agency in modernity. While modernity disempowers individuals within alienating systems and structures, transgression allows individuals to feel utterly in control, utterly 'sovereign' (Bataille 1993) over their being through practices that resist instrumental rationality. As I argued in Chapter 2, whereas pre-modern societies contained spaces for transgression, such as the carnival, transgression has been pushed to the margins of society in modernity. This marginalization has made transgression all the more alluring and consequently all the more threatening. Transgression can produce complete exclusion from mainstream society, and those who practise it risk state and other surveillance. At the same time, the opposite process also occurs in which transgression is assimilated to the point where it is no longer transgressive. Weber shows how the transgressive potential of charisma becomes 'routinized' in modernity. Subcultural theory shows how symbolic challenges to the capitalist order are transformed into popular styles repackaged for utilitarian consumption. Further, as the Frankfurt School recognized, revolutionary movements can become as alienating and disempowering as that which they initially oppose.

The centrifugal forces that either assimilate or marginalize transgression in modernity make transgression an unstable practice on which to base life in modernity. In any case, mundane participation in capitalist society potentially offers comfort and security, at least for those in developed countries with a certain minimum income. A relatively stable existence, built around clearly demarcated patterns of work and leisure, may bring contentment through the mundane pleasures of quietly 'getting on with life'. The problem is that there is a thin line between comfortable mundanity and disempowered alienation. Furthermore, capitalist modernity offers comfort at the expense of a critical outlook on everyday life and mutes any commitment to address forms of oppression in society as a whole.

One way of enjoying the mundane comforts of modernity without alienation and disempowerment may be to participate in modernity within a community. Community is a concept with a long and diverse history in the social sciences (see, for example, Agamben 1993; Bauman 2001; Cohen 1985; Park 1952; and Tönnies 1955). Community is a concept with positive connotations of an enduring space of solidarity, closeness and mutual support. Community is often represented as a bulwark against the onslaught of an atomizing modernity, if perhaps a fragile one. Communities are potentially less alienating than impersonal social structures and may provide the mutual support and meaningful interaction that is threatened by modernity. At the same time, communities may themselves prove disempowering through the homogenization and erasing of difference. Communities may simply become a microcosm of an alienating modernity. Furthermore, the comfortable experience of mundanity that community affords may simply become *too* comfortable and may lead people to a passive acceptance of the world as it is.

The main problem with transgression and mundanity as strategies for experiential survival within modernity is that each risks overwhelming the other, yet each tends to be assimilated in the absence of the other. The novelty of the extreme metal scene is that it offers both experiences in such a way that neither overwhelms the other nor loses their potency. It maintains this balance through the production and maintenance of a seemingly oxymoronic 'transgressive community'. The transgressive community of the extreme metal scene provides a means of survival within modernity that ensures a kind of stable equilibrium between experiential necessities. It offers many of the mundane, comforting, non-material rewards (and, for some, the material rewards) of participation in capitalist modernity, but they are experienced through decentralized, communitarian structures that resist alienation and fragmentation. The scene also ensures that individuality, agency and difference live through the practice of transgression. It ensures that participation in communitarian structures never leads to members being crushed by the weight of the collective. Transgression allows members to voice their frustration at the alienation and disempowerment produced by modernity. It produces excitement, unpredictability and joyous experiences of the body.

Reflexive anti-reflexivity is the mechanism through which transgressive community becomes possible. The practice 'defends' the delicate balance between transgression and mundanity by ensuring that the scene is never overwhelmed by extra-scenic discourses and practices. Reflexive anti-reflexivity also produces the pleasurable illusion that the world is an uncomplicated and safe place. As I have argued, modernity is *not* safe, is *not* uncomplicated, is *not* stable. The pleasures of the extreme metal scene lie in the possibilities for members to experience safely the contradictory pleasures of modernity, safe in the fantasy that, within the scene at least, modernity is neither stressful nor difficult.

### A Critical Perspective on the Scene

While it is hard not to be sympathetic to scene members' attempts to have a pleasurable experience of an unhappy world, this is not the end of the story. This book has set out to develop a critical perspective on the extreme metal scene. As I argued in Chapter 1, a critical perspective involves taking a sober, politically aware look at how far the scene is implicated in relations of domination and power. From this perspective, it is clear that while the scene offers many experiential rewards to members, some members may be excluded from some of these rewards. Furthermore, whatever the pleasures of the scene, what occurs within the scene does not simply stay within the scene. All actions have consequences, whether intended or unintended, that can cause harm to others. No individual and no space can ever be truly outside the workings of power and domination. Scene members try to pretend that the scene stands outside modernity, but we do not have to join in this pretence.

While the scene is implicated in global flows of power and capital, few other social spaces are so open to global participation and reflexive, decentralized control. The problem is that the scene is also a space within which power, when it is gained, is rarely effectively challenged. While power and capital from outside the scene are only erratically convertible into power and capital within it, no allowance is ever made for a *lack* of power and capital from outside the scene. Scenic minorities such as women find it more difficult to enter the scene. Scene members compound these difficulties by passively or actively condoning sexism and racism within the scene. The scene is also a space that enables some members to simultaneously access other spaces that concentrate power far more extensively. Those (admittedly few) owners of financially successful scenic institutions and those (admittedly few) members of financially successful bands accumulate power and capital that is readily transferable into power and capital within other spaces. Clearly then, a significant minority does *not* find the scene an easy, comforting space in which to 'have it all'. For those scene members, the negative experiential consequences of modernity are not alleviated to the same extent.

Other music scenes also mute the exercise of power, while at the same time reproducing it in subtle ways (e.g. Cohen 1991; Thornton 1995). The exercise of power within the extreme metal scene is not necessarily any more severe than in other contemporary music scenes. Although women are marginal within the extreme metal scene, women are also marginal within other music scenes (Cohen 1997). It is true that the extreme metal scene is unique among music scenes in that some members have flirted with far-right discourses. At the same time, the extreme metal scene, in its global extensiveness, is far more heterogeneous than many other scenes.

The scene also both reinforces and ameliorates power in its production of transgression. Extreme metal transgresses many socially sanctioned taboos, particularly with regard to the destruction of the body and to religion. Both Robert Walser (1993) and Deena Weinstein (2000) conclude their studies by arguing that heavy metal provides a way of responding to and challenging the most unpleasant characteristics of contemporary capitalist society. Their findings could potentially be extended to extreme metal. The problem is that transgression within the scene is founded on a preoccupation with control of the 'abject' that associates the abject with female sexuality, homosexuality and blackness. This fear of the abject is at times translated into texts, discourses and practices that openly embrace the most virulent kinds of racism, sexism and homophobia – forms of oppression that are, to a debatable extent, produced by entrenched, large-scale power structures. From this perspective, much of extreme metal merely looks like a self-consciously shocking dramatization of deeply ingrained forms of power.

The extreme metal scene highlights the ironies and limitations of transgression. As Foucault (1977b) points out, no move to transgress one form of discursive 'power/knowledge' can avoid being implicated in the construction of other forms of discursive power. For Foucault, discourse cannot be separated from power and by implication there can be no ultimately 'liberating' discourse. It follows then that, for example, sexist discourses may be transgressive if directed at feminist discourses. From a Foucauldian perspective, sexism, racism and homophobia within the scene must be seen as just as transgressive as those transgressive practices that are more obviously liberating or 'resistant'. If power is 'everywhere', then all attempts at transgression are equally liberating, yet equally futile.

All that said, not all forms of power/knowledge are of equal strength. One can distinguish those forms of power/knowledge that have become institutionalized and embedded in capitalist and state structures. Feminism, for example, is associated with relatively little state power and little financial capital, diminishing the penetration of feminist discourses into everyday life. Thus, when practising sexism, racism and homophobia, scene members transgress relatively weak forms of power/knowledge.

Transgression of anti-sexist and anti-racist discourses would perhaps not be so problematic if it were to take place within a project of 'total' transgression (perhaps similar to the 'aesthetic terrorism' advocated by Parfrey 1990). Such a project would undoubtedly be nihilistic, in that it would render every discourse worthless and all politics impossible. However, nihilism does at least provide a continuous revelation of the fragile discursive underpinnings of the world. This is a similar project to post-structuralism, which has been accused of being nihilistic but, nonetheless, provides one of the most searching critiques of existence ever produced, providing a powerful antidote to intellectual arrogance and essentialism. Moreover, the work of post-structuralist feminists has shown that reclaiming an anti-essentialist politics is still possible (e.g. Butler & Scott 1992).

It would be a relatively small step to take for the transgression practised within the scene to provide a more searching, anti-essentialist critique. Yet this short step has never been taken, even if some scene members may have flirted with the possibility. Something always halts scenic transgression at certain points. The transgressive logic of the scene is limited in two ways. The first limit is where transgression becomes destruction. The work of Bataille shows that the only way to fully experience sovereignty is to kill another or to kill oneself. As we have seen, a very few scene members have done this but, in the process, have brought their scenic careers to a rapid and premature conclusion. If everyone in the scene were to engage in this kind of transgression there would be no scene and this is an intolerable prospect for most scene members. The second limit on transgression is the point where it becomes intolerable either when those outside the scene become alerted to the scene's presence or when transgression involves a painful challenge to fundamental self-interest. Most scene members, most of the time, prefer to practise transgression only in so far as it remains comfortable.

One can imagine an extreme metal scene without racism, sexism and homophobia. While there is a constant slippage from the abject into more concrete notions of gender, sexuality and ethnicity, a dissociation of the abject from these concrete associations is certainly imaginable (if admittedly unlikely). The work of the band Carcass, discussed in Chapter 2 and in Kahn-Harris (2003), demonstrates that within extreme metal there are possibilities for more ambiguous explorations of abjection that are not based on rigid notions of control. The scene produces truly radical transgressions of musical structures and systematic explorations of the boundaries between death, life and the body. Equally radical is the scene's exploration of the boundaries of 'the serious' and its demonstration of how 'play' can be brought into unexpected areas. These explorations are not reliant on the maintenance of 'real world' hierarchies and prejudices.

Perhaps, though, it is in the workings of the scene itself as a transgressive community that the scene's true radical potential lies. The mundane, communitarian, decentralized networks through which extreme metal is reproduced *do* represent an (admittedly uneven) challenge to capitalist monetary accumulation and to homogenizing notions of community. Communities can provide powerful exemplars of alternatives to the supposed inevitability of relations of power and domination. Just as in elements of the scene's transgressive practices there are seeds of a challenging critique of existence, so in the decentralized, globalized structures of the scenic infrastructure there lies potential proof that, as the slogan has it, 'another world is possible'. The extreme metal scene exists on an exceptionally thin line between reproducing a bad parody of the world as it is, and developing a utopian, egalitarian vision of the world as it could be.

## The Future of the Scene

The extreme metal scene will change as all scenes do. The scene is in a constant state of musical and discursive struggle and evolution, bringing about new musical fusions. The institutions of the scene are also in flux, with the Internet threatening to bring about radical change. There are big questions as to whether the scene can manage to maintain its musical and social heterogeneity, whether it can stay creative and dynamic and whether it can continue to bring in new members. These questions are important but for this book the most important question is whether in the future scene members might be willing to engage reflexively with the more problematic aspects of the scene. Given that the fear of 'politics', of certain forms of difference and change, appears central to the scene's existence, it is difficult to imagine such a reflexive engagement.

In considering the possibilities for change then, we first have to consider the possibility of the scene continuing without change of this kind. Would this be such a problem? With certain well-known exceptions, the scene causes little active harm – the worst that happens to marginalized scene members tends to be annoyed disgruntlement. It would be absurd to isolate the extreme metal scene as a crucially pressing social problem. In fact, the scene's marginality is such that we have to ask whether the extreme metal scene really 'matters' at all.

Aside from the principle that political engagement needs to be 'bottom up' tackling the more marginal areas of society, I would argue that it is precisely because the scene is marginal that it matters. The scene has developed potentially important aesthetics, discourses and practices but their significance is lessened by their isolation. The example of the scene has much to contribute to debates about how to form communitarian spaces that allow for difference. The scene's very real 'achievements' are virtually unknown because the scene is so strongly oriented towards maintaining its insularity. In other words, the problem with the scene is that it *doesn't* matter enough, but it definitely *should* matter more. The scene needs to be 'opened up' both so its own practices are challenged and so that the wider world can learn from it. However, this 'opening up' may be extremely difficult to bring about. If the majority of members are contented within the scene, what possible reason might they have for changing it? Furthermore, opening the scene in this way brings with it the very real threat of moral panic and ridicule, which might either destroy the scene or further retrench its isolation.

While external criticism can only exacerbate the isolation of the scene, external praise can have a much more positive effect. Some forms of extreme metal have been praised by music critics. While the occasional positive attention of critics is often treated with cynicism about 'trends', it can also have a rejuvenating effect on the scene. For example, the late 1980s wave of British grindcore bands received considerable praise in the British music press. The highly influential British DJ John Peel would play grindcore and death metal on his show on BBC Radio 1. Such attention (particularly from Peel) was important in developing and expanding the scene at that time. In recent years there has been increased interest in the scene from those interested in the musical avant-garde, for example the earnest journal *The Wire* has shown a sympathetic interest in the more experimental forms of extreme metal (Pouncey 2005).

The potential synergy between extreme metal and the wider arts scene has been sporadically explored. For example, in 1999 the Israeli performance artists Anat Ben-David and Avi Pitchon used extreme metal music in their performance-art piece *Endforever*. In 1998 the Clementine Gallery in New York hosted 'Metal Men', an exhibition of paintings by Amy Hill featuring studies of metal musicians. In 2004, the American photographer Peter Beste produced an exhibition of pictures of members of the Norwegian black metal scene and the British-based photographer Muir Vidler has exhibited photos of Israeli scene members (see Figure 17, p. 112). A number of American visual artists have collaborated on the multimedia 'Slayer Rules' project, focusing on the experiences of Slayer fans. Extreme metal has also been explored in a number of fiction works (Elbom 2004; Richter 1999; White 1999) and was explored in the 2005 documentary film *Metal: A Headbanger's Journey*.

The resituating of extreme metal in the wider arts scene opens up the possibility for extreme metal to become part of networks of avant-garde and oppositional artistic practice. This process may challenge and give new insights to scene members. However, at present, such work is fairly rare and there exists a real danger that extreme metal will become just another artistic resource for non-scenic artists to appropriate while disparaging the scene from which it emerges. Since scene members have little desire to earn cultural capital outside the scene, the scene is ripe for exploitation. 'Cherry picking' certain aspects of the scene ignores that the scene works as an interconnected whole. Critically lauded acts such as Sunn0))) are rooted in a scene of which critically despised music is an intrinsic part.

The mere fact of extreme metal circulating outside the scene is not sufficient to challenge problematic scenic practices and forms of power. Changes in the scene's ability to accept a more critical reflexivity can only come about through the entry of people into the scene with different ideas coming from very different spaces. For example, in 1996 Nick Terry became the editor of *Terrorizer* magazine. Terry's background is very different from that of most scene members. He had been a music journalist for a number of years, writing for magazines such as *Lime Lizard* and *The Wire*. He was imbued with a love of radical musics and had a strong interest in critical and cultural theory. During his time writing for *Terrorizer* (1996–2000) Terry made no obvious efforts to lecture scene members and indeed, as we saw in the previous chapter, the magazine continued to reproduce scenic discourses in all of their reflexive anti-reflexivity. At the same time, his time as editor saw a subtle introduction of a more critical form of music writing that did not undermine existing scenic conventions. Extreme metal was resituated within a wider musical landscape, including radical acts such as Einstürzende Neubauten and Merzbow, while at the same time reinterpreting traditional heavy metal as ironic and burlesque. The example of *Terrorizer* shows how effective a critical approach to the scene can be if it is rooted within the scene itself.

## Conclusion

In *Lipstick Traces*, his study of the interconnections between punk and situationalism, Greil Marcus wrote:

> For a gnomic, Gnostic critique dreamed up by a handful of Left Bank café prophets to reappear a quarter-century later, *to make the charts*, and then to come to life as a whole new set of demands on culture – this is almost transcendently odd. (1989: 19)

No less remarkably, the reverse is true in the case of the extreme metal scene. For a critically derided, unashamedly populist music to commit itself to musical radicalism, *without rejecting its populist roots* – this is at the very least noteworthy.

The extreme metal scene is a powerful example of how popular music can be a source of artistic radicalism that is nonetheless rooted in a lived experience of community. At the same time, the scene is also an example of how popular music has had enormous difficulty in translating its dynamism into a more direct political challenge (Grossberg 1994). The suspicion that scene members have of the political is widely shared throughout popular music culture. For example, *No Direction Home* (2005), the acclaimed documentary on Bob Dylan, shows the singer repeatedly denying that there was any political relevance to his work, despite the evident impact that his music had on the politics of the 1960s. It may be that the de-politicization of the extreme metal scene is simply part of a wider problem with music itself. As Ronald Bogue puts it:

> Music, in short, through its heightened and yet somehow dispersed, intangible sensuality, has the power of undoing the coordinates of the commonsense world But in music's great power as a deterritorializing force lies its danger. Its dissolution of codes, structures and conventions can expand, accelerate and form part of an undifferentiated will to annihilation and destruction. And its abstract, dematerializing affectivity can be channeled into any number of violent, repressive and reactionary circuits of power. (2004b: 114)

Music's abstract power can stimulate fantasies of disconnection from the intricate webs of connection that tie human beings together. This is all the more the case in extreme metal, which ' . . . reorients conventional music listening experiences so radically as to fundamentally disrupt any potential for an identificatory relationship between death metal fans and their music' (Phillipov 2004).

The scene's resistance to politics and to change may therefore seem to be so rooted in the scene's musical nature that change may seem inconceivable. But if music is the problem, perhaps it can also be the solution. It is important to remember that up until the early 1990s, the scene's subsequent musical developments may also have seemed inconceivable. Could anyone have envisaged the use of keyboards and sequencers in black metal? Could anyone have envisaged the use of folk music in extreme metal? Just as the scene was musically enriched in the 1990s through a few scene members 'thinking the unthinkable', so can the scene be socially enriched today if a few prominent scene members would have the will. Extreme metal has always walked a knife-edge – between destruction and continuity, between obscurity and popularity, between unity and fragmentation, between radicalism and conservatism. Perhaps extreme metal is on the edge of a wider social relevance and cultural transformation.

This appendix gives brief details of interviewees quoted in this book. I have omitted details of the sizeable number of interviewees that are not quoted. Interviewees quoted in the book are not necessarily representative of all interviewees, they are simply the most 'quoteable'. All interviews were conducted in English.

Some details are omitted in the case of interviewees who could easily be identified by scene members. All details apply to the time when the interview was conducted.

### Israel Interviewees

[All are male]

Eli:      Mid 30s, Tel Aviv suburbs, long-time scene member
Motti:    23-year-old, Tel Aviv suburbs, plays in death metal band
Raffi:    Early 20s, Tel Aviv suburbs, plays in black metal band
Shimon:   21-year-old, Haifa, plays in black metal band
Yoav:     Mid 20s, Tel Aviv suburbs, highly involved scene member

### Sweden Interviewees

Eric:     25-year-old, Stockholm, plays in black metal band
Goran:    40s, Gothenburg, runs label
Henrik:   23-year-old, Stockholm, edits fanzine
Johan:    26-year-old, Stockholm, record producer and plays in death metal band
Lars:     25-year-old, Stockholm, runs label and distro
Nora:     19-year-old, southern Sweden, writes for fanzine
Ulf:      28-year-old, southern Sweden, plays in various bands

### United Kingdom Interviewees

Dave:     Mid 30s, London, long-time scene member
Elaine:   Early 20s, London, plays in death metal band
Graham:   36-year-old, Midlands, runs label
Jane:     26-year-old, southern England, highly involved scene member
Jason:    30-year-old, Midlands, plays in band and runs label
John:     28-year-old, London, plays in death metal band and edits fanzine
Nathan:   26-year-old, southern England, plays in black metal band and co-runs distro/label

Pauline:  23-year-old, London, scene member
Richard:  19-year-old, London, plays in band
Tom:      36-year-old, southern England, edits fanzine
Tony:     34-year-old, southern England, runs distro
Will:     32-year-old, southern England, runs label/distro
Zara:     23-year-old, London, plays in black metal band

# NOTES

## Introduction

1. Selected significant recordings by extreme metal acts mentioned in this and the following chapters are listed in the discography at the end of the book.

## Chapter 2    The Scene and Transgression

1. Pillsbury (2006) offers a similarly thought-provoking musicological analysis of the work of Metallica. Unfortunately, the book was published too late for its findings to be fully addressed in this book.
2. For more information on the case of the West Memphis 3, see http://www.wm3.0rg/ (accessed November 2005).
3. I am indebted to Professor Philip Tagg for his help in researching this section.
4. All the names of interviewees interviewed by me that are quoted in this book are pseudonyms. For further interviewee details see the appendix.

## Chapter 4    Capital, Power, Infrastructure

1. The addresses of websites quoted in this and other sections appear in the references section. Unless otherwise stated, all websites in this section were accessed in November 2005.

## Chapter 5    Comparing Extreme Metal Scenes

1. I am grateful to Ingemar Grandin and Kosta Economou (personal communication, 4 March 2005) for this figure and for other information in this section.
2. For a more detailed account of the Israeli extreme metal scene see Kahn-Harris (2002).

## Chapter 6    Extreme Metal and Subcultural Capital

1. As the interview quoted in the previous section shows, mundane subcultural capital has currency even in *Isten* 100. As I will show later in this chapter, the logics of mundane and transgressive subcultural capital intermingle in complex ways in the scene.
2. Les Back (personal communication) has drawn my attention to a worrying parallel with the far-right music scene. In the 1990s far-right bands, such as Rahowa and other bands on the US label Resistance records, attempted to purge their music of 'black' influences.

## Chapter 7    Reflexivity, Music and Politics

1. A number of examples in this chapter are drawn from *Terrorizer* magazine in order show that the phenomena discussed are not restricted to the margins of the scene, but occur in even the most prestigious and intellectually rigorous sources of scenic discourse.
2. Unless otherwise stated, all addresses of websites quoted appear in the references section and were accessed in November 2005.

## REFERENCES

**Books and Journals**

Adorno, T. and Horkheimer, M. (1997), *Dialectic of Enlightenment*, London: Verso.

Agamben, G. (1993), *The Coming Community*, London: University of Minnesota Press.

Althusser, L. (1992), 'Ideology and the Ideological State Apparatus', in A. Easthope and K. McGowan (eds), *A Critical and Cultural Theory Reader*, Buckingham: Open University Press.

Anderson, B. (1991), *Imagined Communities*, London: Verso.

Anderson, C. A., Carnagey, N.L. and Eubanks, J. (2003), 'Exposure to Violent Media: The Effects of Songs with Violent Lyrics on Aggressive Thoughts and Feelings', *Journal of Personality and Social Psychology*, 84(5): 960–71.

Arnett, J. J. (1995), *Metalheads: Heavy Metal Music and Adolescent Alienation*, Boulder, CO: Westview Press.

Attali, J. (1985), *Noise: The Political Economy of Music*, Manchester: Manchester University Press.

Atton, C. (2002), *Alternative Media*, London: Sage Publications.

Avelar, I. (2003), 'Heavy Metal Music in Postdictatorial Brazil: Sepultura and the Coding of Nationality in Sound', *Journal of Latin American Cultural Studies*, 12(3): 330–46.

Baddeley, G. (1999), *Lucifer Rising: Sin, Devil Worship and Rock 'n' Roll*, London: Plexus.

Badley, L. (1995), *Film, Horror and the Body Fantastic*, London: Greenwood Press.

Bakhtin, M. (1984), *Rabelais and his World*, Bloomington: Indiana University Press.

Bataille, G. (1985), *Literature and Evil*, London: Marion Boyars.

—— (1993), *The Accursed Share: An Essay on General Economy*, New York: Zone Books.

Baudrillard, J. (1988), *Selected Writings*, Cambridge: Polity Press.

Baulch, E. (2003), 'Gesturing Elsewhere: The Identity Politics of the Balinese Death/Thrash Metal Scene', *Popular Music* 22(2): 195–216.

Bauman, Z. (2001), *Community: Seeking Safety in an Insecure World*, Cambridge: Polity Press.

Bayton, M. (1989), 'How Women Become Musicians', in S. Frith and A. Goodwin (eds), *On Record: Rock, Pop and the Written Word*, London: Routledge.

Becker, H. (1973), *Outsiders: Studies in the Sociology of Deviance*, New York: Free Press.

Beckwith, K. (2002), 'Black Metal is for White People', *M/C: A Journal of Media and Culture* 5(3), http://www.media-culture.org.au/0207/blackmetal.php (accessed 6 December 2005).

Bennett, A. (1999), 'Subcultures or Neo-Tribes? Rethinking the Relationship Between Youth, Style and Musical Taste', *Sociology* 33(3): 599–618.

—— and Kahn-Harris, K. (eds) (2004), *After Subculture: Critical Studies in Contemporary Youth Culture*, London: Palgrave.

Bennett, H. S. (1980), *On Becoming a Rock Musician*, Amherst: University of Massachusetts Press.

Berger, H. M. (1999a), 'Death Metal Tonality and the Act of Listening', *Popular Music* 18(2): 161–78.

—— (1999b), *Metal, Rock and Jazz: Perception and the Phenomenology of Musical Experience*, Hanover, NH: Wesleyan University Press.

Bjornberg, A. (1996), 'Om Tonal Analys av Nutida Populärmusik' *Dansk Årbog for Musikforskning*, 24: 69–84.

Blum, A. (2001), 'Scenes', *Public* 22(3): 7–36.

Bogue, R. (2004a), *Deleuze's Wake: Tributes and Tributaries*, Albany, NY: State University of New York Press.

—— (2004b), 'Violence in Three Shades of Metal: Death, Doom and Black' in I. Buchanan and M. Swiboda (eds), *Deleuze and Music*, Edinburgh: Edinburgh University Press.

Bossius, T. (2003), *Med Framtiden i Backspegelen – Black Metal och Transkulturen. Ungdomar, Musik och Religion i en Senmodern Varld* [With the Future in the Rear-View Mirror – the Black metal and Trance Culture. Youth, Music and Religion in a Late Modern World], Gothenburg: Daidalos.

Bourdieu, P. (1979), *Distinction: A Social Critique of the Judgement of Taste*, London: Routledge.

—— (1989), *Outline of a Theory of Practice*, Cambridge: Cambridge University Press.

—— (1991), *Language and Symbolic Power*, Cambridge: Polity Press.

—— (1993), *The Field of Cultural Production*, Oxford: Polity Press.

Brown, A. (2003), 'Heavy Metal and Subcultural Theory: A Paradigmatic Case of Neglect?' in D. Muggleton and R. Weinzierl (eds), *The Post-Subcultures Reader*, Oxford: Berg.

Burghart, D. (1999), *Soundtracks to the White Revolution: White Supremacist Assaults on Youth Music Subcultures*, Chicago: Center for the New Community.

Burnett, R. (2001), 'Global Strategies and Local Markets: Explaining Swedish Music Export Success', in A. Gebesmair and A. Smudits (eds), *Global Repertoires: Popular Music Within and Beyond the Transnational Music Industry*, Aldershot: Ashgate.

Butler, J. (1997), *Excitable Speech: A Politics of the Performative*, New York: Routledge.

—— and Scott, J. (eds) (1992), *Feminists Theorise the Political*, New York: Routledge.

Campion, C. (2005), 'In the Face of Death', *Observer Music Monthly*, 02/05: 12–17.

Carrabine, E. and Longhurst, B. (1999), 'Mosaics of Omnivorousness: Suburban Youth and Popular Music', *New Formations*, 38: 125–140.

Castells, M. (1996), *The Rise of the Network Society*, Cambridge, MA: Blackwell Publishers.

Cayton, C. (1999), 'Black Metal Unmasked', *Searchlight*, June 1999: 13–17.

Certeau, M. de (1984), *The Practice of Everyday Life*, Berkeley: University of California Press.

Chanan, M. (1994), *Musica Practica: The Social Practice of Western Music from Gregorian Chant to Postmodernism*, London: Verso.

Chastagner, C. (1999), 'The Parents' Music Resource Center: From Information to Censorship', *Popular Music*, 18(2): 179–92.

Christie, I. (2003), *Sound of the Beast: The Complete Headbanging History of Heavy Metal*, New York: Harper Entertainment.

Clarke, G. (1990), 'Defending Ski-Jumpers: A Critique of Theories of Youth Subculture', in S. Frith and A. Goodwin (eds), *On Record: Rock, Pop and the Written Word*, London: Routledge.

Clawson, M. A. (1999), 'Masculinity and Skill Acquisition in the Adolescent Rock Band', *Popular Music*, 18(1): 99–114.

Cloonan, M. (1996), *Banned! Censorship of Popular Music in Britain: 1967–92*, Aldershot: Arena.

—— (1999), 'Pop and the Nation State: Towards a Theorisation', *Popular Music* 18(2): 193–208.

Clover, C. (1992), *Men, Women and Chainsaws: Gender in the Modern Horror Film*, London: British Film Institute.

Cohen, A. (1985), *The Symbolic Construction of Community*, London: Routledge.

Cohen, P. S. (1968), *Modern Social Theory*, London: Heinemann Educational Books.

Cohen, S. (1991), *Rock Culture in Liverpool*, Oxford: Clarendon Press.

—— (1997), 'Men Making a Scene: Rock Music and the Production of Gender', in S. Whiteley (ed.), *Sexing the Groove*, London: Routledge.

Cohen, S. (1987), *Folk Devils and Moral Panics: The Creation of Mods and Rockers,* Oxford: Basil Blackwell.

—— and Taylor, L. (1976), *Escape Attempts: The Theory and Practice of Resistance to Everyday Life,*

London: Allen Lane.

Crafts, S. D., Cavicchi, D. and Keil, C. (1993), *My Music*, Hanover, NH: Wesleyan University Press.

Craib, I. (1984), *Modern Social Theory: From Parsons to Habermas*, London: Harvester Wheatsheaf.

Crane, J. L. (1994), *Terror and Everyday Life: Singular Moments in the History of the Horror Film*, London: Sage Publications.

DeNora, T. (1997), 'Music and Erotic Agency – Sonic Resources and Social-Sexual Action', *Body and Society* 3(2): 43–65.

—— (2000), *Music in Everyday Life*, Cambridge: Cambridge University Press.

Denski, S. and Sholle, D. (1992), 'Metal Men and Glamour Boys: Gender Performance in Heavy Metal', in S. Craig (ed.), *Men, Masculinity and the Media*, Newbury Park: Sage.

Derrida, J. (1990), *Writing and Difference*, London: Routledge.

Douglas, J. (1971), *Understanding Everyday Life: Towards the Reconstruction of Sociological Knowledge*, London: Routledge and Kegan Paul.

Douglas, M. (1984), *Purity and Danger: An Analysis of the Concepts of Pollution and Taboo*, London: Ark Paperbacks.

Duncombe, S. (1997), *Notes From Underground: Zines and the Politics of Alternative Culture*, London: Verso.

Durant, A. (1984), *Conditions of Music*, London: Macmillan.

Durkheim, E. (1984), *The Division of Labour in Society*, London: Macmillan.

Elbom, G. (2004), *Scream Queens of the Dead Sea*, New York: Thunder's Mouth Press.

Epstein, J. S., Pratto, D. J. and Skipper, J. K. (1990), 'Teenagers, Behavioural Problems, and Preferences for Heavy Metal and Rap Music: A Case Study of a Southern Middle School', *Deviant Behaviour* 11: 381–94.

Fabbri, F. (1982), 'A Theory of Musical Genres: Two Applications', in D. Horn and P. Tagg (eds), *Popular Music Perspectives*, Gothenburg and Exeter: International Association for the Study of Popular Music.

Finnegan, R. (1989), *The Hidden Musicians: Music-Making in an English Town*, Cambridge: Cambridge University Press.

Fonarow, W. (1997), 'The Spatial Organisation of the Indie Music Gig' in K. Gelder and S. Thornton (eds), *The Subcultures Reader*, London: Routledge.

Fornäs, J. (1995), 'The Future of Rock: Discourses that Struggle to Define a Genre', *Popular Music* 14(1): 111–25.

—— (1997), 'Text and Music Revisited', *Theory, Culture and Society* 14(3): 109–23.

Foucault, M. (1977a), *Discipline and Punish*, London: Penguin Books.

—— (1977b), *Language, Counter-Memory, Practice: Selected Essays and Interviews*, Oxford: Basil Blackwell.

Fox, K. J. (1987), 'Real Punks and Pretenders: The Social Organisation of a Counterculture', *Journal of Contemporary Ethnography* 16(3): 344–70.

Frisby, D. (1985), *Fragments of Modernity*, Cambridge: Polity Press.

Frith, S. (1983), *Sound Effects: Youth, Leisure and the Politics of Rock 'n' Roll*, London: Constable.

—— (1996), *Performing Rites*, Oxford: Oxford University Press.

—— (2004), 'Does British Music Still Matter? A Reflection on the Changing Status of British Popular Music in the Global Music Market', *European Journal of Cultural Studies* 7(1): 43–59.

Gaines, D. (1990), *Teenage Wasteland: Suburbia's Dead End Kids*, New York: Harper Collins.

Gelder, K. and Thornton, S. (eds) (1997), *The Subcultures Reader*, London: Routledge.

Giddens, A. (1984), *The Constitution of Society*, Cambridge: Polity Press.

—— (1990), *The Consequences of Modernity*, Cambridge: Polity Press.

Giovanni, J. di (1997) 'A Deadly Divide', *The Guardian Magazine,* 4 October 1997: 21–4.

Goodrick-Clarke, N. (1985), *The Occult Roots of Nazism: The Ariosophists of Austria and Germany 1890–1935*, Wellingborough: The Aquarian Press.

Greene, P. (2001), 'Mixed Messages: Unsettled Cosmopolitans in Nepali Pop', *Popular Music* 20(2): 169–88.

—— (In Press), 'Electronic and Affective Overdrive: Tropes of Transgression in Nepal's Heavy Metal Scene' in H. M. Berger, P. D. Greene and J. Wallach (eds), *Metal Rules the Globe*.

Griffin, C. (1991), 'The Researcher Talks Back: Dealing With Power Relations in Studies of Young People's Entry into the Job Market', in W. B. Shaffir and R. A Stebbins (eds), *Experiencing Fieldwork: An Inside View of Qualitative Research*, London: Sage Publications.

Gross, R. L. (1990), 'Heavy Metal Music: A New Subculture in American Society', *Journal of Popular Culture* 24(1): 119–29.

Grossberg, L. (1992), *We Gotta Get Out Of This Place: Popular Conservatism and Postmodern Culture*, London: Routledge.

—— (1994), 'Is Anybody Listening? Does Anybody Care? On Talking about 'The State of Rock'', in A. Ross and T. Rose (eds), *Microphone Fiends: Youth Music and Youth Culture*, London: Routledge.

Habermas, J. (1989a), *The Structural Transformation of the Public Sphere*, Cambridge: Polity Press.

—— (1989b), *The Theory of Communicative Action Volume 2: Lifeworld and System: A Critique of Functionalist Reason*, Cambridge: Polity Press.

Hakanen, E. A. and Wells, A. (1990), 'Adolescent Music Marginals: Who Likes Metal, Jazz, Country and Classical', *Popular Music and Society* 14: 57–66.

Hall, S. (1993), 'Encoding, Decoding', in S. During (ed.), *The Cultural Studies Reader*, London: Routledge.

—— and Jefferson, T. (1976), *Resistance Through Rituals: Youth Subcultures in Post-War Britain*, London: Hutchinson.

Hamm, C. (1994), 'Genre, Performance and Ideology in the Early Songs of Irving Berlin', *Popular Music* 13(2): 143–50.

Harrell, J. (1994), 'The Poetics of Deconstruction: Death Metal Rock', *Popular Music and Society* 18(1): 91–107.

Harris, K. D. (1997), '"Music is my Life"? Discourse Analysis and the Interview Talk of Members of a Music-Based Subculture', Working Paper Number 4, Department of Sociology, Goldsmiths College, London.

—— (2000), '"Roots"? The Relationship Between the Global and the Local Within the Global Extreme Metal Scene', *Popular Music* 19(1): 13–30.

—— (2001), 'Transgression and Mundanity: The Global Extreme Metal Music Scene', PhD Thesis, Goldsmiths College, London.

Harvey, D. (1990), *The Condition of Postmodernity*, Oxford: Blackwell Publishers.

Hebdige, D. (1979), *Subculture: The Meaning of Style*, London: Methuen.

Hecker, P. (2005), 'Taking a Trip to the Middle Eastern Metal Scene: Transnational Social Spaces and Identity Formations on a Non-National Level', *NORD-SÜD Aktuell* 19: 57–66.

Heller, Z. (1992), 'Teenage Monsters', *The Independent on Sunday Magazine*, 6 September 1992: 15–16.

Hemming, J. (2003), 'Hard Rock, Heavy Metal and Punk: Comparing Psychological Findings with Cultural Studies Accounts', Paper Presented at the 5th Triennial Conference of the European Society for the Cognitive Sciences of Music, Hanover.

Hesmondhalgh, D. (2005), 'Subcultures, Scenes or Tribes? None of the Above', *Journal Of Youth Studies* 8(1): 21–40.

Hodkinson, P. (2002), *Goth: Identity, Style and Subculture*, Oxford: Berg.

Hunter, S. (2004), *Hell Bent for Leather: Confessions of a Heavy Metal Addict*, London: Fourth Estate.

Irwin, J. (1997), 'Notes on the Status of the Concept Subculture', in K. Gelder and S. Thornton (eds),

*The Subcultures Reader*, London: Routledge.

Jackson, B. (1987), *Fieldwork*, Urbana: University of Illinois Press.

Jenks, C. (1998), 'Cultures of Excess', Inaugural Professorial Lecture, Goldsmiths College, London.

—— (2005), *Subculture: The Fragmentation of the Social*, London: Sage Publications.

Jervis, J. (1999), *Transgressing the Modern*, London: Blackwell.

Kahn-Harris, K. (2002), '"I hate this fucking country": Dealing with the Global and the Local in the Israeli Extreme Metal Scene', *Critical Studies* 19: Music, Popular Culture, Identities: 133–151.

—— (2003), 'Death Metal and the Limits of Musical Expression', in M. Cloonan, and R. Garofalo (eds), *Policing Popular Music*, Philadelphia: Temple University Press.

—— (2004a), 'The "Failure" of Youth Culture: Reflexivity, Music and Politics in the Black Metal Scene', *European Journal of Cultural Studies* 7(1): 95–111.

—— (2004b), 'Unspectacular Subculture? Transgression and Mundanity in the Global Extreme Metal Scene', in A. Bennett and K. Kahn-Harris (eds), *After Subculture*, London: Palgrave.

—— (2005), 'The Meaning of Strife', *Terrorizer*, February 2005: 128.

Kearney, M. C. (1997), 'The Missing Links: Riot Grrrl – Feminism – Lesbian Culture', in S. Whiteley (ed.), *Sexing the Groove*, London: Routledge.

Keith, M. and Pile, S. (eds) (1993), *Place and the Politics of Identity*, London: Routledge.

Klosterman, C. (2001), *Fargo Rock City: A Heavy Metal Odyssey in Rural North Dakota*, New York: Scribner.

Kristeva, J. (1982), *The Powers of Horror: An Essay on Abjection*, New York: Columbia University Press.

Kruse, H. (1993), 'Subcultural Identity in Alternative Music Culture', *Popular Music* 12(1): 31–43.

Laing, D. (1985), *One Chord Wonders: Power and Meaning in Punk Rock*, Milton Keynes: Open University Press.

Lash, S. (1994), 'Reflexivity and its Doubles: Structure, Aesthetics, Community', in U. Beck, A. Giddens and S. Lash, *Reflexive Modernization: Politics, Tradition and Aesthetics in the Modern Social Order*, Cambridge: Polity Press.

—— and Urry, J. (1994), *Economies of Signs and Space*, London: Sage.

LaVey, A. S. (1969), *The Satanic Bible*, New York: Avon Books.

LeBlanc, L. (1999), *Pretty in Punk: Girls' Resistance in a Boys' Subculture*, New Brunswick: Rutgers University Press.

Lefebvre, H. (1971), *Everyday Life in the Modern World*, London: Allen Lane.

—— (1991), *The Production of Space*, Oxford: Blackwell Publishers.

Leonard, M. (1997), '"Rebel Girl, You Are The Queen Of My World": Feminism, 'Subculture' and Grrrl Power', in S. Whiteley (ed.), *Sexing the Groove*, London: Routledge.

—— (1998), 'Paper Planes: Travelling the New Grrrl Geographies', in T. Skelton and G. Valentine (eds), *Cool Places: Geographies of Youth Cultures*, London: Routledge.

Lowney, K. S. (1995), 'Teenage Satanism as Oppositional Youth Subculture', *Journal of Contemporary Ethnography* 23(4): 453–84.

Lynskey, D. (2005), 'I'm Going to Jail? That's Great!', *The Guardian*, 2 September 2005.

Maffesoli, M. (1996), *The Time of the Tribes: The Decline of Individualism in Mass Society*, London: Sage Publications.

Marcus, G. (1989), *Lipstick Traces: A Secret History of the Twentieth Century*, Cambridge, MA: Harvard University Press.

Marx, K. (1976), *Capital: A Critique of Political Economy*, Harmondsworth: Penguin.

Massey, D. (1994), *Space, Place, Gender*, Cambridge: Polity Press.

McClary, S. (1991), *Feminine Endings: Music, Gender and Sexuality*, Minnesota: University of Minnesota Press.

McIver, J. (2000), *Extreme Metal*, London: Omnibus Press.

McRobbie, A. (1991), *Feminism and Youth Culture*, London: Macmillan.

—— and Thornton. S. (1995), 'Rethinking 'Moral Panic' for Multi-Mediated Social Worlds', *British Journal of Sociology* 46(4): 559–74.

Merton, R. K. (1957), *Social Theory and Social Structure*, 2nd ed, New York: The Free Press.

Miles, C. (1998), 'Spatial Politics: A Gendered Sense of Place', in S. Redhead, D. Wynne and J. O'Conner (eds), *The Clubcultures Reader: Readings in Popular Cultural Studies*, Oxford: Blackwell Publishers.

Miller, D. S. (1988), 'Youth, Popular Music and Cultural Controversy: The Case of Heavy Metal', PhD Thesis, University of Texas, Austin.

Moynihan, M. and Søderlind, D. (1998), *Lords of Chaos: The Bloody Rise of the Satanic Metal Underground*, Venice, CA: Feral House.

Mønk, G. (In Press). 'Why Didn't the Churches Begin to Burn a Thousand Years Later', in T. Bossius, A. Häger and K. Kahn-Harris (eds), *Religion and Popular Music in Europe*.

Mudrian, A. (2004), *Choosing Death: The Improbable History of Death Metal and Grindcore*, Los Angeles: Feral House.

Muggleton, D. (1998), 'The Post-Subculturalist', in S. Redhead, D. Wynne, and J. O'Conner (eds), *The Clubcultures Reader: Readings in Popular Cultural Studies*, Oxford: Blackwell Publishers.

—— (2000), *Inside Subculture: The Postmodern Meaning of Style*, Oxford: Berg.

—— and Weinzierl, R. (eds), (2003), *The Post-Subcultures Reader*, Oxford: Berg.

Nahum, D. (2004), 'Transgression in the Metal Subculture: A Terror Management Perspective', BSc Thesis, Macquarie University, Sydney.

Negus, K. (1992), *Producing Pop: Culture and Conflict in the Popular Music Industry*, London: Routledge.

—— (1999), *Music Genres and Corporate Cultures*, London: Routledge.

Niketta, R. (1998), 'Rock Musicians in Germany and Ideas for their Promotion', *Popular Music* 17(3): 310–25.

Oakes, J. L. (2004) 'Pop Music, Racial Imagination, and the Sounds of Cheese: Notes on Loser's Lounge', in C. J. Washburne and M. Derno (eds), *Bad Music: The Music We Love to Hate*, London: Routledge.

O'Conner, A. (2000), 'An Anarcho-Punk Gathering in the Context of Globalisation.' Paper Presented at the Third International Crossroads in Cultural Studies Conference, University of Birmingham.

—— (2002), 'Local Scenes and Dangerous Crossroads: Punk and Theories of Cultural Hybridity', *Popular Music* 21(2): 225–36.

Olson, M. J. V. (1998), '"Everybody Loves Our Town": Scenes, Spatiality, Migrancy', in T. Swiss, J. Sloop and A. Herman (eds), *Mapping the Beat: Popular Music and Contemporary Theory*, Oxford: Blackwell.

Parfrey, A. (ed.) (1990), *Apocalypse Culture*, Venice, CA: Feral House.

Park, R. (1952), *Human Communities*. New York: Free Press.

Partridge, C. (2005), *The Re-Enchantment of the West: Alternative Spiritualities, Sacralization, Popular Culture, and Occulture*, London: Continuum.

Petrov, A. (1995), 'The Sound of Suburbia (Death Metal)', *American Book Review* 16(6): 5.

Phillipov, M. (2004), 'A Gateway to Annihilation? Death Metal and the Reorientation of Listening', Paper Presented at the CSAA Annual Conference, 'Everyday Transformations: The Twenty-First Century Quotidian', Freemantle.

Pillsbury, G. (2006), *Damage Incorporated: Metallica and the Production of Musical Identity*, London: Routledge.

Potter, J. and Wetherell, M. (1987), *Discourse and Social Psychology: Beyond Attitudes and Behaviour*, London: Sage Publications.

Pouncey, E. (2005), 'Subterranean Metal', *The Wire*, February 2005: 36–43.

Purcell, N. (2003), *Death Metal Music: The Passion and Politics of a Subculture*, Jefferson: McFarland and Company.

Redhead, S. (ed.) (1993), *Rave Off: Politics and Deviance in Contemporary Youth Culture*, Aldershot: Avebury.

—— (ed.) (1998), *The Clubcultures Reader: Readings in Popular Cultural Studies,* Oxford: Blackwell.

Regev, M. (1997), 'Rock Aesthetics and Musics of the World', *Theory, Culture and Society* 14(3): 125–42.

—— and Seroussi, E. (2004), *Popular Music and National Culture in Israel*, Berkeley: University of California Press.

Reynolds, S. and Press, J. (1995), *The Sex Revolts: Gender, Rebellion and Rock n Roll,* London: Serpent's Tail.

Richardson, J. T. (1991), 'Satanism in the Courts: From Murder to Heavy Metal', in J. T. Richardson, J. Best and D. Bromley (eds), *The Satanism Scare*, New York: Aldine de Gruyter.

Richter, S. (1999), 'Goal 666', *Granta* 66: 147–61.

Roach, D. (1999) 'The Revolution Will Not Be Amplified', *The Big Issue*, 10 May 1999: 19–20.

Roccor, B. (2000), 'Heavy Metal: Forces of Unification and Fragmentation within a Musical Subculture', *The World of Music* 42(1): 83–94.

Rodel, A. (2004), 'Extreme Noise Terror: Punk Rock and the Aesthetics of Badness', in C. J. Washburne and M. Derno (eds), *Bad Music: The Music We Love to Hate*, London: Routledge.

Schofield Clark, L. (2003), *From Angels to Aliens: Teenagers, the Media, and the Supernatural*, Oxford: Oxford University Press

Sennett, R. (1996), *The Fall of Public Man*, New York: WW Norton.

Shank, B. (1994), *Dissonant Identities: The Rock n Roll Scene in Austin, Texas,* Hanover, NH: Wesleyan University Press.

Shepherd, J. (1991), *Music as Social Text*, Cambridge: Polity Press.

Simmel, G. (1971), 'The Metropolis and Mental Life', in *On Individuality and Social Forms: Selected Writings*, Chicago: University of Chicago Press.

Skelton, T. and Valentine, G. (eds) (1998), *Cool Places: Geographies of Youth Cultures*, London: Routledge.

Soja, E. (1989), *Postmodern Geographies: The Reassertion of Space in Critical Social Theory*, London: Verso.

Sontag, S. (1982), 'Notes on "Camp"', in *A Susan Sontag Reader*, London: Penguin.

Stallybrass, P. and White, A. (1986), *The Politics and Poetics of Transgression*, London: Methuen.

Steinke, D. (1996), 'Satan's Cheerleaders', *Spin*, February 1996: 62–70.

Stokes, M. (ed.) (1994), *Ethnicity, Identity and Music: The Musical Construction of Place*, Oxford: Berg.

Straw, W. (1991), 'Systems of Articulation, Logics of Change: Communities and Scenes in Popular Music', *Cultural Studies* 5(3): 368–88.

—— (1997), 'Sizing up Record Collections: Gender and Connoisseurship in Rock Music Culture', in S. Whiteley (ed.), *Sexing the Groove*, London: Routledge.

—— (2001), 'Scenes and Sensibilities', *Public* 22(3): 245–57.

Swedenburg, T. (2000), 'Satanic Heavy Metal in Egypt', Paper Presented at the American Anthropological Association Annual Meeting, San Fransisco.

Swiss, T., Sloop, J. and Herman, A. (eds) (1998), *Mapping the Beat: Popular Music and Contemporary Theory*, Oxford: Blackwell.

Tagg, P. (1994), 'Subjectivity and Soundscape, Motorbikes and Music', in H. Jarvilouma (ed.), *Soundscapes: Essays on Vroom and Moo*, Department of Folk Traditions, Institute of Rhythm Music, University of Tampere.

—— (1998), 'Tritonal Crime and 'Music as Music'', in S. Miceli, L. Gallenga and L. Kokkaliari (eds),

*Norme Con Ironie: Scritti Per I Settant' Anni Di Ennio Morricone*, Milan: Suvini Zerboni.

Taylor, T. D. (1997), *Global Pop: World Music, World Markets*, London: Routledge.

Terry, N. (1998), 'It's The End of the World As We Know It (And I Feel Fine)', *Terrorizer*, December 1998: 61.

Theweleit, K. (1987), *Male Fantasies Volume 1: Women, Floods, Bodies, History*, Minneapolis: University of Minnesota Press.

Thornton, S. (1995), *Club Cultures: Music, Media and Subcultural Capital*, Cambridge: Polity Press.

Tsitsos, W. (1999), 'Slamdancing, Moshing and the American Alternative Scene', *Popular Music* 18(3): 397–414.

Tönnies, F. (1955), *Community and Association*, London: Routledge and Kegan Paul.

Toynbee, J. (1993), 'Policing Bohemia, Pinning Up Grunge: The Music Press and Generic Change in British Pop and Rock', *Popular Music* 12(3): 289–300.

Turner, V. (1974), *Dramas, Fields and Metaphors: Symbolic Action in Human Society*, London: Cornell University Press.

Udo, T. (2002), *Brave Nu World*, London: Sanctuary.

Virilio, P. (1986), *Speed and Politics: An Essay on Dromology*, New York: Columbia University Press.

Wallach, J. (2003), '"Goodbye My Blind Majesty": Music, Language and Politics in the Indonesian Underground', in H. M. Berger and M. T. Carroll, *Global Pop, Local Language*, Jackson: University Press of Mississippi.

—— (In Press), 'Unleashed in the East: Metal Music, Masculinity, and Malay Identity in Indonesia, Malaysia, and Singapore', in H. M. Berger, P. D. Greene and J. Wallach (eds), *Metal Rules the Globe*.

Waksman, S. (2001), 'Into the Arena: Edward Van Halen and the Cultural Contradictions of the Guitar Hero', in A. Bennett and K. Dawe (eds), *Guitar Cultures*, Oxford: Berg.

Walser, R. (1993), *Running With The Devil: Power, Gender and Madness in Heavy Metal Music*, Hanover, NH: Wesleyan University Press.

Weber, M. (1964), *The Theory of Social and Economic Organisation*, New York: Free Press.

—— (1976) *The Protestant Ethic and the Spirit of Capitalism*, London: Allen and Unwin.

Weinstein, D. (2000), *Heavy Metal: The Music and its Culture* 2nd ed, New York: Da Capo Press.

—— (In Press), 'The Globalization of Metal', in H. M. Berger, P. D. Greene and J. Wallach (eds), *Metal Rules the Globe*.

Wells, J. (1997), 'Blackness 'Scuzed: Jimi Hendrix (In)Visible Legacy in Heavy Metal', in J. J. Fossett and J. Tucker (eds), *Race Consciousness: African-American Studies for the New Century*, New York: New York University Press.

Wells, S. (1998), 'Is This The Most Evil Man In Rock?', *New Musical Express*, 5 September 1998: 17–20.

White, T. (1999), *Satan! Satan! Satan!* London: Attack!

Widdicombe, S. and Wooffitt, R. (1995), *The Language of Youth Subcultures: Social Identity in Action*, London: Harvester Wheatsheaf.

Willis, P. (1977), *Learning to Labour*, Aldershot: Gower.

—— (1978), *Profane Culture*, London: Routledge and Kegan Paul.

—— (1990), *Common Culture*, Milton Keynes: Open University Press.

Wood, R. T. (1999), 'Nailed to the X: A Lyrical History of the Straight Edge Youth Subculture', *Journal Of Youth Studies* 2(2): 133–51.

**Website References**

All sites were accessed November 2005 unless otherwise stated.

*Aardschok* (accessed July 2005) www.aardschok.com

*American Nihilst Underground Society* www.anus.com

*Anus.com*'s list of 'People Accused of Being Bad Traders' www.anus.com/metal/about/links/traders.html

*Blabbermouth* www.blabbermouth.net

*Blackmetal.com* www.blackmetal.com
*Black Tears* www.blacktears.oskorei.net
*British Northern Metal Web* (accessed July 2005) www.shipley.ac.uk/north
*Burzum* www.burzum.com
*Chronicles Of Chaos* www.chroniclesofchaos.com
*Grimoire Of Exalted Deeds* www.thegrimoire.com
*Hells Laughter* users.belgacom.net/hellslaughter/index.htm
*Infernal Combustion* www.roadrun.com/infernalcombustion
*Isten* www.isten.net
*Mega's Metal Asylum* www-user.lut.fi/%7Emega/music.html
*Metalist* www.metalist.co.il
*Metal Injection* www.metalinjection.net
*MetalTabs.com* www.metaltabs.com
*Metal Trade* (accessed July 2005) www.metaltrade.ws
*Metal Travel Guide* www.metaltravelguide.com
*Metal Underground* www.metalunderground.com
*Northern Heritage* www.cfprod.com/nh
*Official Homme Page of Death Kristjan* www.neovoid.org/deathkristjan
*Plastic Head* www.plastichead.com
*Relapse Records* www.relapse.com
*Snake Net* www.snakenetmetalradio.com
*Terrorizer* www.terrorizer.com
*Unholy Black Metal Songtitle-O-Matic* metalseb.free.fr/index.php
*Where Is Mitch Hale?* (accessed July 2005) www.shipley.ac.uk/north/mitchhale.htm
*Windows 666* www.fortunecity.com/tinpan/motorhead/13

**Discography**
This discography contains details of all recordings referred to throughout the book and selected recordings by particularly significant acts referred to in the book. This list should not be seen as recommending any particular act or recording, nor is it comprehensive. Collectively though, the list does give a flavour of the diversity and development of extreme metal throughout its history.
Absu (1997) *The Third Storm of Cythraul* Osmose
Agoraphobic Nosebleed (2002) *Frozen Corpse Stuffed With Dope* Relapse
Arallu (2002) *Satanic War In Jerusalem* Raven
Arch Enemy (2005) *Doomsday Machine* Century Media
Arcturus (1997) *La Masquerade Infernale* Misanthropy
At The Gates (1995) *The Slaughter Of The Soul* Earache
Bathory (1984) *Bathory* Black Mark
—— (1988) *Blood Fire Death* Black Mark
Black Sabbath (1971) *Paranoid* Vertigo
Blut Aus Nord (2005) *Thematic Emanation Of Archetypal Multiplicity* Candelight
Bolt Thrower (1991) *Warmaster* Earache
Burzum (1992) *Hvist Lyset Tar Os* Misanthropy
Cannibal Corpse (1991) *Butchered at Birth* Metal Blade
—— (1994) *The Bleeding* Metal Blade
Carcass (1989) *Symphonies of Sickness* Earache
Celtic Frost (1987) *Into The Pandemonium* Noise
Cradle Of Filth (1998) *Cruelty And The Beast* Music For Nations
Dark Funeral (1996) *The Secrets of the Black Arts* No Fashion

Darkthrone (1994) *Transylvanian Hunger* Peaceville
Dark Tranquillity (1997) *The Mind's I* Osmose
Death (1986) *Scream Bloody Gore* Combat
Deicide (1990) *Deicide* Roadracer
Demoniac (1999) *The Fire And The Wind* Osmose
Dillinger Escape Plan (1999) *Calculating Infinity* Relapse
Dimmu Borgir (1997) *Enthrone Darkness Triumphant* Nuclear Blast
Discharge (1982) *Hear Nothing, See Nothing, Say Nothing* Clay
Dismember (1991) *Like an Ever Flowing Stream* Nuclear Blast
Dissection (1995) *Storm Of The Light's Bain* Nuclear Blast
Emperor (1994) *In The Nightside Eclipse* Candelight
Entombed (1990) *Left Hand Path* Earache
God Forbid (2005) *IV: Constitution Of Treason* Century Media
Grotesque (1997) *In The Embrace Of Evil* Black Sun
Hammerfall (1997) *Glory To The Brave* Nuclear Blast
Hellhammer (1985) *Apocalyptic Raids* Noise
Helloween (1987) *Keeper Of The Seven Keys* Noise
Immortal (1999) *At the Heart of Winter* Osmose
In Flames (1997) *Whoracle* Nuclear Blast
Iron Maiden (1982) *The Number Of The Beast* EMI
Judas Priest (1978) *Stained Class* CBS
Killswitch Engage (2004) *The End Of Heartache* Roadrunner
Korn (1996) *Life is Peachy* Sony
Led Zeppelin (1971) *Led Zeppelin IV* Atlantic
Limp Bizkit (2000) *Chocolate Starfish And The Hot Dog Flavored Water* Interscope
Machine Head (1994) *Burn My Eyes* Roadrunner
Manowar (1992) *The Triumph of Steel* Atlantic
Marduk (1999) *Panzer Division Marduk* Osmose
Mayhem (1994) *De Mysteriis Dom Sathanas* Deathlike Silence
Megadeth (1986) *Peace Sells . . . But Who's Buying* Capitol
Melechesh (2001) *Djinn* Osmose
Metallica (1983) *Kill 'Em All* Music For Nations
Morbid Angel (1989) *Altars Of Madness* Earache
Mötley Crüe (1983) *Shout At The Devil* Elektra
My Dying Bride (1994) *Turn Loose The Swans* Peaceville
Napalm Death (1987) *Scum* Earache
Neurosis (1996) *Through Silver In Blood* Relapse
Nightwish (2004) *Once* Spinefarm
Nile (2000) *Black Seeds Of Vengeance* Relapse
Nirvana (1991) *Nevermind* DGC
Obituary (1990) *Cause of Death* Roadrunner
Opeth (1999) *My Arms, Your Hearse* Candelight
Orphaned Land (2004) *Mabool* Century Media
Otyg (2000) *Sagovindars Boning* Napalm
Ozzy Osbourne (1980) *Blizzard Of Oz* CBS
Paradise Lost (1991) *Gothic* Peaceville
Pentagram (1985) *Pentagram* Pentagram
Pessimist (1997) *Cult of the Initiated* Lost Disciple

Poison (1986) *Looked What The Cat Dragged In* Capitol
Possessed (1985) *Seven Churches* Combat
Repulsion (1989) *Horrified* Necrosis
Salem (1994) *Kaddish* Morbid
Saxon (1981) *Denim And Leather* Carrere
Sepultura (1989) *Beneath The Remains* Roadrunner
—— (1996) *Roots* Roadrunner
Siege (1984) *Demo* (Version reissued as *Drop Dead* by Relapse in 1998)
Slayer (1983) *Show No Mercy* Metal Blade
Slipknot (1999) *Slipknot* Roadrunner
Sodom (1989) *Agent Orange* Steamhammer
St Vitus (1989) *V* Hellhound
Sunn0))) (2003) *White 1* Southern Lord
The Gathering (1998) *How To Measure A Planet* Century Media
The Haunted (1998) *The Haunted* Earache
The Obsessed (1990) *The Obsessed* Hellhound
Ulver (1998) *Themes From William Blake's The Marriage Of Heaven And Hell* Jester
Unleashed (1993) *Across The Open Sea* Century Media
Various (1997) *Awakenings: Females In Extreme Music* Dwell
—— (1997) *Israheller* Heller Productions
Venom (1981) *Welcome to Hell* Neat
—— (1982) *Black Metal* Neat

# INDEX